Routledge Revision: Questions & Answers

Evidence
2011–2012

Routledge Q&A series

Each Routledge Q&A contains approximately 50 questions on topics commonly found on exam papers, with answer plans and comprehensive suggested answers. Each book also offers valuable advice as to how to approach and tackle exam questions and how to focus your revision effectively. New **Aim Higher** and **Common Pitfalls** boxes will also help you to identify how to go that little bit further in order to get the very best marks and highlight areas of confusion. And now there are further opportunities to hone and perfect your exam technique online.

New editions publishing in 2011:

Civil Liberties & Human Rights	Equity & Trusts
Commercial Law	European Union Law
Company Law	Evidence
Constitutional & Administrative Law	Family Law
Contract Law	Jurisprudence
Criminal Law	Land Law
Employment Law	Medical Law
English Legal System	Torts

For a full listing, visit http://www.routledge.com/textbooks/revision

Routledge Revision: Questions & Answers

Evidence

2011–2012

Christopher Allen LLM, MA, PhD
Barrister, Formerly Senior Lecturer, Inns of Court School of Law

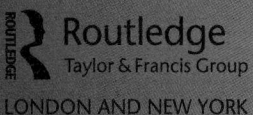
Routledge
Taylor & Francis Group
LONDON AND NEW YORK

Ninth edition published 2011
by Routledge
2 Park Square, Milton Park, Abingdon, Oxon, OX14 4RN

Simultaneously published in the USA and Canada
by Routledge
270 Madison Avenue, New York, NY 10016

Routledge is an imprint of the Taylor & Francis Group, an informa business

© 1994–2011 Christopher Allen

Previous editions published by Cavendish Publishing Limited
First edition	1994	Fourth edition	2000
Second edition	1996	Fifth edition	2002
Third edition	1998	Sixth edition	2005

Previous editions published by Routledge-Cavendish
| Seventh edition | 2007 | Eighth edition | 2009 |

The right of Christopher Allen to be identified as author of this work has been asserted by him in accordance with sections 77 and 78 of the Copyright, Designs and Patents Act 1988.

Typeset in TheSans by RefineCatch Ltd, Bungay, Suffolk
Printed and bound in Great Britain by TJ International Ltd, Padstow, Cornwall

All rights reserved. No part of this book may be reprinted or reproduced or utilised in any form or by any electronic, mechanical, or other means, now known or hereafter invented, including photocopying and recording, or in any information storage or retrieval system, without permission in writing from the publishers.

British Library Cataloguing in Publication Data
A catalogue record for this book is available from the British Library

Library of Congress Cataloging-in-Publication Data
Allen, C. J. W. (Christopher J. W.), 1944–
 Evidence/Christopher Allen.—9th ed.
  p. cm.—(Q&A, Routledge questions & answers series)
 Rev. ed. of: Evidence, 2009–2010. 8th ed. 2009.
 Includes bibliographical references and index.
 ISBN 978-0-415-59830-9 (alk. paper)
1. Evidence (Law)—England. 2. Evidence (Law)—England—Examinations, questions, etc.
I. Allen, C. J. W. (Christopher J. W.), 1944– Evidence, 2009–2010. II. Title.
KD7499.6A43 2011
347.42'06076—dc22   2010040388

ISBN13: 978–0–415–59830–9 (pbk)
ISBN13: 978–0–203–83282–0 (ebk)

Contents

	Table of Cases	vii
	Table of Legislation	xiii
	Guide to the Companion Website	xvii
	Introduction	1
1	Basic Concepts	3
2	Burden and Standard of Proof	17
3	Presumptions, Competence and Compellability	33
4	Hearsay I	47
5	Hearsay II	63
6	Hazardous Evidence	77
7	Confessions and Ill-Gotten Evidence	97
8	Character Evidence I	123
9	Character Evidence II	143
10	The Course of Testimony	163
11	Opinion Evidence	175
12	Privilege and Public Policy	183
13	Revision	197
	Index	209

Table of Cases

A & BC Chewing Gum Ltd, see DPP v A & BC Chewing Gum Ltd
A (No 1) [2001] 2 WLR 1546 **10, 164, 172, 207**
A (No 2) [2002] 1 AC 45 **82, 83, 172**
Abadom [1983] 1 WLR 126 **176, 179**
Agar [1989] NLJR 116; [1990] 2 All ER 442 **191, 192**
Air Canada v Secretary of State for Trade (No 2) [1983] 2 AC 394 **188**
Al-Khawaja [2006] 1 WLR 1078; [2005] EWCA Crim 2697 **49, 51**
Al-Khawaja v UK [2009] All ER (D) 132 (Jan) **51, 54**
Alladice (1988) 87 Cr App R 380 **108, 110**
Allan [1969] 1 All ER 91; [1969] 1 WLR 33 **24**
Alobaydi [2007] EWCA Crim 145 **128**
Anderson [1993] Crim LR 447 **114**
Andreae v Selfridge & Co Ltd [1938] Ch 1 **12**
Andrews [1987] AC 281 **64, 72, 75**
Argent (1997) 2 Cr App R 27 **120**
Ashburton (Lord) v Pape [1913] 2 Ch 469 **195**
Associated Provincial Picture House v Wednesbury Corporation [1948] 1 KB 223 **204**
Attorney-General of Hong Kong v Lee Kwong-Kut [1993] 3 All ER 939 **20**
Aziz and Others [1995] 3 All ER 149, HL; [1996] 1 AC 41 **82, 83, 107, 172, 207**
B (C) [2004] EWCA Crim 1254 **146, 155**

Bailey and Smith (1993) 97 Cr App Rep 365 **121**
Barclays Bank v Eustice [1995] 1 WLR 1238 **190**
Bathurst [1968] 2 QB 99 **101, 102**
Batt [1994] Crim LR 592 **69**
Batt [1995] Crim LR 240 **98, 121**
Beck [1982] 1 WLR 461 **79, 85**
Beckles [2004] EWCA Crim 2766 **121**
Bentley (DW) (Deceased) [2001] 1 Cr App R 307 **23**
Betts and Hall [2001] EWCA Crim 224 **121**
Birks [2003] All ER (D) 155 (Jan); [2002] EWCA Crim 3091 **75**
Blake and Tye (1844) 6 QB 126; 115 ER 49 **98**
Blastland [1986] AC 41 **8, 15, 74, 86, 148**
Boardman, see DPP v Boardman
Bowman v DPP [1990] Crim LR 600 **11**
Boyson [1991] Crim LR 274 **133**
Bratty v Attorney-General for Northern Ireland [1963] AC 386 **25**
Brigden [1973] Crim LR 579 **101**
Britzman [1983] 1 WLR 350 **160**
Brown; Daley (1987) 87 Cr App Rep 52 **191, 193**
Buckley (1873) 13 Cox CC 293 **75**
Burge and Pegg [1996] 1 Cr App Rep 163 **15, 57, 80, 87, 171, 201**
Byrne [1960] 2 QB 396 **179**
C [2006] EWCA Crim 197 **67**
Calcraft v Guest [1898] 1 QB 759 **195**
Callender [1998] Crim LR 337 **75**

Campbell [2007] 1 WLR 2798 128–130, 149, 153, 160, 205
Campbell v Tameside MBC [1982] QB 1065 188
Camplin, *sub nom* DPP v Camplin [1978] AC 705 7–9
Carnall [1995] Crim LR 944 72
Carr-Briant [1943] KB 607 24
Chard v Chard [1956] P 259; [1955] 3 All ER 721 36, 41
Chenia [2004] 1 All ER 543, [2003] 2 Cr App Rep 83; [2002] EWCA Crim 2345 118
Chief Constable of the West Midlands, *ex parte* Wiley [1995] AC 274 189
Christie [1914] AC 545 165
Coles [1995] 1 Cr App Rep 157 176
Comptroller of Customs v Western Lectric Co Ltd [1966] AC 367 56
Condron [1997] 1 WLR 827 120
Constantine (Joseph) Steamship Line Ltd v Imperial Smelting Corp Ltd [1942] AC 54; [1941] 2 All ER 165 26
Conway v Rimmer [1968] AC 910 185
Cooke [1995] 1 Cr App Rep 318 117, 120
Cowan [1996] QB 373; [1995] 4 All ER 939 145, 150, 152, 157
Crawford [1998] 1 Cr App Rep 338 155
Crescent Farm v Sterling Offices [1972] Ch 553 190
Crompton (Alfred) Amusement Machines Ltd v Customs and Excise Commissioners (No 2) [1974] AC 405 188
D [2009] EWCA Civ 2577 82, 84, 173, 203
DPP v A & BC Chewing Gum Ltd [1968] 1 QB 159 179
DPP v Boardman [1975] AC 421; [1974] 3 All ER 887 134
DPP v Camplin, see Camplin

DPP, *ex parte* Kebilene (*sub nom* Kebiline) [2000] 2 AC 326; [1999] 3 WLR 972 20, 21, 29, 31
DPP v Majewski, see Majewski
Davies [1962] 3 All ER 97 176
Davies v DPP [1954] AC 378 85
Davies v Health and Safety Executive [2002] EWCA Crim 2949 20, 21, 29, 31
Dervish [2001] EWCA Crim 2789; [2002] 2 Cr App Rep 105 111
Desmond [1999] Crim LR 313 161
Devonport and Pirano (1996) 1 Cr App R 221 70
Dillon v R [1982] 2 WLR 538 37
Dix (1981) 74 Cr App Rep 306; [1982] Crim LR 302 178
Donald [2004] EWCA Crim 965 132
Duff Development Co Ltd v Government of Kelantan [1924] AC 797 12
Duncan (1981) 73 Cr App R 359 107
E [2005] Crim LR 227 173
Edwards [1975] QB 27 29, 30
Edwards [1991] 2 All ER 266 164
Edwards [2006] 1 Cr App Rep 31; [2005] EWCA Crim 1813 124
Elson (1994) *The Times*, 30 June 104
Evans [1965] 2 QB 295 85
Everett [1988] Crim LR 826 114
Exall (1866) 4 F & F 922 141
Fernandez, *ex parte* (1861) 10 CBNS 3 39, 40, 42, 43
Forbes [2001] 1 All ER 686 91, 92, 94
Foster [2009] EWCA Crim 353 130, 153
Fowler (1988) 86 Cr App Rep 219 135
Fulcher [1995] 2 Cr App R 251 124
Fulling [1987] QB 426 99, 105, 110, 114, 122
Gadsby [2005] EWCA Crim 3206 155
Gayle [1999] 2 Cr App R 130 92, 94

George v Davies [1911] 2 KB 445 12
Gilfoyle [1996] 3 All ER 583 75
Gill [1963] 1 WLR 841 117
Gill [2001] 1 Cr App R 160 118, 168
Glendarroch, The [1894] P 226 28
Goddard v Nationwide Building Society [1987] QB 670 195
Goldenberg (1988) 88 Cr App R 285 112, 114
Goss [2005] Crim LR 61; [2003] EWCA Crim 3208 123
Gowland-Wynn [2002] 1 Cr App Rep 569; [2001] EWCA Crim 2715 118
Grannell (1990) 90 Cr App Rep 149 89, 99
Grant (1996) 1 Cr App R 73 7, 8, 13, 14, 69, 70
Grant v The Queen [2007] 1 AC 1; [2006] 2 WLR 835 49
Gray [2004] EWCA Crim 1074 123, 125, 128, 161
Gray, Liggins, Riding and Rowlands (1995) 2 Cr App R 100 69, 98, 99
Grayson [1993] Crim LR 864 99
Griffiths [1998] Crim LR 567 9, 69
Gummerson and Steadman [1999] Crim LR 680 92, 94
Gunewardene [1951] 2 KB 600 66, 98, 100, 108
Guney (1998) 2 Cr App R 242 7, 8, 69
H and Others (Minors) (Sexual Abuse: Standard of Proof), Re [1996] 1 All ER 1 27
Hacker [1994] 1 WLR 1659 136
Halpin [1996] Crim LR 112 7, 8, 13, 15
Hanson [2005] 1 WLR 3169 124–127, 129, 130, 133, 136, 138, 140, 141, 146, 148, 151, 154, 159, 161
Harvey [1988] Crim LR 241 113, 114
Hasson [1997] Crim LR 579 70
Hayes [1977] 1 WLR 234 39, 40

Hennessy (1978) 68 Cr App Rep 419 191, 192
Hepworth [1955] 2 QB 600 24
Hersey [1998] Crim LR 281 92, 94
Hetherington v Hetherington (1887) 12 PD 112 35
Hickin and Others [1996] Crim LR 584 95
Highton [2006] 1 Cr App Rep 125; [2005] EWCA Crim 1985 137, 145, 151, 158
Hoare [2004] EWCA Crim 784 121
Hornal v Neuberger Products [1957] 1 QB 247 27
Horncastle [2009] UKSC 14 51, 54
Hoskyn v Commissioner of Police for the Metropolis [1979] AC 474 43, 44
Howell [2003] EWCA Crim 01 121
Hunt [1987] AC 352 21, 29, 30
Hurst [1995] 1 Cr App Rep 82 175
Islam [1999] 1 Cr App Rep 22 82, 83, 171, 206
Ismail [1990] Crim LR 872 107
Jelen & Katz (1989) 90 Cr App Rep 456 97, 99
Johnson [1988] 1 WLR 1377 191, 193
Johnson [1995] 2 Cr App Rep 41 87, 133
Johnstone [2003] 1 WLR 1736 20–22, 29, 31
Jones and Others [1997] 2 Cr App R 119 99
Kearley [1992] 2 AC 228 48, 52–54, 72, 74
Kebilene, see R v DPP, *ex parte* Kebilene
Kelly [1992] Crim LR 181 90, 92, 94, 95
Khan (1981) 73 Cr App Rep 190 40
Khan (Sultan) [1997] AC 558; [1996] 2 Cr App Rep 440 121
Knight [2003] EWCA Crim 1977 121
Kritz [1950] 1 KB 82 23, 24
L [2008] 2 Cr App R 18 203

TABLE OF CASES

L v DPP [2002] 2 All ER 854 **24, 25**
Lambert [2001] 3 All ER 577; [2002] 2 AC 545 **19–21, 24, 29, 31**
Lee [1996] 2 Cr App Rep 266 **133**
Levison v Patent Steam Carpet Cleaning Ltd [1978] QB 69 **28**
Lilley [2003] EWCA Crim 1789 **57, 74**
Lobban v R [1995] 1 WLR 877 **117**
Lobell [1957] 1 QB 547 **25, 203, 204**
Lovelock [1997] Crim LR 821 **70**
Lowery v R [1974] AC 85 **180**
Luca v Italy (2003) 36 EHRR 46 **49, 50**
Lucas [1981] QB 720 **15, 57, 80, 87, 91, 92, 171, 201**
Lupien (1970) 9 DLR (3d) 1 **180**
Lydon [1987] Crim LR 407 **56**
M (T) and Others [2000] 1 All ER 148 **124**
M [2009] EWCA Crim 618 **82, 173, 203, 204**
Majewski [1977] AC 443 **7–9**
Makanjuola (Oluwanfunso) [1995] 1 WLR 1348 **79, 80**
Makanjuola v Commissioner of Metropolitan Police [1992] 3 All ER 617 **188**
Makin v Attorney-General for New South Wales [1894] AC 57 **131**
Malashev [1997] Crim LR 587 **95**
Malindi v R [1967] 1 AC 439 **150, 159**
Maqsud Ali [1966] 1 QB 688 **61, 121**
Marcus [2005] Crim LR 384 **95**
Marks v Beyfus (1890) 25 QBD 494 **191–193**
Martinez-Tobon [1994] 2 All ER 90; (1993) *The Times*, 1 December **101, 102**
Mason [1988] 1 WLR 139 **97, 106, 114**
Matto v Wolverhampton Crown Court [1987] RTR 337 **119**
Mawaz Khan v R [1967] 1 AC 454 **57, 60, 86**

McGovern [1991] Crim LR 124; (1990) 92 Cr App R 228 **104, 106, 112–114**
McIntosh [1992] Crim LR 651 **60, 200**
McQuaker v Goddard [1940] 1 KB 687 **12**
Mertens [2004] EWCA Crim 2252; [2005] Crim LR 301 **146, 155**
Michael, The [1979] 1 Lloyd's Rep 17; [1978] 1 WLR 411 **27**
Middleton [2000] All ER (D) 453 **87**
Miller v Howe [1969] 3 All ER 451 **56**
Miller v Minister of Pensions [1947] 2 All ER 372 **27**
M'Naghten's Case [1843–60] All ER Rep 229 **177**
Moghal (1977) 65 Cr App Rep 56 **75, 86**
Mountford [1999] Crim LR 575 **118**
Mullen v Hackney LBC [1997] 1 WLR 1103 **11**
Murray v DPP (1993) 97 Cr App Rep 151 **101, 102**
Murrell [2005] EWCA Crim 382 **146, 155**
Myers v DPP [1965] AC 1001 **52, 53**
Napper [1996] Crim LR 591 **144**
Nash [2004] EWCA Crim 2696 **93**
Neil [1994] Crim LR 441 **104, 107, 114**
Nelson [1998] 2 Cr App Rep 399 **107**
Nickolson [1999] Crim LR 61 **118**
Nye v Niblett [1918] 1 KB 23 **12**
O [2006] 2 Cr App R 405 **171**
Oyesiku (1971) 56 Cr App Rep 240 **167, 168**
PS v Germany [2002] Crim LR 312 **75**
Paraskeva (1982) 76 Cr App Rep 162; [1983] Crim LR 186 **166**
Paris [1994] Crim LR 361; (1992) 97 Cr App Rep 99 **103**
Parker [1995] Crim LR 233 **99**
Patel v Comptroller of Customs [1966] AC 356 **56**
Patrick [1999] All ER (D) 532 **87**

Pattinson and Exley [1996] 1 Cr App R 51 **92, 93**
Payton [2006] EWCA Crim 1226 **123**
Pearce (1979) 69 Cr App R 365 **69, 207**
Peart v Bolckow Vaughan & Co Ltd [1925] 1 KB 399 **11**
Perry [1984] Crim LR 680 **136**
Petkar [2003] EWCA Crim 2668; [2004] 1 Cr App Rep 270 **87, 111, 118, 120, 167, 168, 198**
Phillips (1936) 26 Cr App Rep 17 **166**
Pieterson [1995] 1 WLR 293 **60**
Podola [1960] 1 QB 325 **24**
Popat (1998) 2 Cr App Rep 208 **94**
Popat (No 2) [2000] Crim LR 54 **93, 94**
Price [2004] EWCA Crim 1359; [2005] Crim LR 304 **146, 155**
Qadir [1998] Crim LR 828 **92, 93**
Rankine [1986] QBD 861 **191, 193**
Redgrave (1981) 74 Cr App Rep 10 **147**
Renda [2005] EWCA Crim 2826; [2006] 2 All ER 553 **124**
Rennie [1982] 1 All ER 385 **108, 110**
Reynolds [1989] Crim LR 220 **180**
Reynolds v Llanelly Tinplate Co Ltd [1948] 1 All ER 140 **11**
Rice [1963] 1 QB 857 **56**
Roberts [1942] 1 All ER 187 **165, 167**
Roberts [1997] 1 Cr App R 217 **97**
Robertson [1968] 3 All ER 557 **24**
Robinson (Dennis) [2005] EWCA Crim 3233; [2006] 1 Cr App Rep 480 **146, 155**
Robinson (Wayne) [2006] Crim LR 427 **58**
Robinson [2003] EWCA Crim 2219 **121**
Rodley [1913] 3 KB 468 **138, 139**
Rogers v Home Secretary [1973] AC 388 **188**
Romeo [2004] 1 Cr App R 417 **171**
Rowton (1865) Le & Ca 520 **147, 148, 165**

Rudd (1948) 32 Cr App Rep 138 **100**
Rush & Tompkins Ltd v Greater London Council [1989] AC 1280 **184**
Ryder [1993] Crim LR 601 **134**
Salabiaku v France (1988) 13 EHRR 379 **19, 20**
Samuel [1988] QB 615; [1988] 2 WLR 920 **117**
Sang [1980] AC 402 **57, 124, 125, 127, 133, 137, 140, 143, 146, 151, 153, 158, 160**
Savage v Chief Constable of the Hampshire Constabulary [1997] 2 All ER 631 **188**
Sellick [2005] 1 WLR 3257 **49, 51**
Selvey v DPP [1970] AC 304 **154**
Senat v Senat [1965] 2 WLR 981 **168**
Sharp [1988] 1 All ER 65 **82, 83, 99, 100, 104, 107, 108, 207**
Shaw (1888) 16 Cox CC 503 **166**
Sheldrake v DPP [2004] QB 487; [2003] EWHC 273 (Admin) **20, 21**
Silverlock [1894] 2 QB 766 **180**
Singh [2006] EWCA Crim 660 **48, 54, 73, 75**
Slater [1995] 1 Cr App R 584 **92, 93**
Slowcombe [1991] Crim LR 198 **191, 192**
Smith [1976] Crim LR 511 **136**
Somanathan [2005] EWCA Crim 2866; (2005) *The Times*, 18 November **133**
Sparks v R [1964] AC 964; [1964] 1 All ER 727 **52, 54, 74**
Spencer [1987] AC 128; [1986] 2 All ER 928 **79**
Stagg (1994) unreported **106**
Stanton [2004] EWCA Crim 490 **91, 93**
Stone [2005] EWCA Crim 105 **79, 85**
Subramaniam v Public Prosecutor [1956] 1 WLR 965 **48, 73**
T(D) [2009] EWCA Crim 1213 **50, 54**
T and H [2001] EWCA Crim 1877; [2002] 1 All ER 683 **84, 173, 203, 204**

Tahed [2004] EWCA Crim 1220 83
Taylor (Stuart) [2006] 2 Cr App R 14 66
Taylor v Chief Constable of Cheshire [1987] 1 All ER 225; [1986] 1 WLR 1479 61
Taylor, Weaver and Donovan (1928) 21 Cr App Rep 20 59
Teeluck and John [2005] 1 WLR 2421 123
Teper v R [1952] AC 480 52
Thomas v UK (2005) 41 EHRR SE 11 50
Thompson (1976) 64 Cr App Rep 96 169
Thompson v R [1918] AC 221 134
Thomson [1912] 3 KB 19; 7 Cr App Rep 276 75
Thornton [1995] 1 Cr App R 578 92, 93
Tomlin v Standard Telephones and Cables Ltd [1969] 3 All ER 201 184
Toohey v Commissioner for Metropolitan Police [1965] AC 595 180
Toussaint-Collins [2009] EWCA Crim 316 61
Tripodi v R [1961] 104 CLR 1 98
Truscott, Re [1967] SCR 309 139
Turnbull [1977] QB 224 1, 80, 89, 91–95, 132, 198
Turner [1975] QB 834 7, 126, 127, 178

Valentine (1996) 2 Cr App R 213 171
Vye [1993] 1 WLR 471 123, 126, 128, 147, 149, 150, 152, 162, 172
Wainwright (1875) 13 Cox CC 171 75
Walsh (1989) 91 Cr App Rep 161 110
Walters [1979] RTR 220 64
Walters v R [1969] 2 AC 26 23, 24
Ward [2001] Crim LR 316 74
Warner (1993) 96 Cr App R 324 70
Watkins, Re [1953] 2 All ER 1113 41
Waugh v British Railways Board [1980] AC 521 194, 195
Weir [2005] EWCA Crim 2866; [2006] 2 All ER 570 124, 126, 127
Wetherall v Harrison [1976] 1 QB 773 11
Wickham (1971) 55 Cr App Rep 199 144
Wilkins [1975] 2 All ER 724 136
Willis [1916] 1 KB 933 85
Woolmington v DPP [1935] AC 462 17, 19
Wright [1994] Crim LR 55 13, 14, 68, 69
Wright v Doe d Tatham (1837) 7 Ad & El 313 72
Xabri [2006] 1 All ER 776; [2005] EWCA Crim 3135 49, 50
Y [2008] EWCA Crim 10 65, 66, 98, 110, 117

Table of Legislation

STATUTES

Children Act 1989—
  s 96(2) 39, 40
Civil Evidence Act 1972—
  s 1(1) 176
  s 3(2) 176
Civil Evidence Act 1995 63
  s 1(1) 47
  s 1(2) 47
Civil Partnership Act 2004—
  s 84(1) 34
Civil Procedure Rules 1998—
  r 31.20 184, 195
Contempt of Court Act 1981—
  s 10 184
Coroners and Justice Act 2009 164
Criminal Evidence Act 1898 123, 154, 159–161
  s 1(f)(ii) 150, 151, 154, 159
  s 1(f)(iii) 155
Criminal Justice Act 1967—
  s 10 14
Criminal Justice Act 1988 55, 80
  s 23 63, 74, 167
  s 24 63
  s 25 63, 74, 76
  s 26 63, 74, 76
  s 30 176
  s 34(2) 79
  s 139 24
Criminal Justice Act 2003 13, 14, 51, 52, 54, 55, 64, 66, 69, 70, 73–76, 82, 123, 124, 126, 132, 136, 202
  Pt 11, Ch 1 123, 125, 129, 143, 150
  Pt 11, Ch 2 47, 63
  s 98 126, 127, 129, 132, 134, 140
  s 99(1) 155
  s 100 141, 145, 166, 203, 205
  s 100(1) 145
  s 100(1)(a) 166
  s 100(1)(b) 166, 205
  s 100(4) 145, 166
  s 101 141, 203, 205
  s 101(1) 134, 137
  s 101(1)(a) 124
  s 101(1)(b) 124
  s 101(1)(c) 124, 129, 132, 141
  s 101(1)(d) 15, 124, 127, 128–130, 132, 133, 136, 138, 140, 145, 146, 148–160
  s 101(1)(e) 124, 146, 153–155, 161
  s 101(1)(f) 124, 150, 151, 157–159
  s 101(1)(g) 124, 137, 145, 150, 152–154, 156, 158–161, 166
  s 101(3) 124, 127, 130, 132, 133, 137, 145, 146, 149, 152, 153, 155, 157–159, 161
  s 101(4) 124
  s 102 124, 129, 132, 141
  s 103 124, 146
  s 103(1)(a) 15, 127, 129, 130, 153, 154, 158
  s 103(1)(b) 126, 128, 129, 153, 154, 158–160
  s 103(2) 153, 160

s 103(3) 124, 136, 138, 140, 146, 157–160
s 103(4) 124
s 103(4)(b) 160
s 103(5) 160
s 104 124, 155
s 105 124
s 105(1) 150
s 105(2) 150
s 105(2)(a) 150
s 105(3) 151, 158
s 105(4) 151
s 105(5) 151
s 105(6) 158
s 106 124, 154
s 106(1)(b) 158
s 106(2) 160
s 109 134
s 112 126, 127
s 112(1) 129, 132, 134, 140
s 114 48–50, 63, 64, 117, 202
s 114(1) 47, 49, 66
s 114(1)(a) 66
s 114(1)(b) 66
s 114(1)(c) 66
s 114(1)(d) 54, 57, 66, 67, 73–75, 98, 110, 203, 204
s 114(2) 54, 66, 75, 76, 203, 204
s 114(2)(g) 203, 204
s 115(2) 47, 90
s 115(3) 47, 48, 54, 58, 61, 74
s 115(3)(a) 72
s 116 48, 49, 55, 57, 63–65, 67, 72, 74, 81, 201
s 116(1) 57
s 116(1)(a) 57, 81, 82
s 116(1)(b) 57, 74
s 116(2) 57
s 116(2)(a) 82, 200, 201
s 116(2)(c) 67, 76, 206
s 116(2)(d) 67, 76, 206
s 116(2)(e) 75, 169
s 116(4) 75, 76, 169
s 117 63–65, 67
s 117(2)(c) 67
s 117(7) 75
s 118 63, 64, 66, 74, 75, 86
s 118(1) 86
s 118(1), para 4(a) 201
s 118(1), para 4(c) 200, 201
s 118(1), para 5 66
s 118(1), para 7 70
s 118(1), para 8 180
s 118(1)(a) 66
s 119 67, 163
s 119(1) 169
s 120 67, 163, 171, 173
s 120(1) 89, 90
s 120(2) 168
s 120(3) 169
s 120(4) 82, 83, 89, 90, 164, 165, 170, 171, 206
s 120(5) 89, 90, 165
s 120(7) 82, 164, 170, 206
s 120(7)(c) 170
s 120(7)(d) 73, 75, 164
s 120(7)(e) 82, 171, 206
s 120(8) 164
ss 121–125 64
s 121 65, 82, 206
s 121(1) 55, 67
s 121(1)(a) 67
s 121(1)(b) 67
s 121(1)(c) 67, 76, 200, 206
s 126 76
s 126(2) 130
s 139 90
s 139(1) 168, 169
Sch 37, Pt 6 63
Criminal Justice Act 2003 (Categories of Offences) Order 2004 (SI 2004/3346) 160

Criminal Justice and Public Order Act
 1994 **80, 100, 111, 144**
  s 32 **79**
  s 34 **80, 86, 87, 100–102, 104, 111, 116, 118, 120, 121, 167, 168, 198**
  s 34(2A) **87, 111, 118**
  s 35 **100–102, 156, 157**
  s 35(3) **144, 157**
  s 36 **100, 101, 104**
  s 37 **100, 101, 104**
  s 38 **100**
Criminal Procedure Act 1865—
  s 3 **169**
  s 6 **166**
Criminal Procedure (Insanity)
 Act 1964—
  s 4(1) **24**
European Convention on the
 Protection of Human Rights
 and Fundamental Freedoms **19, 49, 50**
  Art 6 **10, 49–51, 54, 74**
  Art 6(2) **18, 19, 22, 29, 31**
  Art 6(3) **50**
  Art 6(3)(d) **49–51, 54**
Evidence Amendment Act 1853—
  s 1 **39**
Family Law Reform Act 1969—
  s 26 **37, 42**
Fatal Accidents Act 1976 **195**
Health and Safety at Work etc.
 Act 1974—
  s 40 **20**
Homicide Act 1957—
  s 2 **177–179**
Human Rights Act 1998 **10, 18, 19, 32, 48, 50, 52, 62, 207**
  s 2(1)(a) **50**
Law of Property Act 1925—
  s 184 **41, 42**
  s 184(1) **35, 36**

Magistrates' Courts Act 1980—
  s 101 **29–31**
Police and Criminal Evidence Act 1984 **66, 80, 103, 108, 122, 202**
  s 58 **106, 116**
  s 58(8) **109, 116**
  s 58(8)(c) **116**
  s 62(10) **102**
  s 62(11) **80**
  s 66 **89**
  s 67(11) **80, 89**
  s 73 **166**
  s 73(2) **136**
  s 74 **133**
  s 74(3) **135, 137**
  s 76 **90, 92, 97, 100, 104–106, 108, 109, 114–116**
  s 76(1) **66, 207**
  s 76(2) **99**
  s 76(2)(a) **99, 115–117**
  s 76(2)(b) **97, 105, 108–117**
  s 76(4) **110, 115, 117**
  s 76(8) **99, 105, 116**
  s 76A(1) **156**
  s 78 **74, 76, 90–92, 97, 99, 100, 105, 106, 108–110, 112, 114–117, 119, 120, 127, 158**
  s 78(1) **57, 92, 94, 116, 117, 119, 121, 124, 125, 132, 140, 151, 158**
  s 80 **34, 38, 39, 42, 43, 45, 203**
  s 80(3) **43, 204**
  s 80(3)(a) **38, 39**
  s 82(1) **86, 98, 104, 105, 109, 111, 113, 116**
  Codes of Practice—
   Code C **92, 99, 100, 104, 108, 109, 115**
    para 1.1 **106**
    para 4.2 **106**
    para 4.3 **106**
    para 8.1 **110**

para 10.1 **113**
para 11.2 **106**
para 11.5 **114**
para 12.6 **116**
para 12.8 **106, 116**
Annex B **117, 122**
Annex B, para 3 **109, 117**
Note B3 **109**
Code D **80, 88, 89, 91, 92, 94, 95**
para 3 **90**
para 3.2 **90**
para 3.2(d) **91**
para 3.3 **89, 90**
para 3.12 **90, 92, 94, 95**
para 3.13 **91**
para 4 **90**
Annex A **80**
Annex B **80**
Annex E **80, 90, 91**
Code E **111**
Prevention of Crime Act 1953—
s 1 **22–24**
Public Order Act 1986—
s 3(1) **87**
Rehabilitation of Offenders Act 1974 **153, 154, 162**
Sexual Offences Act 2003—
ss 75–77 **34**
s 75 **46**
s 76 **46**
Theft Act 1968—
s 8 **39**
s 27(3) **125, 135, 136**
s 27(3)(b) **135**
Workmen's Compensation Act 1925 **11**
Workmen's Compensation Act 1943 **11**
Youth Justice and Criminal Evidence Act 1999 **34, 38**
ss 41–43 **80, 163, 164**
s 41 **8–10, 15, 82, 83, 172, 173, 207**
s 41(1) **83, 207**
s 41(1)(c) **207**
s 41(3) **172, 207**
s 41(3)(a) **172**
s 41(3)(b) **82, 83, 172, 173, 207**
s 41(3)(c) **82, 172, 173, 207**
s 41(3)(c)(i) **83**
s 41(5) **207**
ss 53–56 **34, 45**
s 53(1) **38, 39, 86**
s 53(2)(a) **38**
s 53(3) **39, 86**
s 55(2) **86**
s 55(2)(a) **38, 39**

Guide to the Companion Website

http://www.routledge.com/textbooks/revision

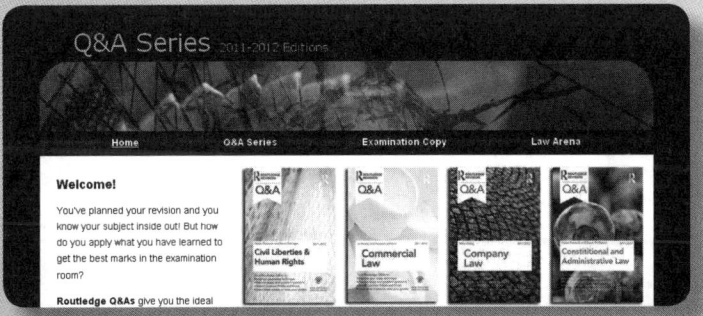

Visit the Routledge Q&A website to discover even more study tips and advice on getting those top marks.

On the Routledge revision website you'll find the following resources designed to enhance your revision on all areas of undergraduate law.

The Good, The Fair, & The Ugly
Good essays are the gateway to top marks. New to this edition, this interactive tutorial provides sample essays together with voice-over commentary and tips for successful exam essays, written by our Q&A authors themselves.

Multiple Choice Questions

Knowledge is the foundation of every good essay. Focusing on key examination themes, these MCQs have been written to test your knowledge and understanding of each subject in the book.

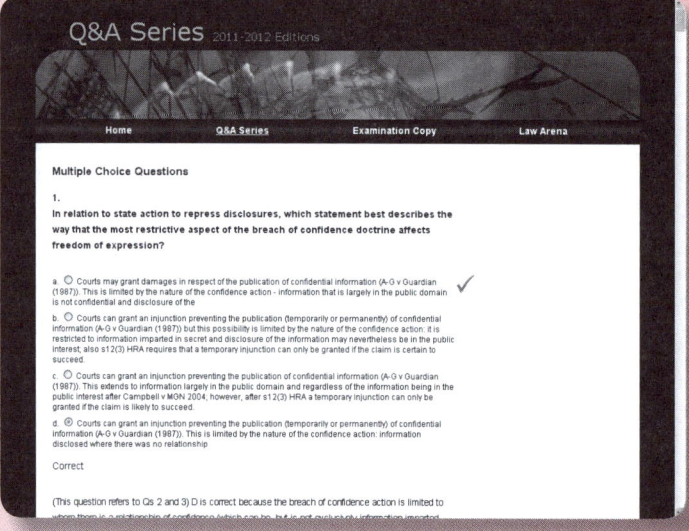

Bonus Q&As

Having studied our exam advice, put your revision into practice and test your essay writing skills with our additional online questions and answers.

Don't forget to check out even more revision guides and exam tools from Routledge!

Lawcards

Lawcards are your complete, pocket-sized guides to key examinable areas of undergraduate law.

Routledge Student Statutes

Comprehensive selections; clear, easy-to-use layout; alphabetical, chronological, and thematic indexes; and a competitive price make *Routledge Student Statutes* the statute book of choice for the serious law student.

Introduction

This book is intended to help students studying evidence law who may feel that they have acquired some knowledge, but do not feel confident about handling it correctly in the examination. The book shows how to apply that knowledge in answering problems and writing answers to essay questions. I have emphasised problem questions in this book in order to give students as much practice as possible in reasoning with facts as well as with law. The practising lawyer is concerned most of the time with facts rather than law. Even in law examinations, analysis of a factual situation is essential to the application of the law, and it is often at this stage that students go astray.

When considering problems of evidence law it may be useful to remember that these can be of two kinds. First, of course, there are questions of admissibility – a traditional concern of evidence law. But the law can also have something to say about how a trial judge should direct a jury in relation to evidence that has been admitted. This was originally a matter for the judge's discretion, but discretion has been giving way to rules. There are now things that a judge must say, for example, about evidence of a defendant's good character, evidence of identification, or about a defendant's silence when questioned by police. If a problem question ends with words such as, 'Discuss the evidential issues that arise,' remember that this requires you to tell the examiner about judicial directions as well as admissibility. Further, you must know not only the principal occasions that require a judicial direction but also the essential elements of the appropriate direction. For example, students who tell the examiner, without more, that a *Turnbull* direction will be necessary, gain little credit. You must be able to say what is required by a *Turnbull* direction.

The book provides examples of the kind of questions that are usually asked in an examination, together with model answers and notes about their structure. I have covered the topics that are usually examined. The answers are about the length of an essay that a good student would expect to write under examination conditions. I am aware, however, that the traditional requirement of answering four questions in three hours may not be universally followed. Accordingly, I have presented a fuller answer where it seemed to be useful to do so. The final chapter has some hints on revision and examination techniques.

I hope that this book may be of value as a way of achieving an overall view of this subject. The emphasis on criminal evidence is intentional; it is here that the subject is most lively and this is reflected in examination questions. I hope that the book will be useful as a means of revision, provided it is remembered that revision of particular topics should be a process that continues throughout the year.

I considered dedicating it 'to those who have better things to do', but gravitas prevailed. I like to think, though, that it will be helpful not only to those whose devotion to their mistress the law is total, but to those who spread their favours more widely: to student poets and musicians, to actors and oarsmen and to many more. Nor do I forget those mature students, often with widely different concerns in their daily work, whose opportunity for study is inevitably limited. To all my readers I wish enjoyment and success.

Christopher Allen
July 2010

1 Basic Concepts

INTRODUCTION

The biggest obstacle to doing well in an evidence examination is failure to realise that this is very largely a practical subject, and that when you are faced with a problem question you need to think as carefully about the facts as about the law – perhaps even more carefully, because quite often what you think about the facts will affect the legal position. It would therefore be a good idea to make it a rule that you think about a problem question first as a story.

Somebody is trying to prove something. How is he doing this? First, he should have in mind a clear idea of what is to be proved. Suppose we take a famous murder trial that took place in 1910 – that of Dr Crippen. The prosecution was trying to prove that Crippen had murdered his wife. The story, according to them, was that Crippen had fallen in love with his young secretary, Ethel Le Neve, and had decided to kill his wife so as to leave him free to marry Ethel. One night, therefore, he put poison in a glass of stout – his wife's regular nightcap. The poison might have been sufficient to kill her, or it might merely have rendered her unconscious. At any rate, by the time Crippen had finished with the body she must have been dead. According to the prosecution, he cut the flesh from the bones and buried it in pieces in the cellar of the house where they lived. He burned the bones, and the head was never found. To explain his wife's absence, he told friends at first that she was staying with relations. Later, when the police began to make inquiries, he told them that she had left him and that he had been too embarrassed to tell people this. Crippen had not yet been arrested, and shortly after his interview with the police, he hurriedly left the country with Ethel Le Neve. Meanwhile, the police dug up the cellar floor and discovered the human remains that had been buried there. Crippen was followed and brought back to England to stand trial.

You know, of course, what constitutes murder in English law. But from the standpoint of someone studying evidence, you must now decide precisely what it was that the prosecution had to prove in this particular case.

The first thing they had to prove was that Mrs Crippen was dead. Crippen maintained throughout that his wife had left him and that he knew nothing of the remains in the cellar. It was therefore necessary for the prosecution to establish that the remains were those of Mrs Crippen. They had also to show that her husband had killed her intentionally.

It is at this stage that the prosecution had to start thinking carefully in terms of relevance. Ideally, each item of evidence they presented should have had a probative job to do in the overall task of proving that Crippen had murdered his wife. For example, by proving that Mrs Crippen had had the mark of an operation on her body, and by showing that one of the pieces of buried flesh had the same mark, the prosecution was able to establish that the remains in the cellar were those of Mrs Crippen and that therefore she was in fact dead.

The evidence of Crippen's flight was also relevant, but it's worth pausing to consider why this was so. What probative job did this item of evidence do for the prosecution? The prosecution suggested that it showed guilty knowledge. But why should it do that? One answer is that people who suddenly leave the country when the police are making inquiries about them are likely to do so because they fear that their criminal activities are about to be discovered.

Notice two important points at this stage. The first is that if you press sufficiently the question why an item of evidence is relevant, your explanation will often take the form of a generalisation about the way things are in the world *which itself may or may not be true*. I tried to make my explanatory generalisation about people who run away appear true by using the words 'are likely to do so'. It leaves room for alternative explanations – they may be innocent but fear that the police will frame them; they may have a rich aunt dying in Brazil – but I put my explanation forward as one that is likely. If I am right in this, it follows that the evidence of the flight was relevant, admissible and had significant probative weight.

Now, let's look at a question of relevance in another famous murder case. Edith Thompson and her husband were not very happily married. They took in a young lodger, Freddie Bywaters. One night, when Mr and Mrs Thompson were walking home, Freddie sprang out from a place where he had been waiting and stabbed Mr Thompson to death. But the prosecution story was that Freddie was not the only culprit. He and Edith, it was alleged, were having an affair, and she had plotted the murder with him and had encouraged him to carry it out.

Among the many items of evidence relied on at trial by the prosecution was the disparity in age between Freddie and Edith. She was 28 years old at the time of the murder; he was only 20. What was the relevance of this? What probative job did this information do? At the time, nobody seems to have had any clear thoughts on the matter. But we need to ask this question: what generalisation about the way things are in the world has to be true for this item of evidence to be relevant? Here is a suggestion: 'In a sexual relationship, an older woman is likely to dominate a younger man.' That, if true, would help the prosecution because it would add to the probability that Edith persuaded Freddie to murder Mr Thompson. But *is* it true? If it is not true, and no satisfactory substitute can be found, then surely the evidence is irrelevant, and so inadmissible. (See Twining, W, *Theories of Evidence: Bentham and Wigmore*, 1985, pp 143–144; and Twining, W, *Rethinking Evidence: Exploratory Essays*, 1994, pp 290–293.)

I said earlier that there were two important points to be made about the sort of answer that I suggested to the question of why evidence of Crippen's flight was relevant at his trial. One was the point that I have just been making about the *form* the answer takes – that of a generalisation. The second important point is this. The weaker a generalisation is, the more likely it is to be true. But the weaker the generalisation, the less probative weight will attach to the item of evidence in question. This may be very important where admissibility depends on assessing the probative weight of a piece of evidence and the improperly prejudicial effect that it might have on a jury if they heard it. For example, some cats are Siamese. I have three cats. But, this is not much evidence that I have a Siamese cat. One or more of them *may* be a Siamese, but the likelihood is not great because there are many other breeds, as well as non-pedigree cats.

Later, you will see the importance in other areas of evidence law of the question: What is the probative job that this item of evidence is put forward to do? (Hearsay is a particularly good example. See Chapters 4 and 5.) But being able to answer this question, and being able to say why an item of evidence is relevant by pointing to an appropriate generalisation, can be done only if you have first thought carefully about the *story* the examiner is telling you in the particular problem question.

If you get a question directly on relevance in the examination, it will almost certainly be an essay question involving theory, and I have tried in the answer to Question 1 to give some idea of how such an essay might be tackled. But you don't *have* to be able to write an answer to a theoretical question about relevance to do well in an examination. What you *do* have to be able to do is understand how the idea *works*.

As well as relevance, there are a few other basic concepts that you ought to know about; I have referred to these in the Checklist and you should find them adequately dealt with in your textbook. You will find that this is a subject that has attracted quite a complicated terminology, about the use of which there is not complete agreement on the part of either judges or writers. A lot of this terminology can in practice be avoided, but you should take care to understand how the writer of the textbook you are using employs his terminology, and you should be particularly careful when reading cases to make sure that you understand what a particular judge is getting at by the language he uses.

Checklist ✔

Students should be familiar with the following areas:

- relevance;
- admissibility;
- what facts are in issue in criminal cases;
- how to discover what facts are in issue in a civil case;
- formal admissions in civil and criminal cases;
- judicial notice.

QUESTION 1

Is a concept of legal relevance useful in the law of evidence?

Answer Plan

Begin by setting out the two different ways in which a legal concept can be 'useful': one is connected with what the law is, the other with what it ought to be. The question raises a classic problem on which the two great American writers on evidence, Thayer and Wigmore, had different views; these are outlined. Note that there are some cases where judges do appear to have laid down rules about what is or is not relevant and at least one occasion where Parliament has tried to do so. Note also the practice of the courts of rejecting evidence of only minimal weight on the ground that it is 'irrelevant'. But, the point is then made that none of this justifies acknowledging a concept of 'legal relevance' in existing law because:

- ❖ such a concept would be impossible to define; and
- ❖ it would be difficult to develop a body of case law on the subject.

In addition, such a concept would be undesirable because:

- ❖ if a body of case law could after all be developed, it would be cumbersome and restrictive;

❖ it would make it even more difficult than it is at present for the law to respond to changing conditions.

In summary, therefore, the essay is constructed as follows:

❖ two ways in which a legal concept can be 'useful';
❖ outline of the argument to be put forward;
❖ Thayer's rejection of 'legal relevance';
❖ Wigmore's contrary view;
❖ judicial decisions about relevance, for example, *DPP v Camplin* (1978); *DPP v Majewski* (1977);
❖ the connection made by courts between relevance and weight;
❖ apparent 'rules' about relevance: *Grant* (1996); *Halpin* (1996); *Guney* (1998);
❖ difficulties presented by 'legal relevance'.

ANSWER

A legal concept may be useful either because it helps us to understand the law as it is, or because if it were to be introduced, it would improve the state of the law. I shall argue that a concept of legal relevance is scarcely to be found in the existing state of the law, and that it would not be useful to introduce it.

Thayer defined the law of evidence as 'a set of rules and principles affecting judicial investigations into questions of fact', but he pointed out that these rules and principles do not regulate the process of reasoning, save to the extent of helping to select the factual material upon which the processes of reasoning are to operate. Chiefly, in addition to prescribing the manner of presenting evidence and fixing the qualifications and privileges of witnesses, these rules and principles determine what classes of things shall not be received in evidence. There is one principle of exclusion, however, which Thayer described as not so much a rule of evidence as a presupposition involved in the very conception of a rational system of evidence: this was the principle which forbids receiving anything irrelevant.[1] But the law, according to Thayer, furnishes no test of relevance. For this, it tacitly refers to logic and general experience, the principles of which are presumed to be known.

Wigmore, on the other hand, questioned the idea that the law furnished no test of relevance. He argued that although relevance is originally a matter of logic and

---

1 Cf *Turner* (1975), *per* Lawton LJ: 'Relevance, however, does not result in evidence being admissible: it is a condition precedent to admissibility.'

common sense, there are still many instances in which the evidence of particular facts as bearing on particular issues has been so often the subject of discussion in courts of law, and so often ruled upon, that the united logic of a great many judges and lawyers may be said to furnish evidence of the sense common to a great many individuals, and so to acquire the authority of law. It is thus proper, he argued, to talk of legal relevance.

It is certainly the case that in some instances, judges have laid down rules about what is relevant or irrelevant. For example, they have decided that age and sex are always relevant when considering the defence of provocation (*DPP v Camplin* (1978)). And intoxication is, as a matter of law, irrelevant in considering whether the *mens rea* for a crime of basic intent was present (*DPP v Majewski* (1977)). And in **s 41** of the **Youth Justice and Criminal Evidence Act 1999** Parliament attempted to lay down what the government minister in the House of Lords referred to as 'a statutory framework for determining relevance' in trials where a sexual offence is alleged.

But, apart from specific rules such as these, it is necessary to take into account the practice of the courts of rejecting evidence that has minimal weight on the ground that it is 'irrelevant'. Is this because the evidence falls short of the minimum requirement of something that can be called 'legal relevance'? There are good reasons why data of very slight weight should be excluded. Doing justice according to law is not the same as doing a piece of historical research. Concessions have to be made to what Justice Holmes referred to as 'the shortness of life', as well as to the financial resources of the litigants or the legal aid fund. Moreover, if the field of judicial inquiry were too wide, it might make decisions more unreliable because a mass of evidence would more readily lead to confusion.[2]

It is also possible for the courts to develop something that can appear at first glance to be a rule about relevance in a particular type of situation, but which is really something else. Over the last few years, there has been a cluster of cases concerned with the precise significance to be attached to the discovery of large sums of cash in the possession of persons charged with possession of drugs with intent to supply. In one of these cases, *Grant* (1996), it was said in the Court of Appeal that if there was any possible reason other than drug dealing for the defendant's possession of cash, the finding of the cash was to be treated as irrelevant, and juries should be so directed. And, in *Halpin* (1996), the Court of Appeal said that evidence of a defendant's possession of large amounts of money, or of his extravagant lifestyle, could not be relevant where the issue in the case was possession, rather than intent to supply. However, this was later rejected in *Guney* (1998), where the Court of Appeal said that although evidence of cash or lifestyle might only rarely be relevant where there was a charge of simple possession of drugs, such

---

2   Cf the observations of Lord Bridge in *Blastland* (1986).

evidence could not be excluded as irrelevant as a matter of law. The relevance of any item of evidence is to be decided 'not on abstract legal theory but on the circumstances of each individual case' (see also *Griffiths* (1998)). It appears that the courts, at any rate, are reluctant to acknowledge a concept of 'legal relevance', higher and stricter than logical relevance. In fact, two main difficulties lie in the way of such development.

The first is that a concept of this kind would defy definition. The second is that since each case would be decided on its own facts, there would be considerable difficulty in developing a body of case law about what was legally relevant. The examples cited earlier of *DPP v Camplin* and *DPP v Majewski* are better seen as defining the substantive law in relation to particular offences than in saying something about a concept called 'legal relevance'.[3]

Not only does there seem to be little support for the proposition that a concept of legal relevance – despite the language of some judges – can be found in the law; there appear to be good reasons why such a concept should not be recognised.

In the first place, there is an inherent conflict between a theory that all logically relevant evidence should be admitted unless excluded by a clear ground of policy, and a theory of legal relevance, which would require a minimum quantity of probative value for each item of evidence in any particular case. There is a danger that a concept of legal relevance, if consistently applied, would exclude logically relevant evidence unless legal precedent authorised its admission. If, despite difficulties, a body of case law were to develop, it would give rise to a large number of cumbersome rules and exceptions.

The second reason why a concept of legal relevance ought not to be recognised is that to fix relevance in a straitjacket of case law would make it even more difficult than it already is to adapt the law to changing circumstances.

Necessarily, judges' decisions about relevance reflect the prevailing value judgments of the society in which they live. Relevance can become a useful instrument for discarding arguments and evidence that challenge important, though perhaps unexpressed, values. Thus, in the 19th century, the courts upheld a notion of freedom of contract, which allowed them to argue that an aggrieved worker could have protected his position by insisting on an appropriate contractual stipulation. Evidence of inequality of bargaining power would have been ruled 'irrelevant'. That what is relevant depends on the basic assumptions of a particular society becomes even clearer when one considers the

---

3   But see **s 41** of the **Youth Justice and Criminal Evidence Act 1999**. It looks very much as if the government accepted that some facts can be *logically* relevant, but, to preserve a 'balance' between the interests of the complainant and the defendant, they are not allowed to be *legally* relevant.

evidential significance of marks on the bodies of those formerly suspected of witchcraft, or of the appearance in their vicinity of such creatures as a cat, a toad or a wasp.[4]

No one, of course, could argue a case from a standpoint wholly outside the beliefs of his own society. And it may well be that arguments about relevance will be constrained by the way in which the substantive law is defined. What one can reasonably hope is that the ability to argue from a critical standpoint in particular cases should not be easily frustrated. A further obstacle in the way of such arguments would be likely to emerge if a concept of legal relevance were to become fully developed in the law of evidence.[5]

A concept of legal relevance could also lead to unfairness to defendants, who might be prevented from adducing relevant and weighty evidence in support of their defence. This was recognised, in effect, by the House of Lords in *A* (2001), when the law lords interpreted **s 41** of the **Youth Justice and Criminal Evidence Act 1999** in the light of the **Human Rights Act 1998** and the defendant's right to a fair trial under **Art 6** of the **European Convention on Human Rights**.

QUESTION 2

How satisfactory is the law on judicial notice?

Answer Plan

The law on this subject is in a mess – albeit an interesting one. The following points should be made:

- the distinction (if any) between taking judicial notice and using local or special knowledge;
- the different rationales that have been suggested for judicial notice;
- the effect of those rationales on the way the law is viewed;
- the failure of English law to commit itself unequivocally to a single rationale;
- the ambiguity of the relationship between judicial notice and evidence.

---

4   Thomas, K, *Religion and the Decline of Magic*, 1971, p 530.
5   See Thayer, JB, *A Preliminary Treatise on Evidence at the Common Law*, 1898, Chapter 6; James, GF, 'Relevancy, probability and the law' (1941) 29 *California Law Review* 689, pp 689–705; Trautman, HL, 'Logical or legal relevancy – a conflict in theory' (1952) 5 *Vanderbilt Law Review* 385, pp 385–413; Weyrauch, WO, 'Law as mask – legal ritual and relevance' (1978) 66 *California Law Review* 699, pp 699–726.

ANSWER

The problem with the law of judicial notice is that it is underdeveloped. As a result of this, there is confusion about the principles on which it rests and about its scope.

There is confusion about its scope because it is unclear whether a distinction should be made between taking judicial notice and using special or local knowledge. In *Wetherall v Harrison* (1976), the Divisional Court held that magistrates were entitled to use their own special or local knowledge when trying cases, but Lord Widgery CJ saw this as a necessary concession to the layman's inability to exclude such factors from his deliberations. He thought that, in this respect, magistrates were unlike trained judges and were more like members of a jury. In line with this approach, the Divisional Court in *Bowman v DPP* (1990) said that a bench of magistrates using its local knowledge of a particular piece of land was not taking 'judicial notice'. But in *Mullen v Hackney LBC* (1997), the Court of Appeal held that a county court judge had been entitled to take judicial notice of his own special or local knowledge about the defendant council's failure to honour undertakings given to the court in other cases. This decision was almost certainly wrong. There is a line of cases to the effect that county court judges can rely on their own local knowledge 'properly and within reasonable limits': see, for example, *Reynolds v Llanelly Tinplate Co Ltd* (1948). But all these cases were decided under the **Workmen's Compensation Acts**, under which the county court judge sat as an arbitrator. There is no doubt that an arbitrator can, in certain circumstances, make use of his own knowledge and experience to determine issues in dispute between the parties to the arbitration, without hearing expert evidence. This was held to be within the judge's powers under those Acts: see, for example, *Peart v Bolckow Vaughan & Co Ltd* (1925). But the cases do not establish that county court judges sitting in any other capacity have the same freedom that they had as arbitrators in workmen's compensation cases. Nor do those cases suggest that judges were taking 'judicial notice' of anything.

There are two main theories about the rationale of judicial notice. On one view, it is a device for filtering out evidence about matters that are really unarguable. If you regard judicial notice in this light, you will tend to want its scope to be restricted to notorious, or readily ascertainable facts; its application to be mandatory rather than discretionary; and the effect of its application conclusive.[1]

Another view is that judicial notice is simply a labour saving device in litigation. If seen in this way, its scope can be wider, and its application discretionary. Its effect can even

---

1 Morgan, EM, *Some Problems of Proof under the Anglo-American System of Litigation*, 1956, p 42.

be defeasible in the light of further evidence.[2] A controversial variant of this view is that any process of judicial reasoning about facts assumes the truth of a mass of material that has not been formally proved. For example, a judge assumes that trains run on rails, that France is outside the United Kingdom, and that there is a law of gravity. If this analysis is right, 'the tacit applications of the doctrine of judicial notice are more numerous and more important than the express ones'.[3] But this is a controversial view. Others have acknowledged that both judges and juries must make use of general knowledge to interpret evidence. But, they argue, this is not a question of judicial notice; it is the tribunal relying on its own experience of the ordinary course of human affairs.[4]

A limited view of judicial notice should require mandatory application. This line has been taken in cases relating to political and constitutional matters. For example, in *Duff Development Co Ltd v Government of Kelantan* (1924), the House of Lords said that where the question of the sovereignty of a foreign State is in issue, it is the practice of the courts to treat as conclusive the information that they obtain on the matter from a Secretary of State. But in other cases the courts have taken the view that they have discretion whether or not to take judicial notice of a particular fact. In *George v Davies* (1911), for example, it was tacitly accepted by the Divisional Court that a judge had discretion to decide whether to take judicial notice of an employment custom that had been established by evidence in earlier cases.

A further problem with judicial notice is its relationship to evidence. Where judicial notice is taken without inquiry, for example, that cats are kept for domestic purposes (*Nye v Niblett* (1918)) or that people who go to hotels do not like having their nights disturbed (*Andreae v Selfridge & Co Ltd* (1938)), it is clear that no process of proof is involved, because no material containing information is produced by either party. But is judicial notice after inquiry based on a process of proof? The opinions of judges have been divided. In *McQuaker v Goddard* (1940), at least one member of the Court of Appeal (Clauson LJ) took the view that a judge was entitled to disregard the rules of evidence and look at materials that would otherwise have been inadmissible, on the basis that he was merely 'refreshing his memory' about the ordinary course of nature – a subject of which, by a legal fiction, judges had complete knowledge.

It is clearly unsatisfactory to have a situation where it is unclear whether rules about admissibility are going to be applied or not. The truth of the matter is that, in principle, scope and effect, the law about judicial notice is underdeveloped and ripe for clarification.

---

2 Thayer, JB, *A Preliminary Treatise on Evidence at the Common Law*, 1898, p 278.
3 Tapper, C, *Cross & Tapper on Evidence*, 11th edn, 2007, p 93.
4 See, for example, Eggleston, R (Sir), *Evidence, Proof and Probability*, 2nd edn, 1983, pp 143–144.

BASIC CONCEPTS   13

QUESTION 3

The police suspect that Alex and Ben are dealing separately in drugs. They lawfully search Alex's house. There they find a large quantity of cannabis resin hidden behind a wardrobe. They also find £3,420 in cash in Alex's coat pockets, and a pair of diamond earrings worth £35,000 in a jewel box belonging to Alex's wife. Alex tells the police that he frequently smokes cannabis and that the supply was solely for his own use. He adds that he had the cash in his coat because he runs a firm of builders and had to pay his staff their wages that afternoon. He is nevertheless charged with possession of cannabis with intent to supply.

The police lawfully search Ben's house. They find a small amount of cocaine in an old tobacco tin on a shelf in his garage, and £345 in cash in a desk in Ben's study. Ben says, 'I'd no idea there was cocaine in that old tin. It must have been left there by Cedric. He used to be a lodger, and I let him keep his motor cycle in the garage.' The police trace and interview Cedric, who tells them that he has never owned a motor cycle and that he never went into the garage when he was Ben's lodger. Ben is charged with possession of cocaine.

▶ Discuss the evidential issues arising.

Answer Plan

The defendants are not suspected of operating together, so deal with each separately.

Alex

- ❖ You are told that the search was lawful, so there is no point to be taken about improperly obtained evidence. Obviously, evidence of finding the cannabis can be given, and it can be produced as an item of real evidence if necessary. Is there anything the prosecution could do to avoid having to produce the cannabis in court? Is there any reason for the defence to insist that it should be produced?
- ❖ The discovery of the cash in Alex's coat. You must first decide if this is relevant to the prosecution case. If it is relevant, and admissible, what directions should the judge give to the jury about the use they can make of this evidence? The cases of *Wright* (1994) and *Grant* (1996) are helpful here. A first-class answer might refer to the strength of those decisions after the passing of the **Criminal Justice Act 2003**, which has made it much easier to adduce evidence of criminal disposition on the part of the accused.
- ❖ The wife's diamond earrings. Are they relevant? Is there any other evidence of 'lavish lifestyle'? Even if there were, would it be likely to be regarded as relevant? See *Halpin* (1996).

> *Ben*
> - Obviously, evidence can be given of discovering the tin containing cocaine, and it can be produced at trial if necessary.
> - Is the cash in Ben's desk relevant to the charge against him? Remember that though initially he was suspected of supplying, he has been charged with possession only.
> - What is the significance of the evidence that Cedric can give? What direction should the judge give to the jury about it?

ANSWER

The prosecution will have no difficulty in adducing evidence of the search at Alex's house or of the discovery of the cannabis, which should be produced as an item of real evidence, unless the defence is prepared to make a formal admission in respect of its discovery under **s 10** of the **Criminal Justice Act 1967**.

The discovery of the cash in Alex's coat is more problematic. In *Wright* (1994) the discovery of £16,000 in cash and a gold necklace worth about £9,000 was held to be relevant and admissible where the defendant was charged with possession of cocaine with intent to supply. In *Grant* (1996) the defendant, charged with possession of crack cocaine with intent to supply, was found with just over £900 in cash in his possession. The Court of Appeal held that the finding of money in conjunction with a substantial quantity of drugs was capable of being relevant to intent to supply, and could properly be admitted. But a proper direction must be given to the jury about the use to be made of such evidence. Any innocent explanation for possession of the cash must be rejected before its possession can be relevant to the offence of possession with intent to supply. But if innocent explanations are rejected, and the presence of the cash indicates not merely past dealing, but ongoing dealing in drugs, it can be taken into account in deciding whether the prosecution has proved intent to supply. It seems clear that the discovery of the cash will be relevant and admissible, but the jury will have to be satisfied that Alex did not have it for his stated purpose before they can take it into account in deciding whether the prosecution has proved intent to supply. It is unclear whether the judge should now also direct them to be satisfied that the money does not indicate merely past dealing, but is evidence of ongoing dealing. At the time when *Wright* was decided there were severe restrictions on the use of evidence of past matters to show the accused's disposition to commit the offence charged. Since the **Criminal Justice Act 2003** those restrictions have been substantially reduced,[1] and it may now be sufficiently relevant if the cash is evidence only of past dealing.

The wife's diamond earrings would probably be regarded as either irrelevant, or inadmissible as possessing insufficient probative value. She is not charged, and there is no evidence even that they were a present from her husband. In *Halpin* (1996) the Court of Appeal said that a 'lavish lifestyle' would only rarely be relevant to intent to supply drugs found in the possession of the accused, and there is nothing on the facts to show that there was anything other than the earrings to indicate such a lifestyle.

In Ben's case, evidence will be given of the discovery of the cocaine, which can be produced as an item of real evidence in the same way as the earlier discovery at Alex's house. It appears that Ben has given no explanation for the presence of cash in his desk. But it is a relatively small sum; he is not charged with possession with intent to supply; and it is difficult to see how possession of this money could be relevant to the question whether he was also in possession of the cocaine. Cedric's denials of possession of a motor cycle or of using the garage suggest that Ben might have been lying to the police. Cedric would have to give evidence at Ben's trial and the judge would have to warn the jury, in accordance with *Lucas* (1981) and *Burge and Pegg* (1996), that before they can use Cedric's evidence against Ben, they must be satisfied that Ben had indeed lied, and was not simply mistaken, and that even if he had lied, he might have done so for an innocent reason.[2]

Aim Higher ★

1. Don't assume automatically that every piece of information in a problem question is relevant. Be prepared to argue for relevance or irrelevance, using appropriate generalisations about 'the way things are in the world'.
2. It is important to be able to apply the distinction between logical and legal relevance in a problem question. Candidates often assume that if an item of evidence is logically relevant, that is enough, but this is not so, as can be seen, e.g., from the **Youth Justice and Criminal Evidence Act 1999, s 41,** as well as from decisions such as *Blastland* (1986).

---

1 See **ss 101(1)(d)** and **103(1)(a)**.
2 See Chapter 6.

Common Pitfalls

1. Candidates frequently fail to consider the relevance of an item of evidence before considering its admissibility. Examiners expect you to be aware that irrelevant evidence is inadmissible and to show this in a practical way in problem questions.
2. Candidates often fail, when arguing for the relevance of an item of evidence, to identify the generalisation about human behaviour on which they rely. Always make sure this is clearly stated where relevance is likely to be contested; e.g., 'The prosecution will argue that people with an interest in antique silver are more likely to steal antique silver objects than people without that interest.'

Burden and Standard of Proof

INTRODUCTION

The burden and the standard of proof are matters that must be kept distinct, and judges have a duty to direct the jury in respect of each of them. Problems are therefore most likely to arise in criminal jury trials because a wrong direction, or no direction at all, could provide a successful ground of appeal.

You must be able to distinguish between a legal and an evidential burden. The latter is not strictly a burden *of proof* at all. It is best seen as a rule of common sense which says that there must be *some* evidence for a particular issue to become a live one, so that it is fit for consideration by a jury or other tribunal of fact. Because of this, whether an evidential burden has been satisfied or not in a jury trial is a matter for the judge alone, and consequently there should never be a need to refer to it in a summing up.

In civil cases, it will generally be clear from the statements of case where the burden of proof lies. Although you will find fascinating cases where it wasn't clear at all discussed in the textbooks, don't get bogged down with them when you first approach this topic.

It is important to understand why in criminal cases it is impossible to say for certain when the well known *Woolmington* principle will *not* apply. As you will see from the answer to Question 4, there can be no simple list of exceptions.

The *standard* of proof is less likely to occur as an essay topic because it raises too many theoretical issues. For example, should we reduce the standard of proof in (some) criminal cases if there were to be a significant increase in a particularly unpleasant type of crime? Does it make sense to talk of 'standards' of proof at all? Aren't things either proved or not, more or less easily, depending on their inherent probability? All good fun, but not to be attempted in the examination if you haven't studied these problems as part of your course.

What you may get is a 'dud direction' question, covering both burden and standard of proof, where you are asked to examine an excerpt from a summing up and say whether there are grounds for appeal. It is important to remember that there is no magic form of words about either the burden or standard of proof that *must* be used, though judges are wise to follow one of the two accepted forms, and it is clear that some directions will not suffice. It's a good idea to look at the cases which have approved various forms of words so as to get their general sense and compare those with cases where there was held to have been a misdirection.

It is particularly important to remember that the legal burden of proof remains with the prosecution where defences such as provocation, self-defence, duress, non-insane automatism and alibi are in issue. In cases where the defendant *does* have the legal burden of proving something, that burden will be discharged if the civil standard of proof is satisfied. Remember also that where there is a burden on the defence on a particular issue, there cannot also be a burden on the prosecution on that same issue. Sometimes, candidates try to have the best of both worlds and say, for example, that the defence in an offensive weapon case has to prove on the balance of probabilities that there was a reasonable excuse, and the prosecution has to prove beyond reasonable doubt that there was not. This is gibberish.

Checklist ✔

Students should be familiar with the following areas:

- the distinction between the burden and standard of proof;
- the meaning of 'evidential burden';
- factors affecting the burden of proof in civil cases;
- the burden of proof in criminal cases;
- the standard of proof in civil and criminal cases.

QUESTION 4

When will the imposition of a legal burden on an accused person be compatible with **Art 6(2)** of the **European Convention on Human Rights**?

Answer Plan

Note, first, that the question is about the developments after the **Human Rights Act**. It should be obvious, therefore, that a discussion of the law before that Act will be irrelevant. And don't try to make it appear relevant by saying that in order to understand recent developments it's necessary to look at the development of the law since *Woolmington*! In this case it's not. The following points could be made:

- the basic principle established in *Salabiaku v France* (1988);
- the six factors that may be taken into account, supported by reference to decided cases, when deciding whether a reverse burden is compatible with the **European Convention on Human Rights**:
  - the distinction between *mala in se* and *mala prohibita* in relation to offences;
  - deference to Parliament's decision;
  - a distinction between elements of the offence and defences;
  - maximum penalties;
  - ease of proof and defendant's peculiar knowledge;
  - the presumption of innocence itself.

ANSWER

Article 6(2) provides that everyone charged with a criminal offence shall be presumed innocent until proved guilty according to law. English law has not consistently followed the 'golden thread' principle referred to in *Woolmington v DPP* (1935). There are statutes expressly providing that an accused shall bear the burden of proof in relation to some matter; other statutes have in the past been interpreted as doing so by implication. Since the passing of the **Human Rights Act 1998**, it has become clear that not every reversal of the burden of proof will infringe **Art 6(2)** of the **European Convention on Human Rights**, but that each statutory provision must be considered on its merits. The European jurisprudence accepts that reverse burdens do not infringe **Art 6(2)** so long as they are confined within reasonable limits, which take into account the importance of what is at stake and maintain the rights of the defence (*Salabiaku v France* (1988)). Prediction has become an uncertain task, but Dennis has identified six elements that may be taken into account in reaching a decision where the court is faced with legislation that apparently reverses the burden of proof in any respect.[1]

The first element is based on a classification of offences that distinguishes, in the traditional terminology, between *mala in se* and *mala prohibita*. For example, in *Lambert* (2002) Lord Clyde said that a strict responsibility might be acceptable in the case of statutory offences that were concerned to regulate the conduct of a particular activity in the public interest. A licence could be required to carry out certain activities,

---

1 Ian Dennis, 'Reverse Onuses and the Presumption of Innocence: In Search of Principle,' [2005] *Criminal Law Review* **901–936**.

or controls might be imposed to promote health and safety and avoid pollution. Such cases, he said, could properly be seen as not truly criminal. Many might be relatively trivial and carry no real social disgrace. This approach was adopted by the Court of Appeal in *Davies* (2002), where the Court upheld **s 40** of the **Health and Safety at Work Act 1974**. This provision imposed a legal burden on a defendant to prove that it had not been reasonably practicable to do more than he had done to ensure that employees were not exposed to risks to their health and safety. The difficulty with classification of offences as a criterion for reverse burdens of proof is, as Dennis pointed out, that the moral quality of regulatory offences is variable. For example, where a regulatory offence leads to someone's death, as was the case in *Davies*, it might not be easy to maintain that the breach involved no real social disgrace. The same could also be true of a regulatory offence that led to widespread pollution of the environment.

A second consideration is the deference that should be shown to Parliament's decision. In *Lambert* (2002) Lord Steyn said that the burden is on the state to show that the legislative means adopted were not greater than necessary. He added that there must be a 'pressing necessity' to impose a legal burden on the accused. But other judges have been more inclined to give weight to the decision of the elected body that passed the legislation. For example, in *R v DPP, ex p Kebilene* (2000) Lord Hope said that such deference would be particularly appropriate where the issues involved questions of social or economic policy. In *Johnstone* (2003) Lord Nicholls pointed out that Parliament had the primary responsibility for deciding, as a matter of policy, what should be the constituent elements of a criminal offence, and courts should reach a different conclusion from the legislature only where it was apparent that the latter had attached insufficient importance to the individual's fundamental right to be presumed innocent until proved guilty.

However, in *Sheldrake v DPP* (2004) Lord Bingham doubted whether there should be an assumption that Parliament would not have made an exception to the basic rule without good reason. Such an approach might lead the court to give too much weight to the enactment under review, and too little to the presumption of innocence. Dennis has suggested that the court's approach should depend on drawing a clear distinction between the two criteria referred to in *Salabiaku*. Deference to the democratic body should be due when considering whether it was in fact pursuing a legitimate aim; less deference should be due when considering whether a reverse onus was a proportionate method of achieving that aim.

A third consideration is based on drawing a distinction between elements of the offence and available defences. For example, in *A-G of Hong Kong v Lee Kwong-Kut* (1993), a decision of the Privy Council, Lord Woolf said that if the prosecution retains responsibility for proving the essential ingredients of the offence, a reverse burden is more likely to be acceptable. But, recognising the difficulty of isolating the essential ingredients, he added that the substance and reality of the language creating the offence should be regarded, rather than its form.

However, the distinction between elements of an offence and defences has often been criticised. Lord Steyn in *Lambert* said that the distinction would sometimes be 'unprincipled and arbitrary'. He observed that sometimes the distinction was based simply on the drafting technique. A constituent element of an offence can be removed from the definition and cast as a defensive issue. Further, any definition of an offence can be reformulated so as to include all possible defences within it. A good example of the difficulty in applying this criterion is *Hunt* (1987), where an element of the offence was found in what appeared at first sight to be a list of exceptions contained in a statutory instrument that had been made pursuant to powers contained in the primary legislation.

Maximum penalties are another consideration. In *Davies* (2002) Tuckey LJ said that the absence of any risk of imprisonment was 'undoubtedly an important factor' in determining whether there was a legitimate reverse burden of proof. Conversely, in *Lambert* Lord Steyn was clearly influenced by the fact that the maximum sentence was life imprisonment. In *Johnstone* Lord Nicholls said that the more serious the punishment, the more compelling must be the reasons for imposing a reverse burden. But in *Sheldrake* the House of Lords upheld a reverse onus where the maximum penalty for the offence was only six months' imprisonment. Dennis has noted that maximum penalties are a very uncertain guide, and that the nature of the penalty, whether custodial or pecuniary, is not conclusive either way.

The ease of proof and the defendant's peculiar knowledge can also be taken into account. For example, in *ex p Kebilene* Lord Hope said that one of the considerations was the nature of the burden on the accused. Did it relate to something that it was likely to be difficult for him to prove, or to something likely to be within his knowledge or to which he had access? The same point was made by Lord Nicholls in *Johnstone*. On the other hand, as Dennis has pointed out, there are very many cases where the accused's state of mind is of crucial importance, but where the burden of proving it is on the prosecution.

A final consideration is the presumption of innocence itself. As Lord Bingham said in *Sheldrake*, the underlying rationale of the presumption is that it is repugnant to ordinary notions of fairness for a prosecutor to accuse a defendant of crime and for the defendant to be then required to disprove the accusation, on pain of conviction and punishment if he fails to do so. The closer a legislative provision is to that situation, the more objectionable it is likely to be. Approaching the problem from a slightly different angle, Lord Nicholls in *Johnstone* said that a sound starting point for considering a reverse burden in the light of **Art 6(2)** is to remember that if a defendant is required to prove a fact on the balance of probability in order to avoid conviction, a conviction can follow in spite of the fact-finding tribunal having a reasonable doubt as to his guilt.

It will be seen that there can be no straightforward answer to the question initially posed. It is possible to identify a number of considerations, but the weight the court will give to them in any particular case is unlikely to be readily predictable. The problem is substantial. In 1996, 40 per cent of offences triable in the Crown Court appeared to violate the presumption of innocence.[2]

QUESTION 5

Answer all FOUR parts of this question:

(a) Alice was convicted of theft. In her summing up, the judge said to the jury: 'The prosecution brings this case and it is for the prosecution to prove it. Unless, having heard all the evidence, you are sure that the defendant is guilty, she must be acquitted.' Advise Alice whether she has grounds for appeal.

(b) Bertha was convicted of having an offensive weapon with her in a public place, contrary to **s 1** of the **Prevention of Crime Act 1953**. In her summing up, the judge said to the jury: 'Members of the jury, it is not contested that this defendant had with her an offensive weapon in a public place. But she says she had it with her for her own protection. She has to satisfy you that that was a reasonable excuse for having the weapon with her, and unless you are satisfied of that, you must convict.' Advise Bertha whether she has grounds for appeal.

(c) Charlene is charged with murder. There is medical evidence suggesting that she is under a mental disability which renders her unfit to plead and stand trial. What is the law relating to the burden and standard of proof in this situation?

(d) Dora was convicted of wounding with intent to do grievous bodily harm. In her summing up, the judge said to the jury: 'The defence in this case is self-defence. That means that the defendant has an evidential burden, but no more, to satisfy you that what she says about acting in self-defence is more probable than not.' Advise Dora whether she has grounds for appeal.

---

2 Andrew Ashworth and Meredith Blake, 'The Presumption of Innocence in English Criminal Law,' [1996] *Criminal Law Review* 306, 314.

Answer Plan

Part (a) obviously deals with the burden and standard of proof. The question is whether the judge has directed the jury adequately. The answer is that she has, but note how you can show your knowledge effectively to the examiner when saying so. Without being at all irrelevant, the following points can be made:

- the need to provide a correct direction on both the burden and the standard of proof;
- the proper direction on the burden of proof;
- the application of that test to what was said in this case;
- the proper direction on the standard of proof;
- it is not a particular formula but the effect of the summing up as a whole that matters;
- *Kritz* (1950) and *Walters v R* (1969).

Don't forget to advise Alice – this is done in the final sentence.

Part (b) is a bit more complicated. You need to know about **s 1** of the **Prevention of Crime Act 1953**, but this is a fairly well cited example of a statutory provision that expressly puts a burden of proof on the defendant. It is important to remember that a direction on the *burden* of proof and a direction on the *standard* of proof are two different things. The following points should be made:

- whether there has been a correct direction on the burden of proof;
- standard of proof where a burden is placed on a defendant in a criminal trial;
- ambiguity of the language used in Bertha's case.

Part (c) provides an example of the operation of different standards of proof, depending on which side raises the issue.

Part (d) requires you to make the following points:

- basic rule about burden of proof;
- self-defence available as a defence;
- no *legal* burden on the accused;
- the evidential burden.

ANSWER

(a) Every summing up should contain a correct direction on both the burden and the standard of proof (*Bentley (Deceased)* (2001)). Here, there is a direction on each. The judge has rightly told the jury, in effect, that the burden is on the prosecution. No particular form of words is necessary, and this is the clear sense of the words actually used. There has also been a correct direction on the standard of proof. Again, it is not the particular formula that matters, but the effect of the summing up (*Allan* (1969)). One of the well established forms of direction, however, is to tell the jury that in order to find the accused guilty they must be 'sure', or 'satisfied so that they feel sure' (*Kritz* (1950); *Walters v R* (1969)). Here, the former expression has been used. It is entirely adequate and Alice has no grounds for appeal on this part of the summing up.

(b) **Section 1** of the **Prevention of Crime Act 1953** provides a defence of reasonable excuse to a charge of having an offensive weapon in a public place, but the section places the burden of proving this defence on the accused. It would be possible to argue, following *Lambert* (2002), that the effect of **s 1** is to impose only an evidential burden on defendants. But this interpretation is unlikely to be applied. In *L v DPP* (2002), the Divisional Court upheld the traditional interpretation of **s 139** of the **Criminal Justice Act 1988**, saying that there was a strong public interest in bladed articles not being carried in public without good reason, and that it was not obviously offensive to the rights of the individual to require him to prove a good reason for carrying one. The same approach is very likely to be adopted towards having an offensive weapon in a public place. The judge has almost certainly got her direction on burden right. However, in all cases where the law puts a burden of proving something on a defendant, it can be discharged merely by proof on the balance of probabilities – the civil, rather than the criminal standard (*Carr-Briant* (1943)). What has happened here is that the judge has told the jury that Bertha has to 'satisfy' them that she had a reasonable excuse. But this is ambiguous, for it could refer either to the civil or to the higher criminal standard (*Hepworth* (1955)). Thus, the jury might have applied the wrong standard in deciding whether Bertha had made out her defence. Accordingly, she has a good ground of appeal.

(c) The answer depends on who raises the issue.[1] If the prosecution says that Charlene is under this disability and the defence disputes this, the burden of proof will be on the prosecution to satisfy the jury beyond reasonable doubt that its contention is correct (*Robertson* (1968)). If, on the other hand, it is the defence which puts forward this contention and the prosecution disagrees, the defence will have the burden of proof, but only to the civil standard – on a balance of probabilities (*Podola* (1960)).

(d) Where the defendant is charged with wounding with intent to cause grievous bodily harm, the burden of proof, as is usual in criminal cases, rests throughout on

---

1 Either the prosecution or the defence may do so: see **s 4(1)** of the **Criminal Procedure (Insanity) Act 1964**.

the prosecution. In certain circumstances, self-defence may be a defence to this charge, but the accused bears no legal burden on the issue. Thus, in *Lobell* (1957), where the appellant had been convicted on such a charge after the trial judge had directed the jury that it was for the defence to establish its plea of self-defence, the conviction was quashed on the ground that there had been a misdirection. What the defendant does have is an evidential burden, but this means no more than that he must be able to point to some evidence in the trial which makes self-defence a live issue for the jury's consideration. As Lord Morris put it in *Bratty v Attorney-General for Northern Ireland* (1963), where the accused bears the evidential burden alone, he must adduce such evidence as would, if believed and left uncontradicted, induce a reasonable doubt in the mind of the jury as to whether his version might not be true.[2]

Whether a party has discharged an evidential, as opposed to a legal, burden is a matter for the judge and not the jury. It was therefore wrong of the judge to refer to the evidential burden in her summing up. If possible, it was even more wrong to refer in that connection to the standard of proof that is applicable where a defendant has a *legal* burden. The jury have been misled, and Dora has a good ground of appeal.

QUESTION 6

Annie hired a removal firm, XY & Co, to move the contents of her house in Plymouth to a house which she had bought in Worcester. The removal van and all its contents were destroyed by fire in a layby just outside Exeter. Some time after the loss, Annie was told by an employee of XY & Co that the van had been deliberately set on fire so that XY & Co could claim from their insurers for its loss.

Annie is suing XY & Co for the value of her destroyed property, which she estimates to be £250,000. She claims first in respect of their deliberate destruction by the defendants; alternatively, she alleges that they were destroyed by reason of the defendants' negligence. By their defence, XY & Co deny deliberately setting fire to the van and plead that their contract with Annie had an exclusion clause, which said that they would not be liable for loss by fire provided that their servants were not negligent. They also plead that it was a term of the contract that they would not be liable for any loss in excess of £5,000. Annie says that she never agreed to this term and that XY & Co are liable for the full loss.

▶ Discuss the burden and standard of proof in relation to the issues that arise.

---

2 Although Lord Morris used the word 'adduce', this does not mean that the defendant must call such evidence himself. It could be obtained from prosecution witnesses under cross-examination, or it might even emerge during their examination-in-chief. See *L v DPP* (2002).

Answer Plan

The first step is to sort out what the issues are likely to be. A rough and ready way of doing this is to think of what matters each side would have to prove in order to win, assuming there is no response from their opponents.

Annie must prove the existence of the agreement with the defendants for the carriage of her goods, the consignment of her goods to the defendants in accordance with the agreement, the fact that non-delivery was due to deliberate destruction of the goods by the defendants, and the amount of the loss. In view of the exclusion clause, the burden of proof in relation to negligence is uncertain.

The defendants must prove the existence of the exclusion clause and, if need be, that the loss falls within it. They may also have to prove that they exercised all proper care of the goods while they were in their possession. In addition, they will have to show that the provision limiting their liability to £5,000 was part of the contract.

Broadly speaking, it will be seen that this ties in with the maxim that he who asserts must prove, but there are problems with the interpretation of the exclusion clause that require discussion of bailment.

The allegation of arson raises the question of the standard to be applied where a crime is alleged in a civil action.

ANSWER

Although the burden of proof in any particular case depends on the circumstances under which the claim arises, in a civil action, the burden normally lies on the party who affirms something to be the case, and not upon the party who makes a denial. As Viscount Maugham said in *Constantine (Joseph) Steamship Line Ltd v Imperial Smelting Corp Ltd* (1942), it is 'an ancient rule founded on considerations of good sense and it should not be departed from without strong reasons'.

Annie will therefore bear the legal burden of establishing the essential elements of her claim. With one exception, these are readily defined.

She will first have to prove the existence of a contract made between herself and the defendants for the carriage by the defendants of her goods from Plymouth to Worcester. She will then have to prove that, pursuant to this contract, she consigned her goods to the defendants. Her principal claim is that the defendants deliberately destroyed her goods by fire whilst they had possession of them. Clearly, the burden of proving this rests on Annie. She will also have to prove the value of the goods that have been lost.

Since this is a civil action, all these matters will have to be proved according to 'the preponderance of probability' (*Miller v Minister of Pensions* (1947)). Even where Annie is alleging matters that would amount to the criminal offence of arson, she does not have to prove them beyond reasonable doubt. In *Hornal v Neuberger Products Ltd* (1957), the plaintiff was sold a lathe by the defendants. One of their directors was alleged to have stated falsely that the machine had been reconditioned by a named firm. Had this representation been made by the director with knowledge of its falsehood, he would have been guilty of fraudulent misrepresentation. In a civil action for damages for breach of warranty, alternatively for fraud, the trial judge found that the claim in respect of fraud had been proved on the balance of probabilities, but added that he would not have been satisfied had the criminal standard been applicable. The Court of Appeal held that he had correctly applied the civil standard.

In *Hornal*, Denning LJ said that the more serious the allegation, the higher the degree of probability required, and in some later cases, the judge appears to have applied a slightly loaded civil standard.[1] However, Morris LJ said in *Hornal* that the gravity of the allegation was simply part of the whole range of circumstances that had to be weighed when deciding on the balance of probabilities. He did not favour variations of standard in civil cases, and current opinion prefers his view. In *Re H and Others* (1996), the majority of the House of Lords supported the view that the more serious the allegation, the less likely it was to be true, and the weightier the evidence needed for a court to find it proved. But it was emphasised that where a serious allegation was in issue, the standard of proof was not higher than the ordinary civil standard. If a third standard were to be substituted in some civil cases, it would be necessary to identify what that standard was, and when it applied. Confusion and uncertainty would result. Any earlier observations to the contrary were not accurate statements of the law.

As an alternative to deliberate destruction, Annie pleads negligence on the part of the defendants. Does she have the legal burden of proving this? Two arguments might be used to show that she does. It could be said that this is just another instance of the application of the basic maxim that it is for the person who affirms something to be the case to bear the burden in respect of that issue. The defendants might also argue by analogy from the way in which an exclusion clause was interpreted in

---

1 See, for example, *The Michael* (1979).

The Glendarroch (1894). In that case, the plaintiffs claimed damages from shipowners for the latter's failure to carry goods safely. The shipowners relied on an exemption clause that excluded their liability for loss or damage occasioned by perils of the sea. It was held that the defendants had the burden of proving this provision and that the loss fell within it, but that the plaintiffs, who wished to rely on a proviso to the exemption clause that excluded its operation in the event of the shipowners' negligence, had the burden of establishing that the facts were such as to bring the proviso into effect.

There is, however, an argument that, instead of Annie's having to prove negligence, the defendants have a burden to show that they used all proper care in the carriage of the goods. This is the basic common law rule in cases of bailment for reward, of which this contract is an instance. It could be argued that any ambiguity as to the burden of proof should be resolved in Annie's favour because this basic principle has not been clearly excluded, and its rationale is clearly present here: after the goods were consigned to the defendants, they, and not Annie, were in a better position to explain what happened to them. This was a consideration that proved persuasive in *Levison v Patent Steam Carpet Cleaning Ltd* (1978). In this case, the defendant carpet cleaners lost the plaintiff's Chinese carpet in unexplained circumstances. A clause in the contract would have exempted them from liability for negligence, but not for any fundamental breach of contract. The burden of proof on the latter issue was held by the Court of Appeal to lie on the defendants. They had to show that they had not been guilty of fundamental breach because they could more easily discharge this burden than could a plaintiff who had a burden to prove that there had been such a breach.

It will of course be for XY & Co to establish the existence of the exclusion clause and, if need be, that the goods were destroyed by fire. Similarly, if they wish to rely on the limitation of damages clause, they will have to prove it formed part of the contract.

QUESTION 7

After a vigorous press campaign prompted by a sudden increase in accidents to customers in book shops, Parliament passes a new piece of legislation: the **Readers (Protection) Act**. **Section 1** provides: 'A book shop owner shall be guilty of an offence if any person suffers injury while on the book shop owner's premises.' **Section 2** provides: 'No offence is committed under **s 1** if the book shop owner took reasonable precautions to prevent the injury from occurring.' The Act provides that a book shop owner shall be liable on conviction on indictment to an unlimited fine, the closure of his premises for such period as the court shall think fit, and to a sentence of imprisonment for a maximum of two years. Fergus, the owner of a book shop, has been charged under **s 1** of the Act after Gerald, a customer, fell downstairs and broke three ribs while moving from one floor of Fergus's shop to another. Fergus says that he took reasonable precautions to prevent injury to customers by ensuring that the stairs were well lit. He says that when he went to Gerald's assistance he could smell alcohol on Gerald's breath. He suspects that the reason for Gerald's fall was that he was unsteady on his feet after drinking too much at lunch on the day in question.

◗ Advise Fergus on the burden of proof.

Answer Plan

The problem raises two substantial questions of interpretation; you are going to have to be selective in the amount of law to which you refer. At the same time, you must be careful to apply the law to the facts that you have been given.

The first question to deal with is whether the statute imposes an implied reversal of the burden of proof. At this stage you do not have to consider **Art 6(2)** of the **European Convention on Human Rights**. If you can persuade the judge that the effect of **s 2** is to provide an essential element of the offence, the prosecution will have to prove that Fergus failed to take reasonable precautions; there will be no burden on the defendant at all.

Start with **s 101** of the **Magistrates' Courts Act 1980**, and show by reference to *Edwards* that its principles apply in this case. *Hunt* is an obvious case on which to rely so as to show that there is some flexibility in applying the **s 101** principles. Refer to Lord Griffiths's guidelines and try to apply them in this situation.

Then turn to the problem that will arise if the judge holds that the effect of **s 2** *is* to impose a reverse burden on the defendant. Will that be compatible with **Art 6(2)**? Again, there are guidelines to which you can refer, and which can be found in cases such as *ex p Kebilene*, *Lambert*, *Davies*, and *Johnstone*. Remember to try to apply these guidelines to the facts that you have been given. You should come to some conclusion, but there can be no question of its being right or wrong. The decision could go either way.

ANSWER

The first question that arises is whether **s 1** of the Act creates an offence to which **s 2** can be relied on as a defence, or whether the sections must be read together, so that the book shop owner's failure to take reasonable precautions is one of the elements of the offence. If the latter is the correct interpretation, the prosecution will have the burden of proving beyond reasonable doubt that there had been a failure to take reasonable precautions. If the first suggestion is correct, the court will have to consider whether any, and if so what, burden has been imposed by Parliament on the defendant.

Section 101 of the **Magistrates' Courts Act 1980** can be taken as a convenient starting point. Although the offence with which Fergus is charged is triable only on indictment, it was held in *Edwards* (1975) that **s 101** was a statutory statement of the common law applicable in all criminal courts. **Section 101** provides that where the defendant relies for his defence on any 'exception, exemption, proviso, excuse or qualification', whether or not it is part of the description of the offence, the burden of proving such a defence shall be on him.

However, as Lawton LJ observed in *Edwards*, when applying this principle it is necessary to 'construe the enactment under which the charge is laid'. This was subsequently emphasised by the House of Lords in *Hunt* (1987). In that case the prosecution proved that the defendant had been in possession of powder containing morphine, but their evidence did not prove whether the quantity of morphine was more than 0.2 per cent. The relevant legislation exempted from its provisions preparations containing not more than that quantity. The House of Lords held that, on a correct interpretation of the statute, the rule contained in **s 101** of the **Magistrates' Courts Act 1980** did not apply because the 0.2 per cent provision was part of the definition of the offence. The burden therefore lay on the prosecution to prove that the powder contained more than that quantity of morphine. It was not for the defence to show that it contained only 0.2 per cent or less. In reaching this conclusion, the House of Lords said that the classification of defences was not constrained by the form of words used or their location in the statute creating the offence.

Lord Griffiths suggested certain guidelines for interpretation. First, he said that courts should be very slow to classify a defence as falling within **s 101**, because Parliament can never lightly be taken to have intended to impose an onerous duty on a defendant to prove his innocence. Probably the **Readers (Protection) Act** does not impose an onerous duty on owners of book shops. They are the persons most familiar with their premises and are in the best position to do what needs to be done to ensure the safety of their customers. Making sure that your premises are safe can hardly be regarded as an onerous duty.

Secondly, Lord Griffiths said that the ease and difficulty to be encountered by the parties in discharging the legal burden are of great importance. Probably it is no more difficult for a book shop owner to show what precautions he took than for the prosecution to establish that he did not take all reasonable precautions. It may indeed be easier for the book shop owner to establish that he took all reasonable precautions because he is likely to be aware of current practices in his trade. Although following common practice will not conclusively establish that all reasonable precautions were taken, it may go some way towards doing so.

Thirdly, the gravity of the offence should be considered. The more serious the offence, the more likely it will be that any ambiguity will be resolved in favour of the defendant. In this case we note that the offence is triable only on indictment; that an unlimited fine can be imposed; that the premises can be forced to close indefinitely; and that a sentence of imprisonment of two years can also be imposed. The financial penalties are potentially very severe; in contrast the maximum term of imprisonment is light. Taking these matters into consideration, the offence seems not to be among the gravest, though it is by no means trivial.

Although a court might well interpret **s 2** as an essential element of the offence, to be proved by the prosecution, there is some danger that it will be regarded as falling within the **s 101** rule. The question that would then arise is whether it imposes a legal burden on the defendant, or only an evidential burden. If the imposition of a legal burden would infringe **Art 6(2)** of the **European Convention on Human Rights**, it is likely to be interpreted as imposing an evidential burden only.

It was suggested in *Lambert* (2002) and in *Davies* (2002) that a strict responsibility might be placed on a defendant where the legislation was concerned to regulate the conduct of a particular activity in the public interest, for example, to promote health and safety. This might suggest that a legal burden on Fergus would not infringe **Art 6(2)**. On the other hand, it was said in *Davies* that the absence of a risk of imprisonment was an important factor in deciding whether a reverse burden was legitimate. In this case there is a danger of imprisonment.

Deference should be shown to Parliament's decision. In *Johnstone* (2003) Lord Nicholls pointed out that Parliament had the primary responsibility for deciding what should be the constituent elements of an offence, and the courts should depart from this only if satisfied that the legislature had attached insufficient importance to the presumption of innocence. Ease of proof and a defendant's special knowledge can also be taken into account, as Lord Hope observed in *ex p Kebilene* (2000).

It seems on balance likely that if a court decides that the statute does impose a reverse burden on the defendant, it will decide that this is a legal, not just an evidential, burden.

Aim Higher ★

1. Be ready to summarise the principles that the courts take into account when deciding whether to 'read down' a statutory provision that apparently imposes a legal burden of proof on a defendant in a criminal case. Make sure that you can apply those principles to the facts in a problem question.
2. In a question that contains quotations from a fictitious summing-up or ruling on a point of law during the course of a trial, make sure you understand the significance of everything that the judge has said before considering whether it accords with the law. For example, if the judge has given a correct direction on the burden of proof in a criminal case, make sure that he does not later in the quotation say something that is at odds with this direction; e.g., that the defendant has to 'establish' an alibi, when all the defendant has in respect of such a defence is an evidential burden.

Common Pitfalls

1. Far too many candidates fail to recognise an express reversal of the burden of proof when it is stares them in the face in a problem question. If a fictitious statute in a question uses words such as 'the proof whereof shall lie on the defendant' in relation to a defence, it is a waste of time to go into cases on implied reversals.
2. Remember that the leading cases on reverse burdens fall into two categories: those that help the court to decide whether there has been an implied reversal, and those that help the court decide whether to 'read down' a reverse burden – whether express or implied – so as to give effect to the **Human Rights Act 1998**. In each category the cases are usually important for the guidelines and principles that can be found in them, not for the decision on their particular facts.

3 Presumptions, Competence and Compellability

INTRODUCTION

Presumptions fit awkwardly into an evidence course. When lawyers first started to write books on evidence, they used to include large amounts of substantive law on such subjects as trespass, nuisance, bailment, actions on the case, and so forth. The object of these writers was to include not only what we should recognise as rules of evidence, relating to such matters as the competence of witnesses and hearsay, but rules about what had to be proved in order to establish particular claims or defences. There was no unifying principle other than the convenience of the arrangement for practitioners. (See, for example, Gilbert's *The Law of Evidence*, 2nd edn, 1760. This was the leading work on the subject in the second half of the 18th century; the last edition was published in 1801. See generally William Twining, 'The Rationalist Tradition of Evidence Scholarship', in *Rethinking Evidence: Exploratory Essays*, 2nd edn, 2006 pp 35–98.)

Modern evidence textbooks deal with some, but by no means all, presumptions. (See the Checklist for details.) However, this is really no more than a hangover from the older way of writing. No successful attempts have been made to find an all-embracing theme that would make 'presumptions' a true part of evidence law. What you will be looking at will be several quite distinct bits of substantive law that have little or no connection with each other.

Because this is an area where attempts to find unifying features have been made so unsuccessfully, you may find classification confusing. When a writer refers to a presumption, you need to be sure about how he is using the word. The sort of presumption that you will be trying to learn about (of death, legitimacy, etc) is what is often called a 'rebuttable presumption of law'. In my view, it confuses things to talk about anything else as a 'presumption'. If someone refers to a 'presumption of fact' he should mean an *inference* about facts, which is part of an ordinary reasoning process, having nothing specially to do with law at all. And, if he refers to an 'irrebuttable presumption of law', that is just the same as referring to some rule of substantive law.

Thus, to refer to 'the presumption of innocence' is the same thing as referring to the rule that places the burden of proof on the prosecution.

Questions of competence and compellability are mainly governed by statute. You should note that the **Youth Justice and Criminal Evidence Act 1999** contains new provisions relating to the competence of witnesses and their capacity to be sworn in criminal trials (**ss 53–56**). It also amends **s 80** of the **Police and Criminal Evidence Act 1984**. Spouses and children are the obvious subjects for examination questions; for details, see the Checklist.

But note that the protection given to spouses has been extended to civil partners by the **Civil Partnership Act 2004, s 84(1)**.

Checklist ✔

Students should generally be familiar with the following areas but check your syllabus, because it may provide a narrower or wider range:

- classifications of presumptions;
- presumption of marriage;
- presumption of legitimacy;
- presumption of death;
- presumption of regularity;
- *res ipsa loquitur*;
- conflicting presumptions;
- presumptions under **Sexual Offences Act 2003, ss 75–77**;
- general rule of universal competence and compellability;
- how a co-accused can become competent for the prosecution;
- comment on an accused's failure to testify;
- competence and compellability of an accused's spouse: for the prosecution, the accused or a co-accused;
- competence of children in civil and criminal cases.

QUESTION 8

'The theoretical basis for recognising presumptions is that the presumed fact would, in the usual course of events, flow naturally from the existence of the primary fact, so that there is a rational connection between the two so strong that it is unnecessary to require evidence of the presumed fact in the absence of unusual circumstances.'

▸ Discuss.

Answer Plan

This is an essay question that requires you to consider a subject that has already been referred to in the 'Introduction'. Is it possible to say something that is true about the way in which all rebuttable presumptions of law behave? If it is, is this the common factor that is to be found? It is important to emphasise that this question, like many other essay questions, cannot be answered on knowledge of statutes and cases alone. You need to have read something of the theory of the subject, and in order to answer this question, you should at least have read what is said in Tapper, C, *Cross & Tapper on Evidence*, 11th edn, 2007, pp 144–148, and Roberts, P and Zuckerman, A, *Criminal Evidence*, 2004, pp 329–344.

You need to cover the following topics:

- the superficial attractiveness of the proposition;
- presumptions that appear to increase artificially the probative worth of the basic facts, for example, presumption of death;
- presumptions designed simply to resolve difficulties of proof, for example, **s 184(1)** of the **Law of Property Act (LPA) 1925**;
- the argument that all presumptions may operate simply as techniques for allocating the burden of proof;
- the diversity of ways in which the 'same' presumption can operate.

The conclusion is that, at best, the quotation tells only part of the story and it may be positively misleading.

ANSWER

The theoretical basis suggested in the quotation is superficially attractive. For example, according to the presumption of legitimacy, it is presumed that a child born during lawful wedlock is legitimate in the absence of evidence to the contrary (*Hetherington v Hetherington* (1887)). Given the fact of a birth in those circumstances, it would seem most unreasonable not to presume the legitimacy of the child.

But not all presumptions provide such a ready illustration of this sort of rational process. According to the presumption of death, a person will be presumed to have died if it is proved that: (a) there is no acceptable evidence that he has been alive at some time during a continuous period of at least seven years; (b) there are persons likely to have heard of him, had he been alive, who have not heard of him during that period; and (c) all due inquiries have been made with a view to finding the person in question, but without success (*Chard v Chard* (1956)).

The presumption in this case appears to operate so as to increase artificially the probative value of the basic facts in the absence of any contrary evidence. So far as probative worth goes, there is nothing special about seven years' absence as opposed, say, to one of six years. Yet, the former period gives rise to a rebuttable presumption of law, while the latter gives rise to no more than an inference of fact that may be made or not.

In other cases, it seems clear that a presumption has been designed simply in order to resolve a difficulty of proof. An example is **s 184(1)** of the **LPA 1925**. This provides that where two or more persons have died in circumstances rendering it uncertain which of them survived the other or others, such death shall (subject to any order of the court), for all purposes affecting the title to property, be presumed to have occurred in order of seniority and, accordingly, the younger shall be deemed to have survived the elder. Here the probative worth of the basic fact is non-existent; the whole effect of the presumption is to allocate the burden of proof.

It has been suggested in fact that a presumption is in all cases simply a technique whereby the substantive law distributes the risk of losing on a given issue, and that it is misleading to try to develop a rationale based on the probative force of the basic facts of the presumption. This misleading approach, it is argued, leads to the conclusion that presumptions such as that of death are simply presumptions of fact to which the law gives artificial weight. If, however, the rationale of presumptions is to be found in the allocation of the burden of proof, the charge of artificiality is misconceived. The rights of someone who has disappeared cannot remain suspended indefinitely; what the law does is to provide, by a rule affecting the burden of proof, a limitation period. The basic fact may, of course, have some probative weight, but it has this by virtue of common sense and experience rather than by virtue of the presumption.[1]

This view of presumptions as devices for allocating the burden of proof receives considerable support from the fact that a particular presumption does not always affect the burden of proof in exactly the same way; the way in which a presumption

---

1 Paul Roberts and Adrian Zuckerman, *Criminal Evidence* (Oxford: Oxford University Press, 2004) p 343.

operates depends on the context in which it may be relevant. This would not be the case if, from a primary fact, there flowed naturally in the usual course of events a particular presumed fact. One would expect a rational process such as that to operate regardless of context.

That this is not the case is shown by the operation of presumptions in a criminal context. According to the presumption of regularity, upon proof of the fact that some official or public act has been performed, or that a person acted in an official capacity, it is presumed that the act which was done complied with any necessary formalities, or that the person so acting had been properly appointed. In *Dillon* (1982), a police officer had been charged in Jamaica with the offence of negligently permitting two prisoners, lawfully in his custody, to escape. The prosecution failed to call any evidence to show that the officer had authority to hold the prisoners in custody, a matter which they had the burden of proving. On a defence submission of no case to answer, the magistrate held that the prosecution was entitled to rely on the presumption of regularity to establish that such authority existed. This decision was upheld by the Court of Appeal of Jamaica but rejected by the Privy Council, which held that the prosecution was not entitled to rely on a presumption to establish a central element of the offence.

There seems little doubt that the presumption of legitimacy would also affect the burden of proof in different ways, depending on the nature of the proceedings. In a civil case, once birth in lawful wedlock is established, the court must find the child legitimate unless the party opposing legitimacy proves on the balance of probabilities that the child is illegitimate.[2] But suppose a defendant is charged with committing incest with his daughter and his defence is that, though conceived and born in wedlock, she is actually the child of another man. It is most unlikely to be held that the defendant has a legal burden of proof on that issue. It would surely be enough to raise in the minds of the jury a reasonable doubt about whether the woman in question might have been the daughter of another man.[3]

It might be objected that in these criminal examples, there is a conflict of presumptions which produces a different outcome, the presumption with which the others conflict being the presumption of innocence. But this would be to mislead by language. The so called presumption of innocence is not a rebuttable presumption of law like the others, but is simply a way of stating the rule that in criminal cases the burden of proof is on the prosecution.

---

2 **Section 26** of the **Family Law Reform Act 1969**.
3 *Andrews and Hirst on Criminal Evidence*, 4th edn, 2001, para 4.17.

At best, therefore, it appears that the theoretical basis for recognising presumptions that is suggested in the quotation does not tell the whole story. At worst, it may be positively misleading.

QUESTION 9

Charlie, while driving his motor car, was involved in a collision with Doris, a cyclist aged 14, who suffered a broken leg as a result.

(a) Charlie is charged with dangerous driving. The CPS wish to call the following, both of whom have made statements to the police, as witnesses for the prosecution:
   (i) Ethel, Charlie's wife. She was travelling in the car with Charlie. Shortly after the accident, she made a statement saying that her husband was distracted by a violent argument with her just before he hit Doris's bicycle. Recently, she has been in touch with the officer in the case and has told him that she does not want to give evidence because she loves her husband despite everything.
   (ii) Freddie, aged nine, who saw the accident while he was waiting for a bus to take him to church, where he sings in the choir.
   Advise the CPS on the competence and compellability of Ethel and Freddie.
(b) Charlie has been prosecuted and acquitted. Civil proceedings have now been begun against him on behalf of Doris for negligence. The claimant's solicitors wish to call Ethel and Freddie as witnesses. Advise the solicitors on the competence and compellability of these potential witnesses.

Answer Plan

This is one of the topics where evidence law depends on whether the proceedings are criminal or civil. Deal with the criminal trial first, and then the civil trial.

The criminal trial
  (i) *Ethel.* For competence, see **s 53(1)** of the **Youth Justice and Criminal Evidence Act (YJCEA) 1999**. For compellability, see **s 80** of the **Police and Criminal Evidence Act (PACE) 1984**, as amended by the **YJCEA 1999**. Is this a 'specified offence'? Note Doris's age at the time of the accident. How should 'involves' in **s 80(3)(a)** be interpreted?
  (ii) *Freddie.* For competence, see **s 53(1)** of the **YJCEA 1999**. Note **s 55(2)(a)**.

The civil trial
(i) *Ethel*. For competence, see *ex p Fernandez* (1861). For compellability, see **s 1** of the **Evidence Amendment Act 1853**.
(ii) *Freddie*. Note the possibility of giving sworn evidence. Your starting point will be the *Hayes* test, with **s 96(2)** of the **Children Act 1989** as a fall-back position.

ANSWER

THE CRIMINAL TRIAL

Ethel is competent by virtue of **s 53(1)** of the **YJCEA 1999**, which provides that, at every stage in criminal proceedings, all persons are (whatever their age) competent to give evidence.

Her compellability will be governed by **s 80** of the **Police and Criminal Evidence Act (PACE) 1984**, as amended. She will be compellable only if the offence with which her husband is charged is a 'specified' offence. At the time of the accident, Doris was under the age of 16. It might be arguable that the offence fell within **s 80(3)(a)**, and so was a specified offence, because it involved injury to a person who was at the material time under the age of 16. The interpretation of 'involves' in this provision is uncertain. It might mean 'involves as a matter of legal definition', as robbery, for example, involves the use of force or a putting in fear of force.[1] If this approach is adopted, dangerous driving is clearly not a specified offence. On the other hand, 'involves' could mean 'involves as a matter of fact in the circumstances of the particular case'. If that were the interpretation adopted, the offence with which Charlie is charged would be a specified offence, and Ethel would be compellable.

Freddie is in principle competent by virtue of **s 53(1)** of the **Youth Justice and Criminal Evidence Act 1999**. There is nothing to suggest that he falls into the category of persons who are not competent that is set out in **s 53(3)**. However, because he is under 14, his evidence will be given unsworn: see **s 55(2)(a)**.

THE CIVIL TRIAL

The basic rule, set out in *ex p Fernandez* (1861), is that all persons are competent to give evidence and may be compelled to testify. By **s 1** of the **Evidence Amendment Act 1853**, it is specifically provided that the husbands and wives of the parties to civil

---

1 See **s 8** of the **Theft Act 1968**.

proceedings are competent *and compellable* to give evidence on behalf of *any* of the parties to the proceedings. Ethel will therefore be a compellable witness for the claimant.

Because this is a civil action, Freddie may give either sworn or unsworn evidence. The question whether he understands the nature of an oath so as to be able to give sworn evidence will presumably be decided by applying the tests formerly used when children gave evidence in criminal proceedings. The judge will question Freddie in open court before he gives evidence. In *Khan* (1981), the Court of Appeal said that although much depended on the type of child before the court, generally, inquiry should be made in the case of a child under 14. The conditions to be satisfied were stated in *Hayes* (1977) to be that the child had a sufficient appreciation of the solemnity of the occasion, and understood that an oath involved an added responsibility to tell the truth over and above the social duty to do so. Understanding of a divine sanction is not required.

If these conditions are not satisfied, Freddie may give unsworn evidence. **Section 96(2)** of the **Children Act 1989** provides that a child's evidence may be heard, even if he does not understand the nature of an oath, if he understands that it is his duty to speak the truth, and he has a sufficient understanding to justify his evidence being heard. Freddie is likely to be competent, and so also compellable (*ex p Fernandez* (1861)).

QUESTION 10

Eight years ago, Mr and Mrs Austin set off from England to spend an indefinite period of time travelling in South America. They left behind them three adult children: Basil, Cynthia and Darren. At first Mr and Mrs Austin wrote regularly to all the children, but after a time they did so erratically and infrequently. After two years, nothing further was heard from them by any of the children. The letters that had been received showed that Mr and Mrs Austin were travelling through parts of South America where from time to time there was civil unrest and also danger from natural disasters such as flooding and earthquakes.

Some years before leaving England, both Mr and Mrs Austin had made wills. Mr Austin left everything to his wife, but he also provided that, if she should predecease him, his estate should be divided equally between 'the legitimate children of my family'. Mrs Austin left everything to her husband; in the event of his predeceasing her, the estate was to be divided between various charities.

Basil and Cynthia say that their parents must by now have died and wish to know what rights of inheritance they have. They say also that Darren, though born to

Mrs Austin during her marriage, was not the child of Mr Austin but of a man with whom Mrs Austin was having an affair while their father was in prison.

▶ Discuss the evidential issues that arise.

> ### Answer Plan
> Three problems of law need to be considered here:
>
> ❖ the presumption of death;
> ❖ the presumption created by **s 184** of the **Law of Property Act 1925**;
> ❖ the presumption of legitimacy.
>
> In dealing with these points, you should bear in mind the inferences that might be drawn from the evidence without the aid of presumptions, and also any gaps there may be that necessitate requests for further information.

ANSWER

A person will be presumed to have died if it is proved that:

(a) there is no acceptable evidence that he has been alive at some time during a continuous period of at least seven years;
(b) there are persons likely to have heard of him, had he been alive, who have not heard of him during that period; and
(c) all due inquiries have been made with a view to finding the person in question, but without success (*Chard v Chard* (1956)).

In the case of Mr and Mrs Austin, nothing has been heard for the last six years only, so the presumption cannot be applied. In any case, it does not appear whether there are any other persons who might have heard from Mr and Mrs Austin, or what inquiries, if any, have been made. Thus, even if Basil and Cynthia were to wait for a period of seven years to have elapsed, a court might not be satisfied that all conditions for the operation of the presumption had been complied with.

Quite apart from the presumption, it would be open to a court to infer from appropriate circumstantial evidence that Mr and Mrs Austin had died, but Basil and Cynthia would have the burden of proving their parents' death on the balance of probabilities. Thus, if the evidence were sufficient, there would be no need to wait for the expiry of seven years.[1] Whether the evidence is sufficient is likely to depend largely

---

1 See, for example, *Re Watkins* (1953) for a case where the presumption of death could not be applied, but where the fact of death was nevertheless inferred.

on what inferences can be drawn as to the presence of Mr and Mrs Austin in areas of natural disaster or insurrection and their likelihood of survival in such circumstances.

Section 184 of the **Law of Property Act 1925** provides that, in all cases where two or more persons have died in circumstances rendering it uncertain which of them survived the other or others, such death shall (subject to any order of the court), for all purposes affecting the title to property, be presumed to have occurred in order of seniority, and accordingly the younger shall be deemed to have survived the elder. For the children to inherit, it would be necessary for Mr Austin to have survived his wife. By **s 184**, he will be presumed to have done so if he was the younger of the two; it will therefore be necessary to discover their respective ages. There appears to be no reason why **s 184** should not apply where the court makes a finding of death by virtue of the presumption of death.

On the assumption that Mr Austin was younger than his wife and that he therefore survived her, the question of Darren's legitimacy arises. There is a presumption of legitimacy in respect of any child who is proved to have been born or conceived in lawful wedlock. However, **s 26** of the **Family Law Reform Act 1969** provides that this presumption may be rebutted by evidence that shows that it is more probable than not that the person in question is illegitimate or legitimate as the case may be. Darren will have the advantage of the presumption because he was born while his parents were lawfully married. It will therefore be for Basil and Cynthia to prove on the balance of probabilities that he is illegitimate in order to exclude him from sharing in the distribution of Mr Austin's estate.

One item of evidence in their favour may be the provision itself in Mr Austin's will; it suggests that he believed that there was at least one child of the family who was not legitimate. Clearly, the evidence of his imprisonment will be of the utmost importance. If, for example, Darren were conceived at a time when Mr Austin could have had no access to his wife, this would seem to rebut the presumption conclusively.

QUESTION 11

Should spouses and civil partners be compellable for the prosecution to testify against each other in criminal trials?

Answer Plan
Your starting point here should be reference to the law as it stands at present. Reference to **s 80** of **PACE** is essential, and there should also be reference to the general rule of compellability, as expressed, for example, in *ex p Fernandez* (1861).

> To advance very far in your answer it is necessary to say something about the reasons for the old rule that one spouse could not testify against the other. These are, roughly, fourfold: the obsolete idea that husband and wife together have only one legal personality; the avoidance of 'implacable discord and dissension' between husband and wife; the harshness of compelling one spouse to testify against the other; and the public interest in maintaining stable marriages. It will help if you can tie these various arguments into decided cases, particularly if they are fairly recent. To conclude, you need to consider the arguments on each side, to realise that we are dealing with conflicting interests, and to provide reasons, in the light of this conflict, why non-compellability should prevail over compellability, or vice versa. Finally, it is worth noting that the scope of this question is a very general one. Other questions could be posed that require a more detailed consideration of the existing law; you might, for example, be asked to consider whether, if some degree of non-compellability is suitable, the existing legislation in **s 80(3)** should be amended, so as to provide a wider or narrower range of 'specified' offences where the spouse will be compellable.

ANSWER

Under **s 80** of the **Police and Criminal Evidence Act (PACE) 1984**, spouses and civil partners are compellable for the prosecution to testify against each other in only limited circumstances. In this way the Act has made some inroads on the common law privilege of spouses to refuse to testify for the prosecution against each other. The question is whether this is a privilege that should be relegated to history, so that spouses, and now civil partners as well, have no special protection against the general rule, stated for example in *ex p Fernandez* (1861), that all competent witnesses are compellable.

The reasons for the general exception have varied to some extent over time. Originally, a wife was not even competent to testify for or against her husband, and vice versa. Thus the question of compellability did not directly arise, but the justifications expressed in that context were later used in relation to a spouse's general non-compellability for the prosecution. At least one justification, the theoretical unity of husband and wife in one person,[1] is now obsolete. Other justifications may still be operative. Coke was of the opinion that without the exception there might result 'implacable discord and dissension' between husband and wife and be 'a means of great inconvenience'. Hale, Hawkins and Blackstone followed Coke's reasoning. Gilbert provided an additional argument. According to him, it would be 'very hard' for a wife

---

1   Co. Litt. 6 b, quoted by Lord Wilberforce in *Hoskyn v Metropolitan Police Commissioner* (1979).

to testify against her husband because it would damage their shared interest in maintaining the marriage.

Not everyone accepted the rule uncritically. Bentham pointed out in his *Rationale of Judicial Evidence* that human families living together illustrated a variety of relationships, every one of which would be liable to suffer damage were one person to testify against another. It was illogical, he argued, to identify the relationship of husband and wife as requiring special protection, and for this situation he blamed 'the heroic dimensions given to the conjugal flame by the sentimentality of English lawyers.'[2] Its persistence amounted, he argued, to a great injustice, because it could be an encouragement to crime. The argument that it was particularly harsh for a wife by her testimony to bring about the conviction of her husband was not one that should prevent her from testifying; it was one that the husband should have had in mind as part of his likely punishment when considering whether to commit the offence.

The interests of the public in protection from crime were considered by Geoffrey Lane LJ when giving judgment in *Hoskyn* (1979) in the Court of Appeal. Even where the wife herself is a victim of the crime, there is a public element. It is in the public interest that evidence of a crime should be freely available to the court that tries the offence. In some cases it might well be that the spouse is the only person who is able to provide evidence for the prosecution. The criminal law serves a dual purpose: to help citizens who themselves seek its protection, but also to protect other citizens.

At the root of the problem presented by any spousal non-compellability are certain conflicting interests. Clearly, the public has an interest in seeing that crimes are successfully prosecuted. A guilty man who goes free because of a spouse's non-compellability is likely to be encouraged in his criminal activities. To that extent, members of the public may be at risk of further crimes from him. Further, the fact that a man or woman has gone 'scot free' in this way may bring the law itself into disrepute. On the other hand, stable relationships are good for the individuals who are in them, and it is widely accepted that they are good for society as a whole. It may be anomalous that two particular stable relationships, those of marriage and civil partnership, are protected when others, such as parent and child, are not. But if such relationships ought to be protected for society's good, that is an argument to extend the exception to the general rule of compellability rather than an argument for total abolition.

---

2 *Rationale of Judicial Evidence*, Book 9, Part 4, Chapter 5, in *The Works of Jeremy Bentham*, edited by John Bowring (Edinburgh: William Tait, 1838–1843), vol. 7. Accessed from http://oll.libertyfund.org/title/1998/131157.

The question must be whether the encouragement of stable marriages is so important as to outweigh the benefit to the public from securing a conviction in a proper case. Marriage today is not, in many cases, the stable relationship that it once was. Many marriages will potentially last far longer than marriages in other centuries when life expectancy was shorter. Marriages that are not harmonious can be readily dissolved. Divorce has been easily obtainable for some decades; when spousal non-compellability was initially recognised, divorce was impossible without a private Act of Parliament. There is wide recognition today that the absence of a parent can be harmful for a child and that a substitute for a missing parent is not always satisfactory. Unfortunately, modern marriages are often so fragile that to try to avoid marriage break-up by suspending the general rule about compellability is likely to strengthen the institution of marriage only minimally, but do rather more harm to society by removing an opportunity for its protection and, possibly, by bringing the law into disrepute where a case attracts sufficient publicity.

It is understandable that since Parliament has decided that civil partnerships should be given so far as possible the same advantages as marriages, the benefits of **s 80** of **PACE** should have been extended to take this into account. It is not known what proportion of these partnerships are the basis for bringing up children, and it may be difficult for that reason to assess the public interest in maintaining their stability. It is suggested, however, that it is unlikely to be greater than the benefit of maintaining marriages, so that, on the argument above, the removal of non-compellability in those cases would also follow.

Aim Higher ★

1. Make sure that you distinguish the correct rules about competence in civil cases from those in criminal cases. Remember that civil trials are governed mainly by the common law, while criminal trials are governed in this respect by the **Youth Justice and Criminal Evidence Act 1999, ss 53–56**.
2. Make sure that you are able to recognise 'specified offences' for the purpose of compellability in criminal cases. It is easy, for example, to miss this point where the defendant is charged with committing a non-sexual assault against someone who at the relevant time was under the age of 16.

Common Pitfalls

1. Candidates often fail to understand the different ways in which **ss 75–76** of the **Sexual Offences Act 2003** operate. **Section 75** creates an evidential presumption, and no more; **s 76** creates a conclusive presumption.
2. Candidates often get wrong the various relationships where parties are generally not compellable. Remember that separation does not end a marriage and that only a decree of divorce does; and that civil partnerships cannot exist between persons of the opposite sex.

Hearsay I

INTRODUCTION

Section 1(2) of the **Civil Evidence Act 1995** defines hearsay, for the purposes of that Act, as 'a statement made otherwise than by a person while giving oral evidence in the proceedings which is tendered as evidence of the matters stated'. That definition is, in effect, adopted in **s 114(1)** of the **Criminal Justice Act (CJA) 2003**, which states, 'In criminal proceedings a statement not made in oral evidence in the proceedings is admissible as evidence of any matter stated if, but only if . . .', and then goes on to set out the circumstances in which such evidence will be admissible.

Different approaches to the rule against hearsay have been taken in civil and criminal proceedings. The **Civil Evidence Act 1995** boldly enacts in **s 1(1)** that 'in civil proceedings evidence shall not be excluded on the ground that it is hearsay'. In criminal proceedings the law is governed by **Part 11, Chapter 2** of the **CJA 2003**. This does not abolish the rule against hearsay. Instead, it defines the rule and codifies the exceptions; but it achieves the latter task in a half-hearted way by preserving a number of existing common law exceptions. At least for criminal trials it is necessary to understand the scope of the rule, because it would be absurd to develop an argument that evidence should be included as a hearsay exception if the rule does not apply in the first place. It is necessary to concentrate on two features in order to understand the scope of the rule: the definitions of 'statement' and 'a matter stated', and the purpose for which evidence of an out-of-court statement is being adduced.

Section 115(2) of the **CJA 2003** defines a statement as 'any representation of fact or opinion made by a person by whatever means; and it includes a representation made in a sketch, photofit or other pictorial form'. The representation can therefore be made by any method. Under the common law, sketches and photofit images were held to be unaffected by the rule. This was illogical, and the Act now brings them, and representations by any other pictorial form, within the rule.

Section 115(3) provides as follows:

A matter stated is one to which this Chapter applies if (and only if) the purpose, or one of the purposes, of the person making the statement appears to the court to have been –

(a) to cause another person to believe the matter, or
(b) to cause another person to act or a machine to operate on the basis that the matter is as stated.

The common law rule against hearsay was held in *Kearley* (1992) to cover non-assertive utterances, such as questions, commands and greetings, where the maker did not intend to communicate any information at all, but where inferences as to the existence of some fact could be drawn from what was said. The decision was widely criticised and the Law Commission recommended that this development should be reversed. **Section 115(3)** corresponds to **cl 2(3)** in the bill drafted by the Law Commission to achieve this result. Its effect is to remove 'implied assertions' from the scope of the hearsay rule by making it essential, for the operation of the rule, that the person whose words or actions are reported should have had as at least one purpose that of causing another person to believe the matter that he stated. This effect was confirmed by the Court of Appeal in *Singh* (2006).

The rule against hearsay excludes an item of evidence *only if the purpose of adducing that evidence is to establish the truth of the facts stated*. It follows that in relation to any item of evidence that you suspect may be caught by the rule, you need first to ask: 'What is the *job of proof* that this item of evidence is being put forward to do?' Only when you know what this is can you see whether the evidence is caught by the hearsay rule, which is brought into operation not by any particular form of words, but by the use that is going to be made of them. Putting it another way, you need to know the *relevance* of the evidence being considered.

Don't try to avoid the problem by saying that an item of evidence might be excluded for offending the rule against hearsay, but might be admitted to prove that the assertion was made. This will discredit you in the eyes of the examiner. If you think that somebody might want to show simply that an assertion was made, you must explain to the examiner why that is the case. For example, in a case like *Subramaniam v Public Prosecutor* (1956), you would say that the evidence ought to be admitted because any threats are likely to have affected the mind of the defendant, thus making the evidence relevant to his defence of duress.

This chapter concentrates mainly on the scope of the rule against hearsay, but some reference is also made to the unavailability exception in **s 116** of the **CJA 2003** and to the 'safety-valve' exception in **s 114**.

Checklist ✔

Students should be familiar with the following areas:

- the definition of hearsay reflected in **s 114(1)** of the **CJA 2003**;
- the definitions of 'statement' and 'matter stated';
- statements produced by machines;
- 'negative hearsay';
- the importance of relevance in the rule against hearsay;
- justifications for excluding hearsay evidence;
- the unavailability exception in **s 116** of the **CJA 2003**;
- the 'safety-valve' exception in **s 114** of the **CJA 2003**.

QUESTION 12

What effect does the **Human Rights Act 1998** have on the law relating to hearsay?

Answer Plan

The conclusion that you are aiming for is that **Art 6** of the **ECHR** provides a right for defendants to have witnesses against them cross-examined, but it does not ban hearsay evidence, and may even permit it in certain cases where hearsay is the sole or principal evidence for the prosecution. It's particularly important to plan an essay such as this, and to spell out that plan at the beginning of your essay so that you yourself and the reader can have clearly in mind where the argument is going. If you don't do this, it's all too easy for the essay to degenerate into 'all the cases I can remember about **Art 6**', or even 'all the cases I can half-remember about the **European Convention**'. It's very useful to summarise the argument again at the end of your essay. It will leave a clear impression of your argument in the mind of the examiner.

It would be helpful to include the following points:

- the way in which the **Convention** affects decisions of English courts;
- **Art 6(3)(d)**;
- the limited effect of the Article – *Xhabri* (2005);
- does **Art 6(3)(d)** ban hearsay evidence where it is the sole or principal evidence against a defendant? *Luca v Italy* (2003); *Sellick* (2005); *Al-Khawaja* (2005); *Grant v The Queen* (2006).

ANSWER

I shall argue in this essay that although the English courts are bound by **Art 6** of the **ECHR** to provide defendants with an opportunity to examine witnesses appearing against them, this is only one feature of the right to a fair trial. In appropriate circumstances the interest of the public in general may allow even the sole or principal evidence against a defendant to be given as hearsay. This is particularly likely to be the case where the defendant himself has been responsible for the failure of the witness to appear at trial. It follows that although the **Human Rights Act 1998** enacts principles that limit the use of hearsay evidence, such evidence is in principle admissible and may be so even where it is the sole or principal evidence against a defendant.

One of the effects of the **Human Rights Act 1998** is to make the **European Convention on Human Rights** directly enforceable by English courts. Further, by **s 2(1)(a)**, a court determining a question which has arisen in connection with a **Convention** right must take into account judgments of the European Court of Human Rights. These are not binding authorities, but it is expected that English courts will follow them unless restrained from doing so by statute or binding case law.

Among the 'minimum rights' of a defendant in criminal proceedings is the right under **Art 6(3)(d)** of the **Convention** 'to examine or have examined witnesses against him'. Broadly speaking, the effect of this is to give a defendant the right to have a witness who gives evidence against him called to give his testimony and be subjected to cross-examination. It amounts to a *prima facie* prohibition on the admission of hearsay evidence to support the prosecution case, but the considerations that support this prohibition also justify the exclusion of hearsay evidence that supports the defence case (*Thomas v UK* (2005)). In *R v T(D)* (2009) the Court of Appeal acknowledged that there was a right to confrontation under **Art 6**, which should not be departed from lightly.

The right recognised by **Art 6(3)(d)** is, however, limited in its application. First, the European Court has often said that the admissibility of evidence is a matter for national law, and that its own role is to assess the overall fairness of the criminal proceedings in question. The rights set out in **Art 6(3)** are aspects of the right to a fair trial but are not absolute in themselves. Secondly, the Court has recognised the need for a fair balance between the general interest of the community and the rights of individual defendants. It is unsurprising therefore that the Court of Appeal said in *Xabri* (2005) that there is no merit in the argument that **s 114 CJA 2003** is incompatible with **Art 6**.

In *Luca v Italy* (2003) there was a suggestion by the European Court that where a conviction is based solely, or to a decisive degree, on statements made by a person whom the defendant has had no opportunity to examine, the rights of the defendant will have been restricted to such an extent as to be incompatible with **Art 6**. If this is right, there would be conflict with a line of English authority to the effect that even where hearsay evidence is the sole or decisive evidence against a defendant, it is possible to admit it without infringing the defendant's right to a fair trial. In *Sellick* (2005) the Court of Appeal said that where a court was sure that a witness had been kept from giving evidence by a defendant, or by persons acting for him, there would be no infringement of **Art 6** because the defendant would have denied himself the opportunity of cross-examining the witness. It was necessary to bear in mind the rights of victims and of the public in general as well as those of the defendant. The Court said that there would be more difficulty where the evidence was not so clear cut, so that it was only highly probable that a witness had been intimidated.

Hearsay evidence of a complainant was admitted in *Al-Khawaja* (2005). In that case the appellant had been charged with two counts of indecent assault, but one of the complainants had died by the time the trial took place. Her statement was admitted in accordance with legislation then in operation. On appeal, it was argued that this violated **Art 6(3)(d)**. The appeal was dismissed. The Court of Appeal said that the public interest in enabling the prosecution to proceed must not outweigh the defendant's right to a fair trial, but the right of cross-examination was only one element in such a trial. In that case, the appellant had been able to attack the accuracy of the deceased complainant's statement by exploring inconsistencies between it and evidence of recent complaints that she had made. He had also been able to adduce expert evidence to counter her allegations, and the trial judge had pointed out to the jury the difficulties presented by lack of an opportunity to cross-examine the witness. The proceedings as a whole had been fair.

The matter later came before the European Court of Human Rights, which ruled in *Al-Khawaja v UK* (2009) that hearsay was inadmissible where it was the sole or decisive evidence against a defendant. However, in *R v Horncastle* (2009) the UK Supreme Court declined to follow the European Court's decision, on the ground that the rule against using hearsay in such cases had been introduced into European jurisprudence without discussion of its underlying principles, and without consideration of whether there was justification for imposing it on common law systems. The Supreme Court said that the safeguards enacted by the **Criminal Justice Act 2003** made the rule unnecessary.

For the reasons given above, it appears that although the English courts are bound by **Art 6** of the **ECHR** to provide defendants with an opportunity to examine witnesses appearing against them, this is only one feature of a fair trial. In appropriate circumstances the interest of the public in general may allow even the sole or main evidence against a defendant to be given as hearsay. This is particularly likely to be the case where the defendant himself has been responsible for the failure of the witness to appear at trial. The **Human Rights Act 1998** enacts principles that have a limiting effect on the use of hearsay evidence, but such evidence is in principle admissible.

QUESTION 13

Has the hearsay rule been brought closer to its rationale by the reforms in the **Criminal Justice Act 2003**?

Answer Plan

You need to begin by stating the traditional rationale – in fact, a collection of reasons – for having a rule against hearsay. Lord Normand in *Teper v R* (1952) is a useful source. Then go on to show ways in which the rule was formerly applied, despite the fact that the rationale did not operate. It would be helpful to make some reference to challenges to the rationale, and to the effect of *Kearley* in divorcing rule from rationale. Finally, consider the effect of the new provisions in the **Criminal Justice Act (CJA) 2003**.

In summary, the essay is constructed as follows:

- traditional reasons for the rule against hearsay;
- application of the rule when some reasons were absent: *Sparks v R* (1964), *Myers v DPP* (1965);
- questionable validity of some reasons against hearsay;
- effect of extending the rule to implied assertions;
- the suggested rights of confrontation and challenge;
- effect of reforms in the **CJA 2003**.

ANSWER

In *Teper v R* (1952), Lord Normand explained the rationale of the rule against hearsay in this way. Hearsay is not the best evidence, and it is not delivered on oath. The truthfulness and accuracy of the person whose words are recounted by another witness cannot be tested by cross-examination, and the light that the original speaker's demeanour would have thrown on his testimony is lost.

But it is clear that the rule against hearsay has been applied when some of these criticisms have been inapplicable. In *Sparks v R* (1964), for example, the trial judge refused to allow the mother of a girl aged three to give evidence that her daughter had told her that she had been assaulted by 'a coloured boy'. This decision was upheld by the Privy Council. But there was no significant hearsay danger. The child's statement was unambiguous, she was unlikely to have been mistaken, and the danger that she might have lied was surely non-existent.

Another example is *Myers v DPP* (1965). In order to show that cars sold by the defendant had been stolen, the prosecution wished to call an employee who was in charge of records kept by the car manufacturers. These records were microfilms of cards that had been filled in by production line workers. They showed details of numbers stamped on the cylinder blocks of the cars on the production line. The House of Lords held that this evidence was hearsay, and so inadmissible. But the manufacturers' records must have been far more reliable than the memories of the workers, even if they could have been identified and called.

It is arguable that the hearsay rule became divorced from some elements of its rationale because those elements had become obsolete, or at least questionable. The argument that hearsay is not the best evidence has always been unsatisfactory. Where hearsay is the only evidence of some matter, it will be the best evidence of that matter. The Law Commission concluded that there is no clear evidence that an oath or affirmation in itself promotes truthful testimony.[1] Wigmore thought that the oath added little to cross-examination, which he thought was the real test.[2] In any case, the argument that hearsay is not on oath addresses only the danger that the person reported might have made a false statement deliberately. It can be no safeguard against an original observation that was mistaken. Opinions have differed about the value of a witness's demeanour in testing reliability.[3] The difficulty in recapturing the emphasis and tone of voice of the original utterance may be a more significant objection to admissibility. The main element in Lord Normand's explanation that survives today is the absence of an opportunity to cross-examine the original speaker.

The extension of the hearsay rule to implied assertions in *Kearley* (1992) divorced the rule even from the rationale based on absence of cross-examination. Lord Normand's objection was that the truthfulness and accuracy of someone whose words are reported by another witness cannot be tested. But where the words relied on are non-assertive, they cannot have a truth value, and this objection cannot apply. The real objection here is that the original speaker may be mistaken (though hardly dishonest) in the underlying belief that prompted the non-assertive utterance. If A is overheard asking B, 'Have you any bananas for sale today?', that utterance cannot be true or false. What is true or false is A's underlying belief that B is in the business of selling bananas.

---

1 Law Com No 245, Cm 3670, para 3.13.
2 *Wigmore on Evidence*, 3rd edn, 1940, vol 5, para 1,362.
3 Law Com No 245, Cm 3670, paras 3.9–3.12.

Lord Normand's explanation of the rule against hearsay relies solely on the limited probative weight to be given to hearsay evidence. A different kind of argument is based not on rectitude of decision, but on concern for procedural rights.[4] There are two rights that may be relied on in support of the hearsay rule. One is the right of confrontation, by which evidence cannot be given against a defendant behind his back. The other is the right of challenge to witnesses. Although these rights make for rectitude of decision, they also maximise the defendant's participation in his own trial and so promote the legitimacy of the verdict in his eyes and in the eyes of the public generally.

Hearsay evidence appears to infringe both the right of confrontation and the right of challenge. There is no absolute right of physical confrontation in English law. Evidence may be given by video link, for example. And European decisions show that hearsay evidence can be used against defendants in certain circumstances, despite **Art 6(3)(d)** of the **European Convention on Human Rights**, which provides that everyone charged with a criminal offence has the right to examine or have examined witnesses against him. Nevertheless, in *R v T(D)* (2009) the Court of Appeal said that there is a right of confrontation under **Art 6** of the **European Convention on Human Rights**, which should not be departed from lightly. In *Al-Khawaja v UK* (2009) the European Court held that hearsay was inadmissible where it was the sole or decisive evidence against a defendant. However, in *R v Horncastle* (2009) the UK Supreme Court declined to follow the European Court's decision, on the ground that the rule against using hearsay in such cases had been introduced into European jurisprudence without discussion of its underlying principles, and without consideration of whether there was justification for imposing it on common law systems.

One of the major reforms effected by the **CJA 2003** was, as the Court of Appeal acknowledged in *Singh* (2006), to remove the concept of 'implied assertions' from the scope of the rule against hearsay. This was done by the definition of 'a matter stated' in **s 115(3)**. In this way the new legislation closed a gap between rule and rationale that the decision in *Kearley* had opened. Further, the decision in *Sparks v R* would almost certainly not be the same today. The reason for this is the existence of the 'safety-valve' contained in **s 114(1)(d)** of the Act, whereby a hearsay statement is admissible either for the prosecution or the defence if the court is satisfied that it is in the interests of justice for it to be admissible. The court must have regard to the factors set out in **s 114(2)**, but this list is intended to focus attention on whether the circumstances surrounding the making of the hearsay statement show that it can be treated as sufficiently reliable to be admitted, despite the fact that its maker cannot

---

4 See Dennis, IH, *The Law of Evidence*, 3rd edn, 2007, secs 16.5–16.7.

be cross-examined. That Parliament – or at least the Law Commission – was conscious of the real dangers of unreliability is shown by the special provisions relating to multiple hearsay contained in **s 121(1)**. The hearsay rule was made to accord more with its rationale by the provisions permitting documentary hearsay in the **Criminal Justice Act 1988**. But the position of oral hearsay remained unchanged until **s 116** of the **CJA 2003** allowed oral as well as written statements to be admissible where a witness was unavailable.

In these respects at least, the **CJA 2003** has brought the law relating to hearsay closer to the traditional rationale for exclusion.

QUESTION 14

Oliver Mellors is charged with the murder in London of Connie Chatterley. The case for the prosecution is that they met at Connie's house, and that during a quarrel Oliver struck Connie repeatedly with a cricket bat, thereby causing her death. There is medical evidence that Connie died between 1 pm and 2 pm. The police found a gold cigarette case engraved with the initials 'OM' beside the body. They subsequently interviewed Mellors, who claimed to have been in France on the day that Connie was killed. Later, a neighbour told the police that she had seen Mellors in London on the day in question, but no written statement was taken and the witness cannot now be traced. Connie's gardener has told the police that at about 10.30 am on that day he overheard a conversation between Connie and a man. He did not see either of them, but he recognised Connie's voice and he thought he recognised that of Mellors. He says that Connie said: 'Don't forget to buy some fish, Oliver.' The man replied, 'I'll get some on the way home.'

▶ Discuss the evidential issues that arise.

Answer Plan

You must first decide what items of evidence have to be discussed. They are as follows:

- ❖ The discovery of the cigarette case. What is its relevance? Is there a hearsay problem? If there is, can it be avoided?
- ❖ The relevance of a false alibi. Is hearsay involved in relating what Mellors said about being in France?
- ❖ Can evidence be adduced of what the neighbour said to establish that the alibi was false?
- ❖ The gardener's evidence. What is its relevance?

ANSWER

The first issue concerns the discovery of the engraved cigarette case. This may assist the prosecution by showing that the defendant was present at the scene of the crime at about the time when the murder took place. For this purpose, it would have to be established that the cigarette case belonged to the defendant, and the engraved initials suggest that this was so. But is there a hearsay problem? It is arguable that the context in which the initials appear shows that their function is to assert ownership; this appears to make the prosecution rely on a statement for the truth of its contents, contrary to the rule against hearsay. A similar situation arose in *Patel v Comptroller of Customs* (1966), where labels on goods that stated the country of origin were held by the Privy Council to be inadmissible as proof of where the goods came from.[1]

The country of origin of the goods was one of the matters in issue in the case of *Patel*, and this serves to distinguish it from *Lydon* (1987). In the latter case, the prosecution wished to adduce evidence that a piece of paper bearing the words 'Sean rules' had been found near the scene of the crime. This was alleged to be relevant because it tended to connect the defendant, whose first name was Sean, with the commission of the offence. The Court of Appeal held that this evidence was admissible because although the words on the paper constituted an assertion, it was not in itself an assertion of anything that was relevant to the facts in issue. The fact that something relevant to a fact in issue might be inferred from this item of evidence did not affect admissibility.

Here, however, the inscription arguably does amount to an assertion of a matter which the prosecution wishes to establish as part of its case – the ownership of the cigarette case. In principle, therefore, admissibility seems to be in doubt because of the rule against hearsay. However, it may be possible for the prosecution to rely on evidence from acquaintances of Mellors who can recognise the cigarette case as one that Mellors used to carry. *Miller v Howe* (1969) suggests that something that is written will not be caught by the rule against hearsay when it is an identifying part of an object, the identity of which is in issue, and not merely an assertion of a characteristic of the object. This was a case where the question arose whether a particular breath testing device had been the one approved by the Home Secretary, an 'Alcotest 80'. The Court of Appeal indicated that a label to that effect on the device would have been sufficient evidence of its identity, and that even the presence of such a label on the box containing the device would have been enough.

The prosecution could also try to rely on the decision in *Rice* (1963) in order to argue that the cigarette case was admissible as an item of original, as opposed to hearsay,

---

1 See also *Comptroller of Customs v Western Lectric Co Ltd* (1966).

evidence, because a cigarette case with those initials engraved on it is likely to belong to someone with those initials. A more recent case is *Lilley* (2003), where the Court of Appeal held that the words 'Sharon's book' on the cover of an exercise book, which had been used to practise forging signatures, were not caught by the rule against hearsay. They operated simply as evidence of the defendant's connection with a conspiracy to defraud.

A last resort would be the 'safety-valve' exception to the rule against hearsay provided by **s 114(1)(d)** of the **Criminal Justice Act (CJA) 2003**.

The giving of a false alibi may be an indication of guilt. The prosecution will have no difficulty in adducing evidence that Mellors told the police that he was in France on the day of the murder. No breach of the rule against hearsay is involved because the prosecution wishes to rely, as in *Mawaz Khan* (1967), not on the truth of what was said, but on its falsity.[2]

The policeman to whom the neighbour spoke might be able to give evidence of what he was told by virtue of the unavailability exception in **s 116(1)** of the **CJA 2003**. The neighbour, had she been available, could have given evidence of having seen Mellors in London on the relevant day, thus satisfying **s 116(1)(a)**. It is assumed that the neighbour can be identified so as to satisfy **s 116(1)(b)**. In the absence of identification the evidence could not be given. The remaining question would then be whether any of the five conditions mentioned in **s 116(2)** is satisfied. The obvious condition on which to rely is condition (d). It would be necessary to show that 'such steps as it is reasonably practicable to take' have been taken to find the neighbour. But even if what the neighbour told the police was admissible in principle under **s 116**, it would be open to the defence to ask the judge to exclude it in the exercise of his discretion, either under the principle confirmed in *Sang* (1980), or under **s 78(1)** of the **Police and Criminal Evidence Act 1984**. Since evidence of identification is regarded as peculiarly hazardous, such an application might well succeed on the basis that the absence of opportunity to cross-examine the identifying witness about the circumstances of the identification would make the proceedings unfair.

The probative force of the gardener's testimony is that Mellors was not in France, but with Connie in London on the day in question. Two factors suggest this. First, the fact that Connie addressed 'Oliver' suggests that it was Mellors to whom she was talking. The fact that the words 'Don't forget to buy some fish, Oliver' were not intended as a statement but as an exhortation, or perhaps a command, means that the words

---

2   For the directions that a judge must give in relation to lies told by a defendant, see *Lucas* (1981), *Burge and Pegg* (1996) **and Chapter 6.**

would not offend the rule against hearsay, because the purpose of uttering them was not to cause the person to whom they were addressed to believe any matter. The words did not, therefore, constitute 'a matter stated' within **s 115(3)** of the **CJA 2003**.

Secondly, however, the fact that the gardener heard a voice that he thought he recognised as that of Mellors also suggests that the latter was in London and not in France. What is relied on here to prove that Mellors was present is not the truth of what the man who made a reply to Connie said, but the fact that whatever words were uttered were in tones which the gardener identified as those of Mellors. No hearsay problem arises, and the gardener should be able to testify that he heard, at the time and place referred to, the voice of Connie and a voice which he thought he recognised as that of Mellors.[3]

QUESTION 15

Percy is being prosecuted for the murder of Edith. He is an Australian visitor to England who was staying in a flat on the third floor of a block known as Shearman Court in West London. Edith lived alone in another flat on the ground floor. The prosecution says that Percy and Edith were having an affair, but that on the evening of 14 July, there was a quarrel between them at Edith's flat, during which Percy strangled her.

Percy was first implicated in the crime when a police tracker dog led detectives to his flat on the third floor. In a properly conducted police interview, he told the police that he had not killed Edith, had never had an affair with her and had never been inside her flat.

Curtis, who lived in another flat on the ground floor of Shearman Court, told police that on the evening of the murder, he had heard a loud argument going on in Edith's flat between Edith and a man with an Australian accent.

When the police lawfully searched Percy's flat, they found an opened letter in a desk drawer. It was addressed to Percy and read as follows: 'Don't be fooled by that tart Edith. She's been screwing Frederick for the last month. Give her up – she's not worth it. With love from Rose.' The prosecution does not wish to call Rose, but it wants to put the letter in evidence as part of its case against Percy.

---

3   For the difficulties with voice identification, see the commentary on *Robinson (Wayne)* (2006) Crim LR 427.

Lilian, a friend of Edith, was interviewed by Percy's solicitor. She told him that after the murder, she took away from Edith's flat a parrot called Max, which Edith had kept as a pet, in order to look after it. She said that during the day Max was silent, but that when evening came, the bird repeatedly called out, 'Frederick, no, no, no!'.

◗ Discuss the evidential issues that arise.

Answer Plan

The first thing to emphasise is that all the evidence you have been asked to consider is circumstantial and highly inconclusive, *but it is not, merely for this reason, inadmissible*. If you think about it, there is no evidence that proves something conclusively, for there will always exist possible alternative explanations for the item of evidence in question. Far too many students think that a defendant cannot be convicted on purely circumstantial evidence, or at least that such evidence is bound by its very nature to be less substantial than direct evidence, such as the evidence given by a witness of what he saw or heard. This too is completely wrong. In *Taylor, Weaver and Donovan* (1928), Lord Hewart CJ said: 'It is no derogation of evidence to say that it is circumstantial.' His words should be remembered.

With this in mind, you need to consider five points:

- *Tracker dog evidence.* There is an English authority on this. Note what has to be proved to establish the reliability of such evidence. Of course, there is no hearsay problem here.
- *What Percy said to the police.* What is the purpose of adducing this in evidence? The answer to that question will solve any hearsay difficulties.
- *Curtis's evidence.* Again, what will the prosecution be adducing this to prove? Your answer should be: (a) There was a quarrel that night. (b) It took place at Edith's flat. (c) It was between Edith and a man. (d) The man was Australian. None of this, of course, points inevitably to Percy, but see the opening paragraph above, and remember that this is only a part of the prosecution case.
- *The letter.* This is an example of what is sometimes called the distinction between hearsay and real evidence. If you treat these expressions as labels that can be instinctively slapped on various items of evidence, you are heading for disaster. The starting point, as always, is not the *label* but the *job of proof* that the evidence can do. Putting it another way, the problem of admissibility can be solved only if you consider carefully what inferences can be drawn from the evidence in question. As part of its case, the prosecution wants to prove a number of propositions. Which of those propositions, if any, does the letter support? The answer to this will tell you

if it is relevant. What arguments are needed to move from the letter to the propositions that the prosecution wants to prove? The answer to this will tell you about admissibility.
- *Lilian's evidence*. Is it relevant? Is there a hearsay problem? If it is relevant and there is no hearsay problem, what is to stop it from being admitted?

ANSWER

The tracker dog presumably led the police to Percy's flat because the animal picked up Percy's scent in Edith's flat. There might have been a perfectly innocent explanation for this but, in view of Percy's denial that he had ever been inside the flat, the evidence is capable of supporting the prosecution case. *Pieterson* (1995) established that evidence of the activities of tracker dogs will be admissible, provided a proper foundation can be laid to establish reliability. The dog's handler should give evidence about its training, and should also establish that over a period of time, it behaved reliably as a tracker during controlled tests.

Evidence can be given of what Percy said to the police. The prosecution will wish to show that Percy lied about his association with Edith and will invite the jury to infer guilt from this. The purpose in adducing evidence of what Percy said will be to show its falsity, not its truth. In these circumstances, the rule against hearsay does not apply (*Mawaz Khan v R* (1967)).

Curtis can give evidence of the sounds that he heard coming from Edith's flat on the evening of 14 July. A jury would be entitled to infer from this that an argument was going on at the time. Curtis could also say that he heard the accents of an Australian male to show that such a person was present on that occasion. Neither of these items of evidence infringes the rule against hearsay because the purpose of adducing the evidence is not to establish the truth of what was said, but the fact that there was an argument and that one of the participants was an Australian man.

The evidential value of the letter found in Percy's desk is not that it establishes the truth about Edith's love life, but that it enables us to infer that Percy had been having some sort of relationship with a woman called Edith and that he probably had a vengeful state of mind towards her. The argument can be put thus: why should Percy have such an interest in the letter that he kept it in his desk if he did *not* have any such relationship? In other words, it is Percy's reaction to what was written that is relied on, not the truth of what was said in the letter. Evidence was admitted for a similar purpose in *McIntosh* (1992) where the defendant was charged with importing drugs. In a house where he had been living before his arrest, the police found a piece of paper which contained calculations, not in the defendant's handwriting, of the purchase and sale prices of 12 oz of an unnamed commodity. The Court of Appeal held that this evidence had been properly admitted as circumstantial real evidence tending to connect the accused with the crime charged. Though not spelled out by the court, the reason appears to have been that the person in possession of the document kept it because he was interested in the information that it contained.

A similar decision in a case closer to the given facts is *R v Toussaint-Collins* (2009), where D was charged with the murder of X. The case for the prosecution was that the murder was a revenge killing, motivated by the belief that X had been responsible for the earlier murder of Y. The question arose whether a letter from another person to D, in which the writer expressed his regret that Y's death had not been avenged, was admissible to prove D's motive for murdering X. D had kept it for some months after receiving it. The Court of Appeal held that this item of evidence was not hearsay, and was admissible, because it helped to show D's vengeful state of mind towards X.

Given that there was a relationship between Percy and Edith, then, *regardless of the truth of what was said about Edith in the letter*, the fact that the allegation was read and the letter kept suggests that Percy took it seriously, and from that it can be inferred that he may have had vengeful feelings towards Edith.

One possible inference from the parrot's behaviour is that the bird was repeating what it heard Edith shout on the evening when she was murdered. From this it could be inferred that, because Frederick is named rather than Percy, it was not Percy who murdered her. The first point to be made is that what the parrot 'said' was not a statement. If Edith uttered those words, she did not do so for the purpose of causing another person to believe anything, as required by **s 115(3)** of the **Criminal Justice Act 2003**. As a non-statement, therefore, what Edith said is not caught by the rule against hearsay. Because some parrots tend to repeat human language that they hear, Max might be seen as a recording device. Had a tape recorder been operating at the time, the tape could well have been admissible as direct evidence of what was going on. In *Maqsud Ali* (1966), the Court of Appeal held that a tape recording is admissible in evidence provided, *inter alia*, the accuracy of the recording can be proved and the voices properly identified.

The real difficulty here is not one of hearsay and, by analogy with *Taylor v Chief Constable of Cheshire* (1987), Lilian should be allowed to give evidence of what she heard if Max is properly seen as a recording device. The prosecution could legitimately object, however, that as a recording device Max is most unreliable. How could the court be satisfied, even on a *prima facie* basis, that Max did not pick up this expression on some quite different occasion or from someone other than Edith? The truth of the matter is that Max is quite different from the sort of mechanical recording devices whose products have been admitted hitherto by the courts as real evidence. Lilian's evidence is therefore most unlikely to be admissible for the defence.

Aim Higher

1. You should always be able to explain the probative job of a particular item of evidence. Only then will you be able to say whether or not it is in principle caught by the rule against hearsay.
2. You should be able to explain what used to be the arguments for the rule against hearsay, and how convincing they are today. Pay particular attention to the so-called 'right of confrontation', which appears to be gaining more ground in England than formerly.

Common Pitfalls

1. Candidates sometimes find it difficult to explain the effect of the **Human Rights Act 1998** on the English law of hearsay. Remember that discussion has centred principally on the extent to which hearsay can be used when it is the only or main evidence against a defendant.
2. Some candidates don't understand how reported speech in a problem question works. In order to apply the hearsay rule effectively, you must be able to turn reported speech into direct speech so as to analyse exactly what was said.

5 Hearsay II

INTRODUCTION

The scope of the rule against hearsay has been much reduced. The **Civil Evidence Act 1995** has abolished the rule completely for civil proceedings. In 1995 the Law Commission published a Consultation Paper on the subject of hearsay in criminal cases, and in 1997 published a Report. The recommendations of the Commission have been very largely incorporated in **Part 11, Chapter 2** of the **Criminal Justice Act (CJA) 2003**, which has created four principal categories of admissibility, all of which are available to both the defendant and the prosecution:

- hearsay admissible by statute;
- hearsay admissible under any preserved common law rule;
- hearsay admissible by agreement;
- hearsay admissible in the interests of justice (the 'safety-valve').

Reference has already been made in Chapter 4 to the unavailability exception in **s 116** of the **CJA 2003** and to the 'safety-valve' exception in **s 114**. It is important to note that hearsay statements under either section can be oral or written.

Under **ss 23** and **24** of the **Criminal Justice Act 1988**, documentary hearsay statements were admissible under certain conditions. However, the interpretation of **ss 23** and **24** gave rise to difficulty, and the powers to admit hearsay statements under them were the subject of a wide judicial discretion, contained in **ss 25** and **26**, that gave rise to accusations of inconsistency and uncertainty. These provisions were repealed **by Sched 37, Part 6** of the **CJA 2003** and replaced by an exception in favour of 'business and other documents' in **s 117**.

With the exception of the rules preserved by **s 118**, the common law rules governing the admissibility of hearsay evidence in criminal proceedings are abolished. As well as some minor exceptions, two major common law exceptions are preserved: *res gestae* statements and statements in furtherance of a common enterprise.

Res gestae statements are generally taken to include four different categories:

(i) Statements that accompany and explain an action of the person making the statement.
(ii) Spontaneous exclamations made in response to an event so dramatic as to rule out any opportunity for concoction. The leading case is *Andrews* (1987), and you should know the tests for admissibility that it establishes.
(iii) Declarations about the maker's contemporaneous state of mind or emotion. The law has developed in a haphazard and unsatisfactory way, and is consequently in a state of some uncertainty (and so is a favourite topic for examination questions). It is odd that the **CJA 2003** did not attempt to clarify it. You should pay particular attention to the cases on statements of intention.
(iv) Declarations about the maker's contemporaneous physical sensations. Note that the declarations cannot be used to prove what caused the sensations.

Statements in furtherance of a common enterprise made by one party to the enterprise are admissible against others, even where they have had nothing to do with making the statement and may not know that a statement has been made. This rule is not confined to conspiracy cases; it applies wherever the prosecution alleges a joint enterprise. But the statement must have been made in furtherance of the enterprise, so it will not apply to the confession of one party after his arrest: *Walters* (1979).

The law relating to confessions is also preserved, but this topic is separately considered in Chapter 7.

Do not neglect the supplementary provisions in **ss 121–125** of the **CJA 2003**. The rules about multiple hearsay are particularly important. You should always be aware that admissible hearsay can still be excluded, either at common law or by statute.

Checklist ✔

Students should be familiar with the following areas:

- the unavailability exception (**s 116**);
- the business and other documents exception (**s 117**);
- the preserved common law exceptions (**s 118**);
- the 'safety-valve' exception (**s 114**);
- the supplementary provisions (**ss 121–125**);
- common law and statutory powers of exclusion.

QUESTION 16

Herbert is charged with the murder of Ivan. The case for the prosecution is that the murder was the result of a street fight. The deceased was accosted by two youths, Joss and Herbert. Herbert attacked Ivan with a garden ornament and a fight ensued between them. In the course of the fight, Herbert called for Joss, who was carrying a knife, to stab Ivan. Joss did so and caused fatal wounds. Joss was arrested several days later. When interviewed under caution he admitted stabbing Ivan at the instigation of another man, whom he did not identify. In due course he pleaded guilty to murder. Before his arrest, Joss had a conversation with Karen, his girlfriend, in the course of which he admitted stabbing Ivan and said that he had done so at Herbert's instigation. After Joss had pleaded guilty to murder, Karen made a written statement to the police giving a full account of what Joss had told her about Herbert's involvement.

Karen is now resident in Australia. Originally she agreed to give evidence at Herbert's trial. The police have recently been told that she has now changed her mind. Joss has refused to cooperate with the police in their investigations concerning Herbert. He refuses to have anything to do with Karen.

▶ Discuss the evidential matters arising.

Answer Plan

The sole question is whether Karen's written statement can be used at Herbert's trial. It is unlikely that a question in the examination would be restricted to such a narrow scope, but the exercise will be useful because it shows how carefully exceptions to the rule against hearsay should be considered.

Note first that the admissibility of the evidence is assessed on the basis that Karen will attend to give oral evidence. There are obvious problems already; note the importance of the Court of Appeal's decision in *Y* (2008). Next, assume that her evidence will be admissible if she attends. What will the position be if she does not attend? In particular, can the prosecution use any of the provisions in **s 116**? Note that **s 117** is not available because of the circumstances in which Karen herself received the information. Now assume that **s 116** can be used. The result will be multiple hearsay. You will have to examine **s 121** to see, finally, if this obstacle can be overcome. Do not expect to be able to come to a firm conclusion.

ANSWER

The availability of Karen seems very uncertain. It will be useful to consider first whether she could give evidence of what Joss told her if she were to give oral evidence at Herbert's trial. If she were to do so, it is clear that she would be repeating what Joss said to her in order to establish the part played by Herbert in Ivan's death. The basic rule, laid down by **s 114(1)** of the **CJA 2003**, is that a statement not made in oral evidence in the proceedings is admissible as evidence of any matter stated if, but only if, one of conditions (a) to (d) inclusive is satisfied. **Subsection (1)(b)** allows such statements if any rule of law preserved by **s 118** makes it admissible. By **s 118(1), para 5**, there is preserved any rule of law relating to the admissibility of confessions or mixed statements in criminal proceedings. **Subsection (1)(a)** allows hearsay evidence if provided for by the **CJA 2003** or by any other statutory provision. By **s 76(1)** of **PACE 1984** a confession made by an accused person may be given in evidence against him in so far as it is relevant to any matter in issue in the proceedings and is not excluded by the court. The difficulty with Joss's statement to Karen is that so far as the proceedings against Herbert are concerned, it is not a confession made by an accused person because Joss has already been dealt with and the only accused person is Herbert. Even if Joss and Herbert had been tried together, what Joss said to the police would have been admissible only against him. **Section 76(1)** explicitly confines admissibility to admissibility against the maker of the statement, and this reflects the pre-**PACE** common law, as expressed in *Gunewardene* (1951). Neither under **s 114(1)(a)** or **(b)** would the evidence that Karen can give be admissible against Herbert. **Subsection (1)(c)** will clearly not apply, and that leaves only **subs (1)(d)**: hearsay evidence will be admissible where the court is satisfied that it is in the interests of justice for it to be admissible. In deciding this question the court must have regard to the factors set out in **s 114(2)**. However, in *Taylor (Stuart)* (2006) the Court of Appeal said that this does not require the judge to embark on an investigation so as to reach a conclusion in relation to any one of them, let alone each one of them. What is required is the exercise of judgment after giving consideration to these factors and to any others that the judge considers relevant.

A further question arises on these facts. Is **s 114(1)(d)** capable of allowing the admission of hearsay material which is contained in a confession by a person other than the defendant, or is it excluded by the presence in the Act of **s 118(1), para 5**? The argument for the defence would be that the preservation of the common law rules relating to the admissibility of confessions preserves, *inter alia*, the rule laid down in *Gunewardene* that a confession is admissible against its maker only.

This question was considered by the Court of Appeal in *Y* (2008). The Court observed that the aim of the Law Commission in proposing the enactment of what is now **s 114(1)(d)** was to provide a residual judicial power to admit hearsay evidence which would not otherwise be admissible. The Court also observed that **s 118** is expressly stated to be concerned with the admissibility, rather than the inadmissibility, of evidence. It concluded that hearsay in the form of a confession is in law as open to admission under **subpara (d)** as any other hearsay. That provision prevails over the general common law rule that hearsay is inadmissible, and so it prevails over the particular common law rule that hearsay contained in the form of a confession is inadmissible against anyone other than the maker.

The position therefore is that Karen's evidence would in principle be admissible if she were to attend in person. The next question is whether her statement could be introduced under **s 116** if she did not attend. The condition set out in **s 116(2)(c)** appears to be the most appropriate, although the prosecution might also have to rely on **s 116(2)(d)**. There is at present no evidence that she is refusing to give evidence through fear.

Section 116(2)(c) was considered by the Court of Appeal in *C* (2006), in which the Court of Appeal said that the expression 'reasonably practicable' has to be judged on the basis of the steps taken, or not taken, by the party who wishes to secure the witness's attendance. The court has to consider what efforts should reasonably be made to secure the attendance of the witness or, at least, to arrange a procedure whereby the contents of his statement can be tested by cross-examination. In Herbert's case, no steps appear to have been taken to discover from Karen herself whether she is willing to attend. What efforts should reasonably be made to secure her attendance? Presumably the prosecution is willing to pay her expenses, though this is not stated. What other steps, such as evidence by video link, could be taken? On the facts as they stand it seems unlikely that a judge could reach a decision to admit Karen's statement under **s 116(2)(c)**.

If **s 116(2)(d)** is relied on, there must be evidence of what steps it is reasonably practicable to take to find her and whether those steps have been taken. If such steps have been taken, what have been the results?

It is possible that a court might be satisfied in due course that Karen's statement was in principle admissible, under either **s 116(2)(c)** or **(d)**. Her statement would then be put forward as hearsay evidence of what Joss said to her about Herbert's part in Ivan's death. The hearsay would be 'multiple', and by **s 121(1)** such a hearsay statement is not admissible unless one of three conditions is satisfied. The first, in **subs (1)(a)**, applies where either of the statements is admissible under **ss 117, 119** or **120**. **Sections 119** and **120** have no application. **Section 117** does not apply because although Karen's witness statement is a document received by a person in the course of police business, she herself is not a person who received the information in the course of a trade, business, etc, as required by **s 117(2)(c)**. For the statement to be admitted, reliance would therefore have to be placed on **s 121(1)(c)**. (**Section 121(1)(b)** can obviously not be relied on.) Without more knowledge of the facts of the case it is not easy to see whether a judge would be prepared to admit the evidence on this basis. The potential value of the evidence is high, but it is impossible to tell, without at least reading the statement, what assessment is likely to be made of its reliability.

QUESTION 17

Adrian, Billy and Charlie are charged with possession of drugs with intent to supply. In the house where all three lived, police found a large quantity of cocaine and £28,000 in used banknotes. When interviewed, all three defendants said that the money had been the proceeds of successful gambling. They said that they had just moved into the house and had no knowledge of the presence of the cocaine, which had been discovered in the loft. The police also found a diary in Adrian's handwriting, in which there appeared inside the back cover a list containing references to first names, to various quantities of something that was unspecified, and to sums of money. Below the list was written: 'Adrian to get half; Billy and Charlie a quarter each.' There were also various entries for the week before the date when all three were arrested. One of these read: 'Billy and Charlie are getting cold feet. I wish they hadn't persuaded me to let them in on the deals.' For two weeks before the arrests were made, DC Kray kept watch outside the house, which was visited by 26 people. He was able to identify 18 of these as persons with previous convictions for the possession of drugs.

▶ Discuss the evidential matters arising.

Answer Plan

There are three items of evidence that need your consideration:

- Is evidence of finding the money admissible? If so, does the judge need to say anything about it in summing up?
- Are the contents of Adrian's diary admissible? Against whom? Don't forget that the entries should be dealt with separately. Will the judge need to give any special direction?
- Is the evidence of DC Kray admissible for the prosecution?

ANSWER

In relation to the cash, two questions arise. Is it relevant to the prosecution case? If it is, what directions should the judge give to the jury about it? In *Wright* (1994), the Court of Appeal held that the discovery of £16,000 in cash in the defendant's flat was admissible to support a charge of possessing cocaine with intent to supply, on the basis that drug dealers are known to deal in large sums of cash. However, in

Batt (1994), the Court of Appeal held that the finding of cash (albeit in that case a much smaller sum) was inadmissible, because it was suggestive only of past dealings. As such, it was unfairly prejudicial because it showed only a disposition to commit such offences. *Batt* seems difficult to reconcile with *Wright*, but later cases have tended to prefer the reasoning in *Wright*. Therefore, the position is that the finding of the cash is likely to be admissible to support the charge, but there are two elements in the charge, both of which the defendants deny. Not only do they deny intent to supply; they also deny *possession* (their case is that they knew nothing of the presence of the cocaine). In *Guney* (1998), the Court of Appeal said that whether evidence is relevant depends on the circumstances of each case. Where possession with intent to supply is charged, there are many circumstances in which evidence of cash and lifestyle might be relevant and admissible in relation to the issue of possession itself, especially to the issue of knowledge as an ingredient of possession. Thus, the discovery of the cash may be relevant to possession as well as intent to supply.[1]

However, a careful direction will have to be given to the jury about the use they can make of this information. In *Grant* (1996), the Court of Appeal said that before relying on such evidence, the jury must be satisfied that the money was not in the defendant's possession for any innocent reason that may have been advanced (in this case, as a result of successful gambling) and that, even if they find that it does relate to drug dealing, they must be satisfied that it relates to an ongoing course of dealing, and is not merely the proceeds of past deals. However, at the time when *Grant* was decided there were severe restrictions on adducing evidence that was relevant only to a defendant's disposition. These were substantially reduced in the **Criminal Justice Act 2003**, and it might now be enough for the cash to be taken only as evidence of past dealing.[2]

In *Pearce* (1979), the Court of Appeal held that wholly exculpatory statements made by suspects when confronted with incriminating evidence are admissible to show their reactions to the accusations being made, but are not evidence of the truth of their contents. Accordingly, the defendants' statements about ignorance of the presence of cocaine, and their explanations for the presence of the money, will be admissible for this limited purpose.

The entries in Adrian's diary should be separately considered. It was held in *Gray and Others* (1995) that a statement made in furtherance of a common purpose by one defendant is admissible as evidence against the others, though made in their absence.

---

1 See also *Griffiths* (1998).
2 See also Question 3.

The reason for this is that a combination of persons for the purpose of committing a crime is regarded as implying an authority to each to act or speak in furtherance of the common purpose on behalf of the others. For example, in *Devonport and Pirano* (1996), where the defendants were charged with conspiracy to defraud a bank, a document drawn up by the girlfriend of one of the defendants, at the latter's dictation, showed an intended division of the proceeds of the offence between all the defendants, who were named. It was held that this was evidence against all the defendants, there being evidence in addition to the document to show that they were all parties to the conspiracy. Since the document was a record of *intended* distribution of the proceeds when the conspiracy had been fulfilled, it had been prepared in furtherance of the conspiracy, and was thus admissible. It would have been different if the document had been merely a record, made when everything was finished, of what had happened. This common law exception was preserved by **para 7** of **s 118(1)** of the **Criminal Justice Act 2003**.

The entries at the back of Adrian's diary show an *intended* distribution between the three defendants, and there is other evidence (the discovery of the drugs and the cash in the house where all three lived) to link Billy and Charlie to a common enterprise, even though not charged as a conspiracy. On this basis, the entry is admissible against all the defendants. But the judge will have to warn the jury that they must be satisfied that the entry was not only evidence of past dealing, but capable of going to intention to supply in the future. In other words, the diary entry must be treated with the same caution as the discovery of the cash: see *Lovelock* (1997). But the reservation noted in relation to *Grant* in respect of such a direction after the passing of the **Criminal Justice Act 2003** might be relevant here also.

The second entry about Billy and Charlie getting cold feet is clearly not made in furtherance of the common enterprise. It is admissible as a confession by Adrian.[3]

The evidence of DC Kray may be relevant because it shows the sort of people frequenting the house, and tends to show that the house was being used for drug dealing. Similar evidence was admitted in *Warner* (1993), where the prosecution's case was that the pattern of visits was consistent with the method of drug dealing testified to by prosecution witnesses. The defence case was that the visitors had been making only social calls but in *Hasson* (1997), evidence that the defendants, who were charged with being concerned in the supply of cannabis resin, had associated with persons with drug-related convictions was held inadmissible. In contrast to *Warner*, it was not part of the prosecution case that the defendants were supplying drugs to those whose

---

3 For confessions, see Chapter 7.

convictions were adduced in evidence. The question on these facts therefore appears to be whether there is a nexus between the defendants' association with these visitors and any specific allegation of dealing made by the prosecution. In the absence of such a nexus, the evidence is likely to be inadmissible.

QUESTION 18

Michael, who runs a car hire firm, is charged with manslaughter. The case for the prosecution is that he rented a car to Nick for one week on 1 April. On 2 April, the car was found at the bottom of a cliff with Nick's body inside. The prosecution alleges that when Michael rented the car to Nick, the steering mechanism was, to Michael's knowledge, so faulty that a driver would be likely to lose control of the car. Michael intends to plead not guilty. He denies that the steering mechanism was faulty. He says that if it was faulty, he had no knowledge of this. He says that fog on the night of the accident made visibility very poor, and that this caused Nick to drive off the road and over the cliff. Another explanation, he says, is that Nick drove over the cliff deliberately because he believed that his wife had left him. Michael wishes to testify that one week before the accident, he rented the same car to Olive, a qualified car mechanic. Michael says that he saw Olive examine the car carefully before getting in and taking it on a test drive by herself. Only when she returned did she allow her children to get in as passengers. Michael also wishes to call Patrick, Nick's best friend, who says that he received a call from Nick's mobile telephone on the night of 1 April. According to Patrick, Nick said: 'I'm driving along a cliff road. The fog is frightening, but I can't find anywhere to stop the car.' The prosecution has disclosed that a note was found on Nick's kitchen table. It was from his wife and was dated 31 March. It said: 'I can't stand living with you any more. I have gone to live with Quentin in Ireland. Don't try to contact me.'

▸ Discuss the evidential issues arising.

Answer Plan

There are three items of evidence, to be considered separately:

- ❖ the incident involving Olive;
- ❖ Patrick's account of the mobile phone call from Nick;
- ❖ the note from Nick's wife.

ANSWER

The significance of the incident involving Olive is that it shows that the car was in good condition only a week before Nick hired it. Olive was a qualified car mechanic, she examined the car carefully before taking it for a test drive, and only on her return did she take her children as passengers. The inference is that she found the car to be in a safe condition. Of course, the fact that the car was safe then does not mean inevitably that there was nothing wrong with it when Nick hired it, but it makes it unlikely.

Under the pre-2003 law, it is possible that evidence about the incident with Olive would have been inadmissible. In *Wright v Doe d Tatham* (1837), Parke B said *obiter* that the rule against hearsay applied to non-verbal conduct. As an example, he envisaged a trial where the seaworthiness of a ship was in issue. Suppose the deceased captain had first examined every part of the ship, and only when his inspection was complete had he embarked on it with his family. Parke B said that this evidence would be affected by the rule against hearsay just as much as a statement by the captain to a bystander to the effect that he had examined the ship and had found it seaworthy. *Wright v Doe d Tatham* was relied on by the House of Lords when it held in *Kearley* (1992) that the rule against hearsay affected non-assertive utterances. Whether it also caught hearsay by conduct was never finally decided. However, **s 115(3)(a)** of the **Criminal Justice Act (CJA) 2003** defines 'a matter stated' as one where the purpose, or one of the purposes, of the person making the statement appears to the court to have been to cause another person to believe the matter stated. The effect of this is to abolish the rule that non-assertive utterances are caught by the rule against hearsay, and its effect must also be to abolish Parke B's notion of hearsay by conduct that was not intended to convey any message to observers. The evidence of Olive's behaviour will therefore be admissible.

Patrick can give evidence of what Nick said during the telephone call by virtue of the unavailability exception in **s 116**, and possibly also by virtue of the preserved *res gestae* exceptions.

If Nick had survived, he could have given evidence of conditions on the cliff road. There are no identification problems, and Nick is unavailable because he is dead. It would be possible to argue, further, that what Nick said amounted to an 'excited utterance'. The leading authority is *Andrews* (1987). This requires that the circumstances provoking the utterance should have been so unusual, startling or dramatic as to dominate the thoughts of the speaker to the extent that the utterance was an instinctive reaction to those circumstances, with no opportunity for reflection or concoction. The difficulty on these facts is that what Nick appears to have been experiencing, though unpleasant, was not a sudden event; it was, apparently, a continuing state of affairs. As such, it could be argued that it lacked the dramatic quality of something like the sudden and violent attack in *Carnall* (1995). Thus, it is difficult to predict with certainty whether or not Patrick's evidence would be admitted under this exception.

The note found on the kitchen table will be admissible. One of the defence theories is that Nick committed suicide when he discovered that his wife had left him. The evidence of the note will be admissible quite simply for the effect it might have had on Nick's mind. In *Subramaniam v Public Prosecutor* (1956), the Privy Council emphasised that a statement will not be caught by the rule against hearsay where it is adduced merely to establish the fact that it was made. This fact, quite apart from the truth of the statement, is frequently relevant in considering the mental state and conduct of someone to whom the statement was made. That is exactly the relevance of the note on these facts. It might have been quite untrue that the wife had gone to Ireland or had decided to leave her husband for another man. The point is that Nick might have believed what he read, and this might have given him a motive for suicide.

QUESTION 19

How successful was the **Criminal Justice Act 2003** in reforming the law relating to hearsay?

Answer Plan

There is a wide range of approaches to this question. But you could make these points, among others:

- abolition of 'implied assertions';
- the 'safety-valve' in **s 114(1)(d)**;
- oral as well as documentary hearsay now available where a witness is unavailable;
- extending the scope of 'recent complaints': **s 120(7)(d)**;
- retention of *res gestae*: a point for criticism;
- the extent of judicial discretion: another possible point for criticism.

ANSWER

Hearsay used to be an essentially common law doctrine with some statutory additions. One critic described it as a 'legalistic backwater' which was 'the home of sophistry and the graveyard of common sense'.[1] Since the **2003 Act** it has become primarily a statutory doctrine with some common law rules preserved.

A major reform has been the abolition, acknowledged by the Court of Appeal in *Singh* (2006), of the concept of 'implied assertions', to which the House of Lords had

---

[1] D. Birch, 'Hearsay: Same Old Story, Same Old Song?' [2004] *Criminal Law Review* 564.

given its authority in *Kearley* (1992). This decision was much criticised for extending the scope of hearsay to such an extent that, in principle, almost any utterance, or even action, could fall within the exclusionary rule on the basis that it reflected a belief of the speaker or agent in a state of affairs that justified the utterance or action in question. The decision was also criticised for its confusion of implications with inferences. **Section 115(3)** of the **CJA 2003** now defines 'a matter stated' as one where the person making the statement appears to the court to have had as one of his purposes either causing another person to believe the matter or causing another person to act (or a machine to operate) on the basis that the matter is as stated. It follows that if A asks B, 'Have you any bananas for sale?' A will not be taken to have had the purpose of asserting that B is a dealer in bananas, and his question, if overheard, can be adduced as evidence of the fact that B is a dealer.

Birch has argued that **s 115(3)** might have been too radical. She has suggested that as the law now stands, the defence will be able to make free play with non-assertive words and conduct, whereas the prosecution, because of **s 78** of the **Police and Criminal Evidence Act (PACE) 1984**, will not.

Another major reform is the availability of the 'safety-valve' in **s 114(1)(d)**, which provides for the admissibility of a hearsay statement where the court is satisfied that it is in the interests of justice for the statement to be admitted. This will not only enable a court to do justice in a case such as *Sparks* (1964); it will make unnecessary the use of 'hearsay fiddles', such as that adopted in *Ward* (2001), where it was held that evidence tending to confirm the defendant's presence near the scene of the crime, but which was *prima facie* hearsay, could nevertheless be admitted because of its weight.[2]

By **s 116**, oral as well as documentary hearsay evidence can now be given where a witness is unavailable; **s 23** of the **Criminal Justice Act 1988** allowed only documentary hearsay to be given in such circumstances. But by **s 116(1)(b)** the person who made the statement must be identified to the court's satisfaction; if this condition is not fulfilled, reliance will have to be placed on the safety valve or on the *res gestae* exception, preserved by **s 118**. The discretion and leave provisions of **ss 25** and **26** of the **CJA 1988** do not appear in the **2003 Act**. But necessity by itself will not eliminate the weaknesses of hearsay evidence.[3] A defence application under **s 78** of **PACE** can be made, and possible breach of **Art 6** of the **European Convention on Human Rights** must also be considered. The European Court has consistently taken the view that a

---

2 See also *Lilley* [2003] EWCA 1789, and D. Birch, 'Hearsay-logic and Hearsay-fiddles: *Blastland* Revisited', in Peter Smith, ed., *Criminal Law: Essays in Honour of JC Smith* (London: Butterworths, 1987).

3 Paul Roberts and Adrian Zuckerman, *Criminal Evidence* (Oxford: Oxford University Press, 2004) p 625.

conviction will not be fair if it is founded 'mainly' on evidence from someone whom the accused has had no opportunity to examine.[4] Further, leave is required by **s 116(2)(e)** where a witness does not give evidence through fear.

A small but significant change in the law appears in **s 120(7)(d)**. Recent complaints are now to be made 'as soon as could reasonably be expected after the alleged conduct'. Formerly, the complaint had also to be 'recent' in relation to the offence (*Birks* (2003)). The probable effect of **s 120(7)(d)** is that this restriction has gone, so that complaints of offences committed against someone who was a child at the time will be more readily admitted. The section extends the scope of recent complaints to offences of any kind. It also provides that previous statements shall now be evidence of the truth of the matters stated, thereby removing a distinction between evidence of truth and evidence of credibility that jurors must have found it hard to appreciate.

A major criticism of the reforms is that they do not go far enough. The retention in **s 118** of the old law relating to *res gestae* is unsatisfactory, in particular because the admissibility of statements about contemporaneous mental states remains underdeveloped and obscure. Cases about statements of intention illustrate this well. In *Buckley* (1873), a decision at first instance, such evidence was admitted, but without reasons. In *Wainwright* (1875), another decision at first instance, such evidence was excluded, but the basis for the decision is unclear. It may well be that admissibility was sought under a different head of *res gestae*. In *Thomson* (1912) the Court of Criminal Appeal held such evidence inadmissible, but the appellant's argument had been based on the much broader proposition that an accused person is entitled to adduce any relevant evidence in his defence, regardless of the rules of evidence. A more favourable view of admissibility was taken, *obiter*, by the Court of Appeal in *Moghal* (1977). A still more favourable view was taken by the Court of Appeal in *Gilfoyle* (1996), which had the apparent effect of removing the requirement of contemporaneity between the utterance and the state of mind under investigation. Another problematic decision is that of the Court of Appeal in *Callender* (1998) where the Court, following a concession by counsel for the appellant, held, contrary to earlier authority, that the *Andrews* (1987) requirement of lack of opportunity for concoction or distortion applied in all the categories of *res gestae*, and not only to excited utterances.

Roberts and Zuckerman have criticised the **2003 Act** on the basis that it creates 'a judicial discretion jamboree'.[5] **Sections 116(4)** and **117(7)** create particular discretions. **Section 114(1)(d)** introduces a radical new inclusionary discretion. This is elaborated in **s 114(2)** by a list of nine factors to structure its exercise. However, in *Singh* (2006) the

---

4   See, for example, *PS v Germany* [2002] **Crim LR 312**.
5   Roberts and Zuckerman, *Criminal Evidence*, p 641.

Court of Appeal held that although all these must be considered, a judge does not have to reach a decision on any one of them. **Section 121(1)(c)** establishes an additional leave requirement applicable to multiple hearsay, apart from business documents. **Section 126** creates a new overriding discretion to exclude hearsay of marginal probative value where its admission would result in undue waste of time. The Act preserves the discretion contained in **s 78** of **PACE**, and the common law discretion to exclude prosecution evidence is also untouched.

It can be argued in favour of so many discretions that they will enable a court to regulate the admissibility of hearsay evidence in a way that takes into account justice and common sense. On the other hand, experience of operating the discretions in **ss 25** and **26** of the **CJA 1988** showed, as the Law Commission noted, such a wide variety of judicial approaches that consistency suffered. Balancing the benefits of being able to do justice in the instant case against the dangers of inconsistency will always be difficult. The **2003 Act**, in this respect, probably achieves as satisfactory a compromise as could be made.

Aim Higher

1. You should always be able to take into account in a problem question the considerations that are meant to guide the judge's judgment about admitting an item of hearsay. So, for example, be prepared to refer to **CJA 2003**, **ss 114(2)** and **116(4)**.
2. Be prepared to assess the advantages and disadvantages of the scheme introduced by the **2003 Act**. One of the most important criticisms is that too much unreviewable discretion is left to the trial judge, and that this makes for uncertainty in the application of the law and the unequal treatment of defendants.

Common Pitfalls

1. It is a sign of weakness if a candidate fails to advise on hearsay in relation to the particular facts of a problem question. So, for example, you should always check that necessary conditions, such as those in **s 116(2)(c)** and **(d)**, have been satisfied, or that in an appropriate case there is admissible evidence to show that a witness does not give evidence through fear.
2. Candidates often miss the presence of 'multiple hearsay'. So, for example, always ask yourself whether an original speaker could have given evidence orally only by relying himself on a hearsay exception.

Hazardous Evidence

INTRODUCTION

All evidence, without exception, is hazardous. There are several reasons for this.

The first is that all evidence emerges as the result of some sort of selection. One kind may be loosely described as 'natural selection'. Not all the evidence that is relevant to a particular inquiry will have survived. Witnesses may have died; documents may have been destroyed; the physical features of a building may have been altered. Another sort of selection is human selection. In any investigation, someone has to gather the evidence that has survived. But to gather evidence effectively, you have to be intelligent enough to recognise what may be significant, and honest enough to do the job without pre-conceived ideas of what the outcome of the investigation should be. Natural selection and human frailty between them ensure that no jury ever sees more than a part of the whole picture, and that part may be a very small and misleading one.[1]

Another reason for the hazardous nature of evidence is that too much has to be taken on trust. It is not always appreciated that the only direct experience upon which a tribunal of fact can depend in a legal inquiry is its perception of witnesses testifying in the witness box, and perhaps also the perceptions that it experiences from its own examination of an item of real evidence. In relation to a testifying witness, two difficulties arise. The first comes from uncertainty as to whether the witness can trust the evidence of his own senses. He may believe that he saw the defendant stab the victim, but what guarantee has he that things were not otherwise? The second difficulty comes from the fact that the jury has to rely on the witness for an insight into what happened on the occasion under investigation. But all the jury can perceive is the witness in the box giving evidence. What is their

---

[1] This is perhaps more obviously true of a historian's work. See Carr, EH, *What Is History?*, 2nd edn, 1987, Chapter 1. But a little reflection should be enough to show that the same is true of the investigation that precedes a criminal or civil trial.

justification for inferring from the witness's testimony that the defendant did in fact stab the victim?

A third reason for the hazardous nature of evidence is that, save for some items of real evidence, it is presented through the medium of language. But language is notoriously ambiguous. 'Words . . . may easily be misunderstood by a dull man. They may easily be misconstrued by a knave. What was spoken metaphorically may be apprehended literally. What was spoken ludicrously may be apprehended seriously. A particle, a tense, a mood, an emphasis may make the whole difference between guilt and innocence.'[2] But more than this, the very adversary system adopted in our courts tends to perpetuate ambiguity. One of the earliest lessons learned by a student of advocacy is how to avoid giving a witness whom he is cross-examining a chance to explain his testimony. Closed, leading questions that require a 'yes' or 'no' answer are recommended. These may be good trial tactics, but they are ill designed for the discovery of the truth.[3]

Politicians and lawyers have generally turned a blind eye to these fundamental defects. Attempts to make verdicts a little more reliable have been made only erratically and on a piecemeal basis. This chapter deals with attempts that have been made to control the way in which juries think about evidence which at various times has been thought to be particularly unreliable. These attempts gave rise to law that compelled judges to warn juries in a particular way when they had to consider certain types of evidence, or evidence from certain types of witness.

MANDATORY WARNINGS TO THE JURY

In the 18th century, when the beginnings of our modern law of evidence can be perceived, both prosecution and defence were often unrepresented by counsel, and the judge played a much larger part in criminal cases than he did in the 19th century and later. In particular, judges had a greater control over juries' deliberations. Summings up could contain much more of the judge's opinion than would now be thought proper. Where it appeared that a deliberation was likely to be short, the jury would often not leave the jury box, and this could provide an opportunity for informal dialogue with the judge about the evidence. Even if a jury

---

2 Macaulay (Lord), *The History of England from the Accession of James the Second*, 1848–1861, reprinted 1880, Vol 2, Chapter 5, p 161. Even more hazardous is evidence of statements alleged to have been made on an earlier occasion by a defendant.
3 See, for example, Stone, M, *Cross-Examination in Criminal Trials*, 1988, p 107; Boon, A, *Advocacy*, 2nd edn, 1999, pp 113–114; cf McEwan, J, *Evidence and the Adversarial Process: The Modern Law*, 1992, pp 16–19.

returned a verdict with which the judge disagreed, he could persuade them to reconsider.

In time, this informal procedure gave way to a system more like the one we are used to today, though there was one major difference: until 1898, there was no general right for a defendant to testify in his own defence. Prosecution and defence came increasingly to be represented by counsel, possibly because of an increase in the size of the Bar, and the judge's control over the jury's deliberations slackened. But because jurors were free to weigh the evidence without judicial intervention, it became more necessary to warn them in a formal way during summing up about the weight to be attached to certain types of witness and testimony, and of the danger in convicting on the basis of such evidence without some independent support. Warnings were thought to be necessary in three main cases: those involving the evidence of children, of accomplices, and of complainants in cases where a sexual crime was alleged.

For a long time, the manner in which a warning was given, and even whether a warning was given at all, was a matter solely for the trial judge's discretion. But when the Court of Criminal Appeal was set up in 1907, discretionary practices tended to harden into rigid rules of law. Before long, a highly complex law of corroboration had developed. Eventually, it was thought to be so unsatisfactory that Parliament very largely abolished it in **s 34(2)** of the **Criminal Justice Act (CJA) 1988** and in **s 32** of the **Criminal Justice and Public Order Act (CJPOA) 1994**.

Alongside the strict law of corroboration, there had also developed a less formal body of law about warnings that should be given to a jury where a witness might be unreliable even though he did not fall within the limited classes to which corroboration law applied. Thus, it was held that an informal warning should be given where witnesses had a purpose of their own to serve in giving evidence, or suffered from mental disorder (*Beck* (1982); *Spencer* (1986)). In *Stone* (2005) the Court of Appeal held that this body of law had not survived the abolition of the former rules of corroboration. In *Makanjuola* (1995), the Court of Appeal emphasised the wide discretion possessed by trial judges to adapt warnings about the testimony of any particular witness to the circumstances of the case. The exercise of that discretion will only exceptionally be reviewed by the Court of Appeal. *Makanjuola* has also been helpful in killing the notion that the old law about corroboration might still somehow apply once the judge had decided to give a discretionary warning.

There remains one common type of evidence where a warning is required which is still governed by a rule-based rather than a discretionary system. Identification evidence that falls within the principles set out in *Turnbull* (1977) and subsequent cases must be the subject of a particular type of judicial warning in the summing up. A body of case law has also developed about warnings that should be given to the jury where a defendant's lies, whether told inside or outside court, could be taken to support the prosecution case. See *Lucas* (1981) and *Burge* (1996).

Code D of the current **(2004) Codes of Practice** made under the **Police and Criminal Evidence Act (PACE) 1984** is likely to be relevant in any problem involving identification. The whole of the Code is important, but you should pay special attention to **Annex A** (video identification), **Annex B** (identification parades), and **Annex E** (showing photographs).

If there has been a breach of the Code, you must be able to advise on the likely consequences. Remember the following:

- What allows the court to look at the provisions of the Code and what makes them relevant? See **s 67(11)** of **PACE**.
- If the quality of the identification evidence is poor and there is no other evidence to support it, the jury should be directed to acquit (*Turnbull* (1977)). Thus, the Code breach may so weaken the identification evidence that a submission of no case to answer will be successful.
- The evidence may be excluded under **s 78** of **PACE**. (See Chapter 7 for further details.)

Checklist ✔

Students should be familiar with the following areas:

- the abolition of corroboration law in the **CJA 1988** and the **Criminal Justice and Public Order Act 1994**;
- the effect of this – see *Makanjuola* (1995);
- the guidelines in *Makanjuola* about discretionary warnings;
- the rules concerning identification in *Turnbull* (1977);
- **Code of Practice D**;
- **s 62(11)** of **PACE**;
- the possible effects of Code breach;
- warnings where a defendant has lied;
- **s 34** of the **CJPOA 1994**, and the directions that must be given where that section is relied on (see Chapter 7);
- **ss 41–43 Youth Justice and Criminal Evidence Act 1999** (see also Chapter 10).

QUESTION 20

Archie is charged with the rape of Clare. Both are aged 20, live in Worcester, and know each other socially. The case for the prosecution is that one evening they were at a party near Worcester given by John, a local politician. Towards the end of the evening Archie offered Clare a lift back to Worcester in his car, which she accepted. It is alleged that Archie stopped the car at some stage during the journey and dragged Clare into a nearby field, where he raped her. Clare says that she was so shocked by what happened that afterwards she returned to the car with Archie and let him drive her home.

Geoff, her elder brother, was at home when she arrived. He noticed that she had mud in her hair and on her clothes and said to her, 'Clare, what has happened? Be sure you tell me the truth, or you are no longer my sister!' Clare then told him that she had been raped by Archie. Geoff later gave a statement to the police reporting what he had seen and heard, but a few days later he was killed in a pub brawl.

When Archie was interviewed under caution by the police he said, 'Look, let me tell you what happened. I wish I'd never offered her a lift. She'd had quite a bit to drink and could talk of nothing except the idea of having sex in the open air. When we reached a road that ran by a field she tried to stop the car; we nearly went into a ditch. I did have sex with her, but I'd never have done so if she hadn't kept on about it.'

Archie wishes to call Ethan and Fergus in support of his account. Each will say that about a month before the alleged rape he had sex with Clare at her suggestion, and that she had insisted on having sex in a park or field.

Archie has recently heard that last year Clare made an allegation of rape against Harry, but that there was no prosecution because of lack of evidence.

▶ **Discuss the evidential matters arising.**

Answer Plan

There are four principal topics for discussion. The first is whether the prosecution can make use of Geoff's statement to the police. You will appreciate from the fact that Geoff is dead that if this statement is to reach the jury at all, it will have to do so on the basis that it is hearsay evidence and that the maker is unavailable. **Section 116** of **CJA 2003** will be applicable, and because of **s 116(1)(a)** you will need to ask whether Geoff could have given evidence in accordance with his statement had he been alive. The statement refers to something observed by Geoff, and clearly he could have given evidence of that. But it also contains an account of what

Clare said to him. This in itself is hearsay, but it is admissible by virtue of **subs (4)** and **(7)** of **s 120**. Remember, however, the warning that must be given to the jury under *Islam* (1999). Since Geoff is not available, this part of his statement will be second-hand hearsay if his witness statement is read in evidence and the multiple hearsay provisions of **s 121** will apply.

The next topic for discussion is what Archie said during his interview with the police. No question of impropriety arises. You are not told about access to legal advice, but don't waste time discussing that if you are not told anything about it. Archie admits having sex but denies rape. It will be to his advantage to be able to show that his defence at trial was raised at the first possible opportunity. Is it admissible? You will need to refer to *Sharp* (1988) or *Aziz* (1995).

Is the evidence of Ethan and Fergus relevant? Clearly it is because it supports Archie's account of events by making it more likely that what he says about Clare's insistence on sex in the field is true. But will this evidence be excluded by **s 41** of the **Youth Justice and Criminal Evidence Act 1999**? The issue is one of consent; **s 41(3)(b)** will not apply because the events took place too long ago, but **s 41(3)(c)** may well do so. There should be some discussion of what amounts to similarity for these purposes. Reference should be made to what was said on this subject in *A* (2002).

The earlier allegation against Harry did not lead to a prosecution, and this might suggest that on that occasion Clare was lying, from which it might be inferred that she is doing so again on this occasion. But this sort of information is strictly regarded by the courts; see, for example, *M* (2009) and *D* (2009).

ANSWER

The first question is whether the prosecution can make use of Geoff's statement to the police. Since Geoff is dead, there appears to be a case for admissibility of the statement under **s 116(2)(a)**. To be admitted, however, the condition in **s 116(1)(a)** must also be satisfied. Could Geoff have given oral evidence of what he saw when Clare returned home? Clearly, he could. But could he also give evidence of what Clare said to him? On the assumption that Clare herself testifies for the prosecution, he can if what she said amounts to an admissible previous statement under **s 120(4)** and **(7)** of the **Criminal Justice Act 2003** (hereafter '**CJA 2003**'). Presumably there will be no difficulty in satisfying the **subs (4)** conditions. The only condition under **subs (7)** that might give rise to argument is **subs (7)(e)**. The words 'you are no longer my sister' could be construed as a threat. Whether they are may depend on how seriously Clare took them. Did she construe them as only an exaggeration that expressed her brother's concern? Or did she take them seriously, perhaps in the light of her brother's previous conduct towards her? If her previous statement is admitted, it will be evidence of the truth of its contents by virtue of **subs (4)**, but the judge in summing up must direct the jury that the earlier statement cannot operate as confirmation from an independent source of the evidence she gives from the witness box. The same direction must also be given in respect of Geoffs evidence about her appearance (*Islam*, 1999).

There is no mention of impropriety in the interview with Archie that the police conducted. What he said amounts to a 'mixed' statement, since it contains an admission that he had sexual intercourse with Clare but also an assertion that this was with her consent. As a mixed statement, it will be admissible and is to be considered by the jury as evidence of the truth of all its contents (*Sharp* (1988); *Aziz* (1995)).

The evidence of Ethan and Fergus is clearly relevant as a matter of common sense. A woman who asks for open-air sex on two fairly recent occasions is likely to have done so again on a third. But admissibility will also depend on whether **s 41** of the **Youth Justice and Criminal Evidence Act 1999** can be satisfied. The issue at trial is one of consent, and **s 41(3)(b)** will not apply because the earlier incidents took place too long ago. The favoured meaning of 'at or about the same time' was accepted in *A* (2002) to be, broadly speaking, within the range of 24 hours on each side of the alleged incident.

But **s 41(3)(c)(i)** is likely to apply. The request made to the defendant for sex in the open air and the act of intercourse with him in the field should be seen as one event. Even if this is not done, the request is clearly 'other sexual behaviour of the complainant' which took place 'at or about the same time as' the alleged rape. The question then will be whether the incidents with Ethan and Fergus are so similar to the events described by Archie that they 'cannot reasonably be explained as a coincidence'. These words have not been precisely defined, and probably are incapable of exact definition. In *A* (2002) it was said by Lord Clyde that the requirement falls short of the earlier test of 'striking similarity', although he added that *mere* similarity would not be sufficient. In *Tahed* (2004), consensual use of the same item of equipment in a park on an earlier occasion was held, with other evidence, to be sufficiently similar to the act complained of. The location on these facts is of a more general nature, but there is at least a reasonable chance of persuading a judge that the condition is satisfied, although the prosecution might pray in aid the illustration of sex in motor cars, which would not be admissible according to Lord Williams during the debate on the Bill in the House of Lords.

On the limited information given, the earlier allegation against Harry will be inadmissible. 'Sexual behaviour' within **s 41(1)** does not include false accusations of sexual offences on earlier occasions (*T; H*, 2002). However, in the same conjoined appeals the Court of Appeal stated that such evidence cannot be admitted unless there are grounds for establishing not only that the earlier allegation was made, but also that it was false. In *D* (2009) it was held that the mere fact that police had decided that there was insufficient evidence to prosecute is not evidence that the earlier allegation was false.

QUESTION 21

Rupert and Edward have been committed for trial, charged with burglary. The case for the prosecution is that they broke into a shop in Brighton owned by Rimsky & Romanov, a firm of jewellers, and there stole a quantity of watches.

Evidence for the prosecution will be given by Tabitha, Rupert's former girlfriend. She has made a statement in which she states that on the evening when the burglary took place, she drove Rupert and Edward to a public house. While drinking there, she overheard Rupert and Edward discussing a plan to break into the premises of Rimsky & Romanov. Later, they all left the public house. Tabitha says that she then drove them in the direction of her house but that on the way Rupert asked her to stop, saying that he and Edward needed to relieve themselves. This was near the rear entrance to the shop owned by Rimsky & Romanov. Tabitha states that she waited in the car for about half an hour until Rupert and Edward returned, and that they then drove to Tabitha's house. Tabitha also states that she helped them with some luggage which they had with them, and that the men left the next day. When the police came to ask for Tabitha's help in this matter, they discovered one of the stolen watches in her bathroom.

The prosecution also have a statement from Tabitha's nephew Archie, aged 10, who says that he found the rest of the stolen goods in Edward's garden shed.

When interviewed by the police without a solicitor, Rupert refused to answer any questions. Edward when interviewed denied having any part in the offence. He said that he spent the evening and the night in question at a hotel in Manchester with a woman called Sheila.

◗ Discuss the evidential matters arising.

Answer Plan
There are six topics that need to be discussed in the answer to this question:

❖ Should there be an informal warning about the reliability of Tabitha's evidence? Note how it is possible to use the old law to argue by analogy,

but be careful to avoid any suggestion that it still has any force as binding authority.
- Sheila's previous convictions.
- Look at the content of Tabitha's evidence. She is reporting what she heard other people say quite a lot. Is all this admissible? Why?
- What is the position about Archie's evidence?
- What is the significance now of Rupert's failure to answer police questions? Try to summarise what the Act says accurately. A student who simply said, for example, that Rupert's silence was evidence of his guilt would not get much credit.
- What are the problems arising from Edward's alibi? Have you read the question carefully enough to deal with this point fully?

ANSWER

The first question that arises is whether the judge should give an informal warning about the reliability of Tabitha's evidence when summing up to the jury. There are two reasons why such a warning might be desirable. We are told that she is Rupert's former girlfriend. Is there any evidence of antipathy towards him that would make it possible that she is implicating him from a desire for revenge? The rule in *Beck* (1982) was that where a witness might have an 'interest or purpose of his own to serve' in giving evidence, the judge should warn the jury about this. Earlier cases such as *Willis* (1916) and *Evans* (1965) established that where a wife gave evidence in support of an accomplice, the jury should be warned of the danger in relying on her testimony because she had an interest to serve. In earlier cases, warnings in situations analogous to those requiring corroboration had been required. In *Stone* (2005) the Court of Appeal held that this requirement had not survived the abolition of the corroboration rules. Nevertheless, it would seem sensible to warn the jury about the different but perhaps equally strong interest of someone giving evidence against a former boyfriend towards whom she felt animosity.

It is worth noting that under the old law, the jury might have had to be warned that Tabitha was an accomplice and that it would be dangerous for them to convict on her uncorroborated evidence (*Davies v DPP* (1954)). This suggests another reason for an informal warning to be given about Tabitha's evidence. It is possible that, although she was never charged, she was an accomplice. She clearly knew of the plan to break into the shop. She stopped the car near the shop and it is unlikely that she believed that Rupert and Edward took half an hour to relieve themselves in its vicinity. She helped them with their 'luggage', and later one of the stolen watches was found in her bathroom.

No special difficulties are presented by the content of Tabitha's evidence. Her report of what she heard Rupert and Edward saying about their plans to break into the shop will be admissible as an exception to the rule against hearsay as showing the contemporaneous state of mind and intentions of the accused. **Section 118(1)** of the **Criminal Justice Act 2003** preserves, *inter alia*, the common law relating to *res gestae* exceptions to the rule against hearsay, including declarations about contemporaneous states of mind such as intention. In *Moghal* (1977), a statement of intention to murder made some six months before the commission of the crime was considered admissible. This particular decision was subsequently criticised by Lord Bridge in *Blastland* (1986) on the ground of relevance. However, the House of Lords emphasised in *Blastland* that such a declaration would be admissible if the state of mind evidenced by it was directly in issue at the trial, or was of direct and immediate relevance to an issue arising in the trial. Clearly, those conditions are satisfied here.

It might also be possible to argue that what was said amounted to a confession by both defendants. A confession is another exception to the rule against hearsay preserved by **s 118**. By **s 82(1)** of the **Police and Criminal Evidence Act (PACE) 1984**, a confession includes any statement wholly or partly adverse to the person who made it, whether made to a person in authority or not. It may be, despite apparent oddity, that things said before the commission of an offence can amount to confessions if the offence is subsequently committed.

Tabitha will be able to report the excuse given by Rupert for stopping the car near the shop because the prosecution will be relying on its falsity, as in *Mawaz Khan* (1967), rather than its truth.

It is just conceivable that the judge would think it appropriate to comment on the weight to be attached to Archie's evidence in view of his relationship to Tabitha if the defence makes a point of this. By **s 53(1)** of the **Youth Justice and Criminal Evidence Act 1999**, at every stage in criminal proceedings all persons are (whatever their age) competent to give evidence. By **subs (3)**, a person is not competent to give evidence in criminal proceedings if it appears to the court that he is not a person who is able to understand questions put to him as a witness and give answers to them that can be understood. There is no suggestion that Archie falls into this category and he will therefore be competent to give evidence. However, his evidence will be unsworn. By **s 55(2)** of the **1999 Act**, a witness may not be sworn unless he has attained the age of 14.

Rupert's failure to answer police questions is now governed by **s 34** of the **Criminal Justice and Public Order Act 1994**. The failure of an accused in such circumstances to mention any fact relied on later in his defence, if it was a fact which in the circumstances existing at the time the accused could reasonably have been expected to mention, will allow the jury in determining whether the accused is guilty of the offence charged to draw such inferences as appear proper. But it is important to know if Rupert was offered a solicitor. **Subsection (2A)** of **s 34** provides that where the accused was at an authorised place of detention at the time of his failure to mention any fact relied on in his defence, no inferences may be drawn unless he was allowed an opportunity to consult a solicitor before being questioned.

If it is an appropriate case for a **s 34** direction, the judge should follow the guidelines set out in *Petkar* (2004). He must identify the facts on which Rupert relies and which were not mentioned on questioning. He must identify the inferences which it is suggested might be drawn from failure to mention such facts, to the extent that they may go beyond the standard inference of late fabrication. The jury should be told that, if an inference is drawn, they should not convict wholly or mainly on the strength of it. They should be told that an inference should be drawn only if they think it is fair and proper, and it should be drawn only if the only sensible explanation for failure to mention facts relied on is that Rupert had no answers, or none that would stand up to scrutiny. Moreover, an inference should be drawn only if, apart from Rupert's failure to mention facts relied on, the prosecution case is so strong that it clearly calls for an answer by him. The jury should be reminded of the evidence on the basis of which they are invited not to draw any inferences from Rupert's silence.

The trial judge should tell the jury that it is for the prosecution to disprove the alibi beyond reasonable doubt (*Johnson* (1995)). In *Burge and Pegg* (1996), it was said that a *Lucas* (1981) direction should be given where, among other cases, the defendant relies on an alibi. However, it is clear that a *Lucas* direction does not have to be given in every case where an alibi is raised by a defendant. For example, in *Patrick* (1999) the Court of Appeal held that there is no need for a direction where the only possible basis for rejecting a defendant's alibi would be acceptance by the jury of the prosecution's identification evidence. A rather similar situation arises on these facts. In effect, the members of the jury have to be satisfied beyond reasonable doubt that Tabitha's account is reliable. If they decide that it is, Edward's alibi must be false. In *Middleton* (2000), the Court of Appeal said that a *Lucas* direction should not be given where it would only confuse the jury, and probably that would be its effect here.

QUESTION 22

Aaron, Bailey and Caleb have been charged with violent disorder, contrary to **s 3(1)** of the **Public Order Act 1986**. The case for the prosecution is that they made a concerted attack on the staff of a gambling club after they had been told to leave.

Dale, a barman, says that he was hit with a bottle by one of the men taking part in the attack. Dale did not recognise the man at the time, but told the police that he would be able to recognise him if he saw him again, despite the fact that the lighting was dim. Eli, another barman, who saw the attack on Dale, also thought he could recognise the culprit if he saw him again. At the police station DS Quelch showed both of them several sets of photographs, each containing ten pictures of men with convictions for crimes of violence. After some discussion, Dale and Eli picked out a photograph of Aaron. They subsequently picked out Aaron again during separate video identification procedures.

Ford, a croupier, says that he also was wounded by one of the men who carried out the attack. He was unable to identify anyone from police photographs, but he was able to give a description of the man to the police, as a result of which a photofit image of his attacker was created. This led to the arrest of Bailey. Ford failed to pick out Bailey during a subsequent video identification procedure. Bailey, however, made several damaging admissions during a properly-conducted police interview, and the photofit bears a strong resemblance to him.

Gabe, a manager, was struck by one of the attackers, who rushed from the building immediately afterwards. Gabe, who was not seriously hurt, ran after him. The man escaped, but Gabe was able to stop a police car that happened to be driving by and explain what had occurred. The officers in the car then drove round some nearby streets to see if Gabe could find his attacker. At one point he saw a man standing in a doorway and asked the police to stop. One of the officers went up to the man and said to Gabe, 'Is that him?' Gabe replied, 'Yes; I'm sure of it.' The man identified himself as Caleb and was arrested. Caleb's solicitor later asked for an identification procedure to be arranged for his client. The police refused, saying that this was not necessary because he had already been positively identified.

Gabe was later invited to the police station to see if he could identify any others who had taken part in the attack. He was shown a selection of photographs, including one of Aaron. Gabe identified him at that stage, and subsequently picked him out during a video identification.

◗ Advise the prosecution on the evidential matters that arise in relation to identification.

Answer Plan

This question is mainly concerned with identifications where there have been breaches of **Code D**. One of the problems is how to order the diverse information that you have been given. Here is a suggestion:

Evidence against Aaron
- Start with the video identifications of Aaron by Dale and Eli, followed by the separate identification which Gabe made.
- Introduce **Code D** and explain its relevance.
- Look at what happened before the video identification, explain the breaches that occurred, and explain how they could be used by the defence.

Evidence against Bailey
- Deal briefly with the way in which the prosecution can use his admissions.
- Deal with the evidential value of the photofit.

Evidence against Caleb
- Gabe's 'on-the-spot' identification of him.
- Refusal of an identification procedure.

All defendants
- *Turnbull* warnings and their contents.

Final check
If there have been breaches of the Code, how will the defence make use of them?

ANSWER

If **Code D** had been followed, Dale, Eli and Ford would give evidence of the assaults committed by Aaron and of their subsequent identification of him during video identifications. Evidence of pre-trial identification is admissible under **s 120(1)**, **(4)** and **(5)** of the **Criminal Justice Act (CJA) 2003**. But there is a difficulty in this case because the identification procedures were vitiated by earlier breaches of **Code D** in relation to the showing of photographs.

Code D is issued pursuant to **s 66** of **PACE 1984**. By **s 67(11)** of that Act, if any provision of a code appears to the court to be relevant to any question arising in the proceedings, it shall be taken into account in determining that question. The court is not obliged to exclude evidence where a breach can be shown; it is necessary to see whether it has caused unfairness (*Grannell*, 1990).

Paragraph 3.3 of **Code D** permits photographs to be shown to a witness where the identity of the suspect is not known. Thus, in principle, it was proper to show photographs to Dale, and if he could not have made an identification from them, to have shown them subsequently to Eli (or vice versa). However, showing photographs has to be done in accordance with **Annex E** of the Code, **paragraph 3** of which states that only one witness shall be shown photographs at any one time. The witness is to be given as much privacy as practicable and not allowed to communicate with any other witness in the case. By **paragraph 4**, the witness shall be shown not less than twelve photographs at a time. The police infringed the provisions of both paragraphs when showing the photographs to Dale and Eli. Since a person who picks out a photograph may later pick out someone during an identification procedure with the photograph in mind rather than what was seen when the offence was committed, particular care is needed to see that the provisions of Annex E are followed. In this case a strong defence argument could be presented that the video identifications of Dale and Eli were contaminated to such an extent that they should be excluded under **s 78** of **PACE**.[1]

Gabe should not have been shown photographs at all. **Paragraph 3.3** of **Code D** provides that a witness must not be shown photographs if the identity of the suspect is known to the police and he is available to take part in an identification procedure. By the time Gabe was invited to look at photographs, the identity of Aaron was known to the police, and presumably he was available, if needed, to take part in an identification procedure. Again, a defence submission to exclude Gabe's video identification under **s 78** could succeed.

Subject to anything that the defence might argue, Bailey's admissions will be evidence against him under **s 76** of **PACE**. The photofit image resembling Bailey is in principle caught by the rule against hearsay under **s 115(2) CJA 2003**. Ford could give evidence describing his attacker, however, and could use the photofit to refresh his memory under **s 139 CJA 2003**. The photofit itself could be put in evidence under **s 120(1)**, **(4)** and **(5)** because it is a 'previous statement' within **s 120(4)** and describes a person, so falling within **s 120(5)**.

In *Kelly* (1992) the Court of Appeal suggested that when a suspect is found within minutes of the crime and close to the scene, it might well be that the provisions of the Code do not apply, and that the best course is for the police to see if the witness thinks that the suspect was the offender. It could also be argued that the Code was followed. By **paragraph 3.2** of **Code D**, where a suspect's identity is unknown, a witness can be taken to a particular neighbourhood or place to see whether he can identify the person he saw committing the offence. But the principles applicable to formal identification procedures are to be followed as far as possible.

Gabe's identification of Caleb is therefore likely to be admissible in principle. But was Caleb entitled to a later identification procedure? **Code D, paragraph 3.12** sets out the circumstances in which an identification procedure must be held. It provides, *inter alia*,

---

1 See Chapter 7.

that where a witness has identified a suspect before a formal identification procedure is held, and the suspect disputes the accuracy of the identification, a procedure shall be held unless it is not practicable or would serve no useful purpose in proving or disproving whether the suspect committed the offence. An example, given in the Code, is where the suspect is already well known to the identifying witness. In *Forbes* (2001) the House of Lords held under a previous version of **Code D** that an identification parade was mandatory where identification was in dispute, save in the circumstances mentioned in the Code or in a case of pure recognition of someone well known to the witness. An earlier identification, however complete, did not mean that a parade could be refused. Under the present Code, by **paragraph 3.2(d)** it is unnecessary, after a witness has made a positive identification and subject to **paragraphs 3.12** and **3.13** for that witness to take part in a further procedure. Although opinion is divided, the better view is probably that *Forbes* has not been impliedly reversed, and that 'no useful purpose' is limited to the most exceptional cases. It may well be, therefore, that Caleb has been wrongfully denied a formal procedure. The defence could argue that Gabe's street identification without further support would so adversely affect the fairness of the proceedings that it should be excluded under **s 78** of **PACE**.

In relation to admissible evidence of all the identifying witnesses the judge will have to direct the jury in accordance with the principles set out in *Turnbull* (1977). So he will warn the jury of the special need for caution before convicting on identification evidence; he must also explain why this warning is needed. He must direct the jury to examine closely the circumstances in which each identification was made and direct the jury to consider whether identification evidence is supported by any other evidence. He should identify what is and what is not capable of providing support. Although in some earlier cases the Court of Appeal said that it is not always necessary to summarise specific weaknesses in the identification evidence, more recent decisions like *Stanton* (2004) show that this is now likely to be treated as an essential part of a *Turnbull* direction.

Aim Higher ★

1. You should be able to show familiarity with the contents of *Turnbull* and *Lucas* directions. Remember that in each case the judge must tell the jury, among other things, why the particular warning is necessary.
2. You should be familiar with the provisions of **Code D** in relation to the conduct of identification procedures, so as to be able to comment in a problem question if anything has been done incorrectly. The same applies to the provisions of **Annex E**, which deals with the showing of photographs to potential witnesses, and is another topic where the setter of a problem question likes to make things go wrong.

> **Common Pitfalls** ✗
> 1. Candidates who refer to the need for a *Turnbull* or *Lucas* direction often do so without saying what these should contain. It is particularly important that you should show your knowledge of the contents of a direction; if you do not, the examiner is likely to assume that you do not know.
> 2. Candidates are sometimes quite good at picking out breaches of **Code C** or **Code D**, but they then wrongly assume that breach leads automatically to exclusion of evidence. You must be ready to show how a breach can be used in an argument grounded on **s 76** or **s 78** of **PACE** to get an item of evidence excluded.

QUESTION 23

'We regard mistaken identification as by far the greatest cause of actual or possible wrong conviction.' (Criminal Law Revision Committee, 11th Report, 1972)

Has enough been done to reduce this risk?

> **Answer Plan**
> Start by identifying the modes of protection: *Turnbull* (1977) warnings and **Code D**. Then deal with the adequacy of *Turnbull* warnings; some reference to voice identification and to 'evidence of description' would be appropriate here. The problems with the application of **Code D** should then be considered.
>
> In summary, therefore, the essay is constructed as follows:
>
> ❖ outline of the two ways of protecting against mistaken identification;
> ❖ the *Turnbull* (1977) guidelines: *Thornton* (1995); *Slater* (1995); *Pattinson and Exley* (1996); *Qadir* (1998);
> ❖ distinction between evidence of identity and evidence of description: *Gayle* (1999);
> ❖ voice identification: *Hersey* (1998); *Gummerson and Steadman* (1999);
> ❖ **Code D**: *Kelly* (1992); use of **s 78(1)** of the **Police and Criminal Evidence Act (PACE) 1984**; **Code D, para 3.12**; *Forbes* (2001).

ANSWER

English law tries to protect defendants from wrongful convictions that are based on mistaken identification evidence in two ways: by a system of judicial warnings to juries, and by a Code of Practice that governs identification procedures.

In *Turnbull* (1977), the Court of Appeal established guidelines that were to apply where the prosecution case depended 'wholly or substantially' on the correctness of one or more identifications of the defendant. The words 'wholly or substantially' have not in practice limited the range of cases in which the guidelines have been considered appropriate. A *Turnbull* direction has to be given in cases where identification is based on recognition as well as in cases where the risk of misidentification might seem greater: for example, where identification is based on a fleeting glimpse. The need for a direction will usually arise when the defendant denies that he was present at a particular place. But the direction may also be necessary where the defendant admits being present at a relevant place but denies involvement in the criminal activity taking place there. So, for example, it was held in *Thornton* (1995), where the defendant was charged with causing grievous bodily harm at a wedding reception, that the *Turnbull* warning ought to have been given because, where others present were similarly dressed, a mistake was clearly possible. As Rose LJ emphasised in *Slater* (1995), the key question is whether there was, in the particular circumstances, the possibility of mistake. Thus, the circumstances in which the warning is required are probably adequate.

Is the nature of the warning adequate? According to *Turnbull*, several stages have to be followed. First, the judge must warn the jury of the special need for caution before convicting on the basis of identification evidence. Secondly, he must tell the jury why such a warning is needed. Some reference should be made to the fact that a mistaken witness can be a convincing one, and that a number of convincing witnesses can all be mistaken. Thirdly, he must direct the jury to examine closely the circumstances in which each identification was made. In *Turnbull*, the court gave examples of topics for comment, such as the light and the length of the period of observation, but in *Pattinson and Exley* (1996), the Court of Appeal said that it was not necessary in every case for the judge to summarise all the weaknesses in the identification evidence. The court added that where the judge does summarise the identification evidence, he should point out strengths as well as weaknesses. In later cases, however, such as *Popat (No 2)* (2000), *Stanton* (2004), and *Nash* (2004), failure to mention weaknesses has given rise to a successful appeal. Fourthly, the judge should direct the jury to consider whether the identification evidence is supported by any other evidence. Fifthly, he should identify the evidence that is capable, and incapable, of providing such support. Not surprisingly, the Court of Appeal has deprecated rigid formulas for the fulfilment of *Turnbull* requirements. Thus, in *Qadir* (1998), it was said that the form and contents of the summing up should, even when identification is in issue, be tailored to the circumstances of the individual case. Nevertheless, the *Turnbull* procedure appears to provide a strong protection for defendants who challenge identification evidence. Further, it was said in *Turnbull* that cases should be withdrawn from the jury where the identification evidence is poor and there is no supporting evidence.

Turnbull almost certainly does not extend to evidence from a witness who says that he would be unable to recognise the person he saw if he were to see him again, but who remembers some identifying features of that person. But there seems to be no reason why it should be extended in this way to such 'evidence of description'. As Henry LJ pointed out in *Gayle* (1999), the danger of an honest witness's being mistaken as to distinctive clothing, or the general description of the person he saw, are minimal.

But *Turnbull* assumes that most identifications are visual. That is so, but sometimes identification may be by the sound of the human voice. On this topic, the law is undeveloped. In *Hersey* (1998), the Court of Appeal showed support for the equivalent of identification parades for voices, and said that juries should be directed as in cases of visual identification, with appropriate modifications. But, in *Gummerson and Steadman* (1999), the Court of Appeal disapproved of 'voice identification parades', and the content of any warning in the summing up remains unclear.

The protection given by **Code D** is less satisfactory. Failure to comply with the appropriate procedure will not lead inevitably to the exclusion of identification evidence (*Kelly* (1992)). What has to be shown is that the breach is sufficiently grave to bring the evidence within the scope of **s 78(1)** of **PACE**.

Code D, **para 3.12** provides that, except in certain stated circumstances, whenever a suspect disputes, an identification procedure shall be held unless it is not practicable, or it would serve no useful purpose in proving or disproving whether the suspect was involved in committing the offence. It has been suggested that the effect is to reverse the decision of the House of Lords in *Forbes* (2001), which held that the identification procedure was mandatory save in very limited circumstances, and to revive the Court of Appeal decision in *Popat* (1998), to the effect that the provision did not apply where a suspect had previously been 'properly and adequately' identified by the witness, or where there had already been an 'actual and complete' identification by the witness. But it is unlikely that **Code D**, **para 3.12** has this effect. If it were otherwise, the problems perceived by the House of Lords in *Forbes* would arise again. First, the police would have to make difficult decisions about the adequacy of earlier identifications. Secondly, to have to make such decisions would be at odds with their primary duty to investigate and prosecute crime. Thirdly, the *Popat* approach overlooked the fact that miscarriages of justice had resulted from identifications that were thought at the time to be satisfactory, but were later proved to be wrong.

It has been argued that the new primacy of video procedures puts a suspect in a more vulnerable position than was the case when identification parades were the primary identification procedure. When a suspect agrees to take part in a parade, he can withdraw his consent if he raises a reasonable objection to its composition or to some other element of unfairness. But once an image has been provided for video procedures, he has no control over the use to which it might be put.[1]

It is too early to say whether enough has been done to reduce the risk of mistaken identification. The contents of a *Turnbull* warning remain uncertain so far as identifying weakness in the identification evidence is concerned, although current authority suggests that this is now an essential feature of the direction. The law relating to voice identification has yet to be developed. The interpretation of **Code D, para 3.12** is open to argument. Subject to this, however, much has been done to allay the fears of the Criminal Law Revision Committee.

It seems clear that the Code does not apply to identifications made only a short time after the commission of the offence. Thus, in *Kelly* (1992), the defendant was charged with attempted rape. The offence took place in a street, and the attacker was distracted before he could commit the full offence. The police arrived soon afterwards, and the victim, while talking to the police, saw the defendant, and told the police that she had seen her attacker. An officer questioned, but did not arrest, the defendant. Meanwhile, the victim was brought closer to him in a police car. She then said that she was sure the man she had seen had been her attacker, and the defendant was arrested. The Court of Appeal rejected the argument that this procedure had denied the defendant the benefit of an identification parade. It added that where a suspect is found within minutes of the crime and close to the scene, it might well be that **Code D** did not apply. Later decisions such as *Hickin and Others* (1996) and *Malashev* (1997) have confirmed this view.

---

1 See the commentary on *Marcus* [2005] **Crim LR 384**.

Confessions and Ill-Gotten Evidence

INTRODUCTION

One of the most important of defence counsel's objectives at trial is to ensure that as little of the prosecution evidence as possible reaches the jury – unless, of course, it happens to favour the defendant. This chapter deals with two important statutory weapons in the defence's armoury: **ss 76** and **78** of the **Police and Criminal Evidence Act (PACE) 1984**. These deal with confessions, and with a discretion to exclude for reasons of fairness evidence on which the prosecution proposes to rely. The sections are very often relied on in the alternative; it was decided in *Mason* (1988) that **s 78** applies to confessions just as much as to any other evidence.

Students of this topic need an important warning. In reading cases where evidence has been excluded under either section, but particularly under **s 78**, you are almost never reading precedents that will have to be followed in later cases. The reason for this is that no situation is ever exactly repeated, defendants are not all alike, and the effect of acts or omissions by the police is likely to vary greatly from case to case. Knowledge of previous decisions cannot be a substitute for rigorous thought about the facts of your own particular case, facts that of course include the personal characteristics of the defendant. This is plain enough from looking at the basic law. **Subsection (2)(b)** of **s 76** – probably the provision in that section which is most relied on – has the effect of requiring the court to attend to the particular circumstances of the individual defendant who relies on the provision. And, in *Jelen and Katz* (1989), the Court of Appeal emphasised that the application of **s 78** was 'not an apt field for hard case law and well founded distinctions between cases'.[1]

It is, of course, in relation to a confession that an argument for exclusion will very often have to be made. When a confession appears in a set of prosecution statements or in an examination question, you need to be able to do three things. You must be able to recognise it when you see it, assess its impact on the case as a whole, and work out what arguments are available to you to get it excluded.

---

1 See also *Roberts* (1997).

RECOGNISING THE CONFESSION

You may think a confession would be easy to spot: 'OK guv; it's a fair cop. You've got me bang to rights.' Perhaps in real life that sort of thing is said more often than we might expect. But because examiners are interested in grey areas, you are not likely to have to deal with anything so simple in the examination. Your starting point is the partial definition contained in **s 82(1)** of **PACE**. With that in mind, you must interpret what has been said. Remember that a favourite topic for questions is the extent to which an accused person can, by something other than an oral statement, *adopt* an allegation against him. Consider some possibilities: he begins to weep; he hangs his head; he blushes violently; he runs away; he says nothing; he attacks the accuser. For a vivid example, see *Batt* (1995).

IMPACT ON THE CASE AS A WHOLE

The obvious impact is that of something said by an accused person which inculpates the maker of the statement in relation to the offence in question. It used to be the case that an out-of-court confession implicating a co-accused, but made in the absence of that co-accused, was admissible evidence only against the maker of the confession. See, e.g., *Gunewardene* (1951). That traditional rule must now be read in the light of *Y* (2008), the effect of which is that such a confession can now, by the operation of **s 114(1)(d) CJA 2003**, be evidence not only against the person making the statement containing the confession, but also against anyone else whom the statement implicates. You should read the case and note the reservations about admitting such evidence as a matter of practice which the Court of Appeal made. These reservations might affect the practical application of the new law, but they don't alter the fact that the law has changed significantly. The result is that it is now wholly unclear in what circumstances the confession of one defendant is likely *in practice* to be admitted against another.

There is a very widespread misapprehension that wherever defendants have embarked on a joint endeavour, anything said at any time by any of them, even after arrest, will be admissible evidence against any of the other absent defendants. The case of *Blake and Tye* (1844) is often cited in this connection. This is a totally false understanding of the law, as a reading of *Blake and Tye* would show. Probably because the report is an old one and not readily available, not many students have read it. Fortunately, to understand the law on this point you do not have to read this case because the matter was dealt with more recently by the Court of Appeal in *Gray and Others* (1995). In that case, the court cited and adopted as an accurate exposition of the law a passage from the judgment of Dixon CJ in the Australian case of *Tripodi v R* (1961). In the course of his judgment, in the passage cited and adopted by the English Court of Appeal, Dixon CJ said that the reason for admitting the evidence of the acts or words of one defendant in a joint enterprise against the others was that the agreement to commit the crime was considered as implying an authority to each to act or speak *in furtherance of the common purpose* on behalf of the others. But from the nature of the case, it could seldom happen that anything said by one of the defendants which was no more than a *narrative or account of events that had already taken place* could be admissible against his companions in the common enterprise, though it might be admissible as a confession against the speaker. Usually, Dixon CJ said, the question of admissibility would relate to directions, instructions or arrangements, or to utterances accompanying acts.[2]

Another favourite topic for questions is the evidential worth of the exculpatory parts of a mixed statement.[3]

EXCLUDING THE CONFESSION

In practice, this will involve the operation of **s 76(2)** of **PACE** and, as a subsidiary argument in case the first should fail, **s 78**. Many candidates lose marks because they fail to construct sensible *arguments* at this point in answering a question. The examiner does not want a string of cases; he wants an argument based on the facts of the particular problem. Note particularly that it is foolish to say much in relation to **s 76(2)(a)** unless there is a proper factual basis for suggesting that there may have been oppression.[4]

In very many cases, you will be relying on breaches of **Code C**. Remember that even though there may have been a breach, you still need to put an argument on paper about why this is relevant to exclusion. Remember also that this is an area where decisions in other cases are of limited use.[5]

This has an advantage for you because it means that you don't have to learn lists of 'authorities'; on the other hand, you will be required to think creatively in the examination about the facts.

Particular attention should be paid to the extent to which the provisions of **Code C** apply to persons who are at a police station 'assisting the police with their

---

2 [1995] 2 CR App R 100, pp 128–129. But it has been said that an account of events narrated by one of the parties to another while the common enterprise was continuing, in order to bring that other up to date, might be regarded as in furtherance of the enterprise, and so admissible against all the parties referred to in it: see *Jones and Others* (1997).
3 See *Sharp* (1988); *Grayson* (1993).
4 See **s 76(8)** and look at what was said about the definition of oppression in *Fulling* (1987) and *Parker* (1995).
5 See, for example, observations to this effect in *Jelen and Katz* (1990) and in *Grannell* (1990).

inquiries' but who, technically, are there voluntarily because they have not been arrested.

> **Checklist** ✔
>
> Students should be familiar with the following areas:
>
> - the definition of 'confession';
> - the adoption by an accused person of allegations made against him;
> - the distinction between *Gunewardene* (1951) and *Rudd* (1948);
> - the principle in *Sharp* (1988);
> - s 76 of **PACE**;
> - s 78 of **PACE**;
> - the provisions of **Code C**;
> - the extent to which **Code C** provisions apply to persons who have not been arrested;
> - ss 34, 35, 36, 37 and 38 of the **Criminal Justice and Public Order Act (CJPOA) 1994**.

QUESTION 24

'The reforms made by the **Criminal Justice and Public Order Act (CJPOA) 1994** to the right of silence in the police station are more extensive and more difficult to defend than those relating to the accused's failure to testify at trial.'

▶ Discuss.

> **Answer Plan**
>
> The question itself contrasts the two different situations where a right to silence has to be considered. In each case, it is necessary to look at the old law to see how much change has been effected by the **1994 Act**. It is probably better to take the right to silence at trial first, as the change in this respect seems, in view of the way the common law was developing, far less radical than the provisions affecting the right to silence in pre-trial proceedings. A good summary of arguments for and against the changes that were being debated before the **1994 Act** can be found in Greer, S, 'The right to silence: a review of the current debate' (1990) 53 MLR 709, pp 709–730.

In summary, therefore, the essay is constructed as follows:

- comments on failure to testify at common law: *Bathurst* (1968); *Brigden* (1973); *Martinez-Tobon* (1993);
- effect of **s 35** of the **CJPOA 1994**: *Murray v DPP* (1993);
- **s 35** and the burden of proof;
- justification of **s 35**;
- effect of **s 34** of the **CJPOA 1994**;
- arguments in favour of **s 34**;
- counter-arguments;
- conclusions on **ss 34, 36** and **37**.

ANSWER

At common law, the trial judge was permitted to comment on the failure of an accused person to testify at his trial, but he was required by *Bathurst* (1968) to emphasise that the jury must not assume guilt from such a failure. In certain cases, provided this basic point had been made, some criticism was regarded as acceptable. For example, in *Brigden* (1973), the accused's case, put to the appropriate witnesses in cross-examination, was that the police had planted incriminating evidence on him. The accused himself did not testify. The Court of Appeal approved the trial judge's comment to the effect that the jury had not heard from the accused, and that this might help them in deciding whether there was any truth in the allegation against the police. The same sort of criticism could be made where the accused did not testify, but relied on facts that must have been within his knowledge. Thus, in *Martinez-Tobon* (1993), the accused was charged with the illegal importation of cocaine in a packet. The defence was that he had thought the packet contained emeralds, but the accused did not testify. The trial judge commented in his summing up that if the defendant had thought the drugs were emeralds, one might have thought that he would be very anxious to say so. On appeal against conviction, it was argued that the judge's comment had gone beyond what was permissible, but the Court of Appeal disagreed. Provided the *Bathurst* essentials were complied with, a judge might think it appropriate to make a stronger comment where the defence case involved alleged facts that (a) were at variance with the Crown's evidence or additional to it and exculpatory, and (b) must, if true, be within the defendant's knowledge.

By **s 35** of the **CJPOA 1994**, the court or jury, in determining whether the accused is guilty of the offence charged, may draw such inferences as appear proper from the failure of the accused to give evidence or his refusal, without good cause, to answer any question once he has chosen to testify. However, the section does not make the accused a compellable witness.

How far does this go beyond the common law? It is likely that the section involves a significant change by making it permissible to infer guilt from failure to testify. In *Murray v DPP* (1993), the House of Lords had to interpret a provision in similar terms to **s 35** in the law of Northern Ireland. It was held that the inferences that could be drawn were not limited to specific inferences from specific facts, but included an inference that the accused was guilty of the offence charged. As Lord Slynn put it, if the evidence clearly calls for an explanation that the accused ought to be in a position to give if an explanation exists, then a failure to give any explanation may as a matter of common sense allow the drawing of an inference that there is no explanation, and that the accused is guilty. This looks very much like the law as it was being developed in *Martinez-Tobon*, minus the protection afforded by the *Bathurst* direction. The effect of *Martinez-Tobon* was to create a situation only too familiar to students of evidence law, where a judge follows an approved formula to save himself from the strictures of the Court of Appeal, gives the defendant protection with one hand, promptly takes it away with the other, and thoroughly confuses any thinking members of the jury.

It was sometimes argued that to change the law in this respect would shift the burden of proof. But, there is no reason why changes in evidence law to help the prosecution *discharge* its burden should have the effect of *shifting* it. Even before the 1994 Act, it was not the case that the prosecution's obligation was to establish the accused's guilt beyond reasonable doubt *without any help from the accused*. If it had been so, evidence of such matters as breath tests, fingerprints and handwriting would have had to be excluded, and **s 62(10)** of the **Police and Criminal Evidence Act (PACE) 1984** provided that such inferences as appeared proper might be drawn from refusal to provide an intimate sample.

Section 35 can be defended on the basis that it makes sense out of a confusing situation at common law and does not affect the burden of proof.

The change in law affecting the right to silence at the police station is both more radical and far less easy to defend. At common law, no inference was permitted from the exercise of the right to silence in the face of questioning by the police or others charged with the investigation of offences. By **s 34** of the **1994 Act**, the failure of an accused in such circumstances to mention any fact relied on later in his defence, if it was a fact that, in the circumstances existing at the time, the accused could reasonably have been expected to mention, will allow the jury in determining whether the accused is guilty of the offence charged to draw such inferences from the failure as appear proper.

The essence of the argument in favour of this change was twofold. First, there was a gut reaction that anyone who was innocent would trust the police and would want to explain things to them as soon as possible. Secondly, although in the past a very few police had misbehaved, the protection given in **PACE** of access to legal advice and recorded interviews meant that no suspect who was innocent now had anything to fear.

Unfortunately, research suggests that this protection is insufficient. It has been proved that the police use a number of devices to discourage access to legal advisers, such as reading the suspect's rights too quickly or failing to mention that legal advice is free. There have been routine breaches of the **Codes of Practice**, such as the holding of improper 'informal' interviews before the recorded interview. The style of questioning in at least one interview was so bullying as to be branded oppressive by the Court of Appeal. Legal advisers may be not only unqualified, but inexperienced and passive, providing no protection at all for the suspect.[1]

Police do not have to be corrupt for the innocent suspect to fear for his safety. They need only to have made some assumptions about the guilt of their suspect and be prepared to use guile to establish what they believe to be the truth. The innocent citizen probably sees the possibility of making a false confession as remote and so, perhaps, it may be. What is far more likely is that he will give an ambiguous answer that will add to the case against him. And how can he avoid giving ambiguous answers? Not only is language riddled by its very nature with ambiguity, but all the circumstances surrounding a police interrogation conspire to increase the risk. The suspect may be in a highly emotional state. He may feel guilty even though he has committed no offence – for example, feelings of anger or guilt are well established reactions to bereavement. He may be ignorant of a vital fact that explains away suspicious circumstances. He may be frightened, confused or forgetful.

Nor does the innocent suspect have to fear anything so horrific as a miscarriage of justice at trial, though past experience has shown that this is all too possible. A mistake or ambiguity in something said to the police can suggest that there is at least a reason for charging the suspect and a case to answer. That may mean a remand in custody. At the very least it is likely to mean months of anxiety whilst on bail awaiting trial. Much is made of the high standard of proof that is required before a court may convict on a criminal charge. But no such standard applies to other decisions made during the pre-trial stages. Yet these decisions may have terrible implications for an

....

1   Greer, S, 'The right to silence: a review of the current debate' (1990) 53 MLR 709, pp 721–722; Sanders, A and Bridges, L, 'Access to legal advice and police malpractice' [1990] *Criminal Law Review* 494, pp 494–509; Hodgson, J, 'Tipping the scales of justice: the suspect's right to legal advice' [1992] *Criminal Law Review* 854, pp 854–862. For a particularly gross example of police oppression, see *Paris* (1993).

innocent suspect's liberty and for his own and his family's financial security and peace of mind.

At the pre-trial stage, a right to silence is, as things stand now in this country, an essential protection for the innocent. The innovations brought about by **ss 34, 36** and **37** of the **1994 Act** are indeed *defensible*, but only on the most short-sighted and crudely utilitarian basis, which accepts that it is expedient that innocent people should suffer for the sake of the majority.

QUESTION 25

Nigel is arrested on suspicion of murdering Olive. At the police station, he is told of his right to a solicitor but says he does not want one because 'they cost too much and waste a lot of time'. His watch and other personal possessions are taken away from him and he is then locked in a cell for five hours. At the end of that time, he is interviewed by DS Lestrade. After three hours of questioning, Lestrade suddenly produces a photograph. 'Just look at that', he says: 'Now, will you tell me the truth, or do I have to get my box of tricks out?' The photograph, which is in colour, shows Olive's mutilated body. Nigel screams and says: 'For God's sake, my nerves can't stand it. I killed her but I never meant to. She drove me to it.' The next day, he is interviewed again by DS Lestrade, but this time in the presence of a solicitor. He again confesses to the murder.

◗ Discuss the evidential issues that arise.

Answer Plan
Here, we have two confessions and the admissibility of each has to be considered.

The first confession
- Application of **s 82(1)** of the **Police and Criminal Evidence Act (PACE) 1984**.
- The possibility of oppression.
- Causation – always vital when considering **s 76**.
- Note the use made of the information about the watch.
- Breaches of **Code C**.

The second confession
- The continuing effect of the first confession – *McGovern* (1991); *Neil* (1994).
- Finally, remember the point based on *Sharp* (1988).

A useful case to remember when dealing with any breach of the Codes is *Elson* (1994), where the Court of Appeal said that the **Codes of Practice** were there to protect the

> individual against the might of the State. The individual, the court said, was at a great disadvantage when arrested by the police, and that was so whether or not the police behaved with the utmost propriety.

ANSWER

Two main questions have to be considered: the admissibility of Nigel's first confession and that of the second confession, made in the presence of a solicitor.

In relation to the first confession, there are two problems: (a) is it likely to be excluded under **s 76** of **PACE**?; (b) if not, is it likely to be excluded under **s 78**? Although the first confession contains exculpatory matter, it is obviously partly adverse to the maker, and so falls within the definition of 'confession' in **s 82(1)**.

Might the first confession have been obtained by oppression? Once the question is raised, the burden is on the prosecution to prove beyond doubt that the confession was not so obtained. The court is likely to be interested in two matters: the reference to the 'box of tricks' and the showing of the photograph. Oppression is partly defined in **s 76(8)** of **PACE** as including 'torture, inhuman or degrading treatment, and the use or threat of violence (whether or not amounting to torture)'. It is possible that 'box of tricks' could have been understood as a reference to equipment designed for torture, or at least violence, so as to make what was said a threat of violence. However, a causative link has to be established between the threat and the confession and Nigel must be able to confirm that this threat, as well as the shock of seeing the photograph, operated on his mind at the time in question.

Showing the photograph to Nigel does not fall within the partial statutory definition of oppression. However, in *Fulling* (1987), the Court of Appeal approved the *Shorter Oxford Dictionary* definition of oppression as the 'exercise of authority or power in a burdensome, harsh or wrongful manner; unjust or cruel treatment of subjects, inferiors, etc, or the imposition of unreasonable or unjust burdens'. The court added that it would be hard to envisage any circumstances in which oppression would not entail some impropriety on the part of the interrogator. Showing the photograph appears to be on the borderline of oppression. It could be argued that it was psychologically burdensome to show it. There appears to be a good chance of persuading the court that the confession *may* have been obtained by oppression, and an even chance that the prosecution would be unable to prove beyond reasonable doubt that it was not.

Even if the argument on oppression failed, the matters relied on could be used to support an argument for exclusion based on **s 76(2)(b)**. Other matters may be relevant under this head. Nigel may well have been suffering from disorientation after the time spent first in his cell and then in being questioned. His watch had been removed, and he was therefore very likely to have been without any means to measure the passing of time. It is possible that the police acted improperly in removing the watch. **Paragraph 4.2** of **Code C** says that a detained person may retain clothing and personal effects unless the custody officer considers that he may use them to cause harm to himself or others, interfere with evidence, damage property or effect an escape, or they are needed as evidence. Did any of these reasons apply? The police might also try to argue that the watch was an 'item of value', and so excluded from the definition of personal effects under **para 4.3**.

The detention for five hours before the interview began may have been a breach of **para 1.1** of **Code C**, which requires that all persons in custody must be dealt with expeditiously. What was the reason for the delay? The three hours of interviewing may have been a breach of **para 12.8**, which requires breaks at recognised meal times and short breaks for refreshment at intervals of approximately two hours, subject to the interviewing officer's discretion. There may also have been a breach of **para 11.2** of **Code C**, which requires the interviewing officer to remind the suspect immediately before the interview begins of his right to *free* legal advice. One of the reasons given by Nigel for not wanting a solicitor suggests that he was not aware of this right.

Section 78 of **PACE** applies to evidence of a confession (*Mason* (1988)). Thus, all the matters referred to in connection with **s 76** could be used, if submissions under that section fail, to support an argument based on **s 78**. But, under this section, there is only a discretion to exclude, and, as the Court of Appeal acknowledged in *Anderson* (1993), it is not entirely clear where the burden of proof lies.[1]

If the first confession is excluded under **s 76**, the question arises whether the second confession was so tainted by the circumstances in which the first was made that it should be excluded also. In *McGovern* (1991), the defendant had confessed in two interviews. The first had been without a solicitor and, because of breaches of **s 58** of **PACE** and for other reasons, that confession was excluded. The Court of Appeal emphasised that when an accused person has made admissions at a first interview, the very fact that those admissions have been made is likely to have an effect on the person during the course of the second interview. It was therefore held that the confession in the second interview should have been excluded, as well as that in the

---

1 However, in *Stagg* (1994), very experienced prosecuting counsel accepted that it was for the prosecution to show either that there was no unfairness, or that its degree did not warrant the exclusion of the evidence.

first (see also *Ismail* (1990)). In *Neil* (1994), the Court of Appeal said that where there is a series of two or more interviews, and the court excludes one on the ground of unfairness, the question whether a later interview which itself is unobjectionable should also be excluded is a matter of fact and degree. It is likely to depend on whether the objections leading to the exclusion of the first interview were of a fundamental and continuing nature and, if so, if the arrangements for the later interview gave the accused a sufficient opportunity to exercise an informed and independent choice as to whether he should repeat or retract what he said in the objectionable interview, or say nothing. There is clearly room for argument in Nigel's case. Much may depend on what he says about his state of mind in the second interview (see also *Nelson* (1998)).

If the confession is admitted, the evidential value of the exculpatory part will have to be considered. This may be particularly important if Nigel chooses not to give evidence at trial. The Court of Appeal in *Duncan* (1981) held that the jury should be directed that both incriminating and exculpatory parts of a confession must be considered in deciding where the truth lies, and that it was not helpful to try to explain that the exculpatory parts were something less than evidence of the facts they stated. The judge may, however, comment on the relative weight of the two parts. This approach was approved by the House of Lords in *Sharp* (1988) and also in *Aziz* (1995).

QUESTION 26

Earlier this year, a painting by the well known modernist painter Bruno Hatte was stolen from a public art gallery in Barchester. Acting on information received, DS Proudie arrested two local men, Josh and Luke, in connection with the theft. When they arrived at the police station, they were placed in separate cells.

After about 10 minutes, Josh was taken to an interview room where Proudie was waiting. Josh said at once: 'I want to see a solicitor.' Proudie replied: 'Look, a valuable painting has been stolen. If there should, at present, be any chance of recovering the painting, that chance will cease to exist if we have to wait for a solicitor. Besides, you know the form. You don't need some pimpled trainee to hold your hand.'

After cautioning Josh, he questioned him for 80 minutes, but all Josh would say in answer to questions was 'No comment'. Finally, Proudie said: 'Right. We'll see what your friend Luke has to say. You won't mind waiting in a cell for a few more hours, will you? You won't be lonely; we've just pulled in a bunch of football supporters for fighting in the street.' Unknown to Proudie, Josh was terrified of football supporters because he had recently been attacked by a group of them. He said to Proudie: 'Look, don't put me with them. Luke and I did it together. But I only got involved because he made me; he's such a bully. We hid the painting in the well in Luke's garden.'

Proudie then visited Luke in his cell. Luke said at once: 'You got nowhere, did you?' Proudie laughed and said: 'In the well in your garden.' Luke shouted: 'Treacherous bastard!' He then refused to say any more.

The painting was found in the well by the police on the following day. Josh and Luke were then offered access to free legal advice, which they both refused. They were then charged with theft of the painting and cautioned. Neither made any reply.

◗ Discuss the evidential issues that arise.

Answer Plan

Josh

- Definition of confession.
- Quick reference to **ss 76** and **78** – need to refer to **Code C**.
- Dispose quickly of the possibility of oppression. Don't waste time by going in detail into what is meant by oppression; there are more important things to write about in an answer to this question.
- What exactly was said about a solicitor? Anchor your argument to the facts and ask for further information, as you would in practice.
- Circumstances in which the police can refuse access to legal advice.
- The *Alladice* point.
- The 'special motive' point – *Rennie* (1982).
- The reliability point – note that the emphasis in **s 76(2)(b)** is on potentiality; it is irrelevant that evidence obtained afterwards confirms the truth of the confession.
- Old favourites: *Gunewardene* (1951) and *Sharp* (1988).

Luke

- Discovery of evidence via an inadmissible confession.
- Is what Luke said a confession within the definition? **Police and Criminal Evidence Act (PACE) 1984**.
- Arguments for exclusion.

Both defendants
Their refusal to answer police questions or to say anything after caution when charged.

ANSWER

THE CASE AGAINST JOSH

Josh has made a statement to the police that is partly adverse to him and is therefore a confession within the definition in **s 82(1)** of **PACE**.

The first matter that has to be considered is whether the confession is likely to be excluded under either **s 76** or **s 78**. In considering this question, it will be necessary to take into account the extent to which there may have been breaches of **Code C** of the **Codes of Practice**.

It does not appear that any question of oppression arises in relation to Josh and, accordingly, I shall consider those matters that would be relevant in arguments based on **s 76(2)(b)** and **s 78**.

The first of these is the refusal to provide an opportunity for Josh to take legal advice. (I assume from the words uttered that this was a refusal and not just discouragement, but I should like to know whether Josh said anything more about having a solicitor after Proudie's remarks.) It is relevant to ask whether Proudie would have been entitled to delay the opportunity for Josh to obtain legal advice if Josh had already been detained. Proudie would have been so entitled if, amongst other things, Josh had been detained for an indictable offence, and an officer of the rank of superintendent or above had reasonable grounds for believing that the exercise of his right to legal advice would, amongst other things, hinder the recovery of property obtained as a result of such an offence.

Theft is an indictable offence. But Proudie would almost certainly not have been justified in refusing Josh access to a solicitor. **Annex B** of **Code C, para 3** provides that authority to delay a detainee's right to consult privately with a solicitor may be given only if the authorising officer has reasonable grounds to believe that the solicitor whom the detainee wants to consult will, inadvertently or otherwise, pass on a message from the detainee or act in some other way that will have any of the consequences referred to in **s 58(8)**. If this is the case, the detainee must be allowed to choose another solicitor. As **Note B3** says, a decision to delay access to a specific solicitor is likely to be a rare occurrence, and on these facts Josh does not appear to have been asking for a specific solicitor. His request could have been met by allowing him access to the duty solicitor.

The question also arises whether, even if delay had not been justified, Josh suffered prejudice as a result. If Josh is experienced in being questioned by the police, the presence of a solicitor might have made no difference. Josh's replies of 'No comment' for 80 minutes suggests that this could well have been the case. In *Alladice* (1988), the appellant admitted that he could cope with being interviewed and said that he was aware of his legal rights. He had requested legal advice because he had wanted a check on the conduct of the police during the interview. The Court of Appeal held that his confession made in the absence of a solicitor was admissible, but the decision in that case was based on findings that the police had made an honest mistake about the appellant's entitlement to legal advice, and that the interview had been properly conducted. It is not clear on the facts given whether the police acted innocently or not.

There is also the problem caused by the suggestion that Josh might share a cell with some football supporters. **Paragraph 8.1** of **Code C** provides that, so far as practicable, not more than one person should be detained in each cell. Was this practicable? Or was the reference to football supporters intended as a threat? If Proudie was acting in bad faith, a court would be more likely to exclude the confession, either under **s 76(2)(b)** or under **s 78**, than if he was not. In *Walsh* (1989), it was said that bad faith might make substantial or significant a breach that might not otherwise be so.

The position is more difficult if Proudie was acting in good faith. A confession will not be excluded under **s 76(2)(b)** merely because the accused had a special motive for making it. As Lord Lane CJ said in *Rennie* (1982), very few confessions are inspired solely by remorse. But what we have here are words uttered by Proudie to Josh which trigger a particular fear, which in turn leads to the confession. **Section 76(2)(b)** can be used even where there has been no police impropriety (*Fulling* (1987)) and it might therefore be applied here. The fact that the confession is in fact proved reliable by the subsequent discovery of the painting is no bar to the operation of **s 76(2)(b)**.

If the confession is admitted, it will be evidence against Josh. But it is now possible to use it against Luke also. In *Y* (2008) the Court of Appeal held that an out-of-court confession was capable of being evidence against persons other than the maker by virtue of the wide scope for admitting hearsay under **s 114(1)(d) CJA 2003**. The court did, however, say that this should not make the police interview of one defendant routinely admissible in the case of another. It remains unclear in what circumstances such evidence, now in principle admissible, will in practice be admitted.

THE CASE AGAINST LUKE

Even if Josh's confession is inadmissible, evidence can be given that the painting was found in the well in Luke's garden (**s 76(4)** of **PACE**).

Has Luke by his reaction to Proudie's taunt produced a confession? It could be argued that Luke's reaction amounts to a confession on the basis that his guilt could be inferred from the words uttered. They would then fall within the partial definition of a confession in **s 82(1)** of **PACE**. However, he does not appear to have been cautioned or offered legal advice, and he was not interviewed and recorded in accordance with **Code E**. For all these reasons, his confession is likely to be excluded under **s 76(2)(b)** of the **1984 Act**.

The prosecution will be unable to rely on Josh's initial refusal to answer police questions. By **s 34(2A)** of the **Criminal Justice and Public Order Act 1994**, inferences cannot be drawn if a suspect has not been allowed an opportunity to consult a solicitor before being questioned. Nor will the prosecution be able to rely on Luke's silence in the face of questions. Not only was no offer of legal advice made, but he does not appear to have been questioned under caution, as is required by **s 34**. However, the prosecution may be able to rely on the silence of both defendants when they were charged if at trial they rely on some fact that they could reasonably have been expected to mention at that stage. In *Dervish* (2002), the Court of Appeal held that the **1994 Act** does not exclude the possibility of drawing an inference from silence on being charged, even if no inferences can be drawn from a suspect's silence on being questioned. The only question would be whether, on the facts of the particular case, it would be fair to draw inferences. The Court of Appeal added that it might not be fair where the police had acted in bad faith by deliberately breaching the Code in the knowledge that an inference could be drawn from a later silence on being charged.

If **s 34** is held to apply, the judge will have to give a careful direction to the jury based on what was said in *Petkar* (2004). He must identify the facts on which each of the defendants relies and which were not mentioned on questioning. He must identify the inferences which it is suggested might be drawn from failure to mention such facts, to the extent that they may go beyond the standard inference of late fabrication. The jury should be told that, if an inference is drawn, they should not convict wholly or mainly on the strength of it. They should be told that an inference should be drawn only if they think it is fair and proper, and it should be drawn only if the only sensible explanation for failure to mention facts relied on is that the defendant had no answers, or none that would stand up to scrutiny. Moreover, an inference should be drawn only if, apart from a defendant's failure to mention facts relied on, the prosecution case is so strong that it clearly calls for an answer by him. The jury should be reminded of the evidence on the basis of which they are invited not to draw any inferences from silence.

QUESTION 27

Benson is charged with obtaining property by deception. The case for the prosecution is that he deceived Miss Prism into agreeing that he should repair some of the windows in her house by falsely telling her that they were in an unsafe condition and that £7,000 was a reasonable price for the work that he did.

After receiving a complaint from Miss Prism's brother, DS Japp went to an address in Anglebury where he saw Benson. Japp told him that he wanted to ask some questions about work that Benson had done for Miss Prism. At that moment, Mrs Benson entered the room and shouted at her husband: 'Tell the copper how you cheated the old girl, you bastard! Tell him you'd cheat your own mother for a fiver!' Benson began to weep and said: 'All right. I'll tell you the truth. I cheated her. I told her she couldn't get a cheaper job anywhere else and it wasn't true.'

Benson was then arrested and cautioned and taken to Anglebury police station. He was offered legal advice but said that he did not need any. He was interviewed shortly afterwards.

When the interview began, Benson said: 'I must get a drink soon. I've got the shakes and I'm feeling sick. If I make a statement will I get bail?' DS Japp replied: 'You know I can't make any promises, but it costs a lot to keep someone in custody.' Benson then fully admitted the offence.

◗ Discuss the evidential issues that arise.

Answer Plan

The two confessions should be dealt with separately. Some comment is needed on the content of the first confession – it is certainly not a full one but is clearly adverse to Benson. The following points should then be made:

- the importance of whether Japp should have cautioned Benson at an earlier stage;
- a quick dismissal of the possibility of oppression;
- the application of **s 76(2)(b)**.

In relation to the second confession, you should make these points:

- the possibility that if the first confession is excluded, the second one might be also, on the principle in *McGovern* (1991);
- the effect of Benson's need for more alcohol – see *Goldenberg* (1988); **s 78 PACE**;
- the conversation about bail.

ANSWER

In relation to the charge against Benson, his words 'I cheated her . . . and it wasn't true' appear to be at least partly adverse to him, although they do not amount to an admission of the whole of the prosecution case. They therefore constitute a confession under **s 82(1)** of the **Police and Criminal Evidence Act 1984**, and the question of admissibility arises.

Presumably, the prosecution will submit that when Japp went to make inquiries of Benson, he did so only to obtain information or his explanation of the facts, and that he did not at that stage have grounds to suspect him of an offence. By **Code C, para 10.1**, a person whom there are grounds to suspect of an offence must be cautioned before any questions about an offence are put to him, if either his answers or silence are to be given in evidence in a prosecution.

On the facts given, the complaint was not made by Miss Prism, but by her brother, who presumably related his sister's account of what Benson had said and how much she had paid. Had Japp obtained this information directly from Miss Prism, and had he perhaps had this substantiated by a receipt or bank statement to show the sum paid, it is likely that a court would find that he did suspect a crime to have occurred, and Benson to have committed it. Is the position likely to be different where the information came second-hand through Miss Prism's brother, apparently without any supporting evidence? This might well change the view a court would take of Japp's state of mind. What may also be of significance is the reason for the complaint coming from Miss Prism's brother rather than from herself. Was it because Miss Prism was too old or ill to be able to make a complaint herself? If so, might she have been muddled about what happened? This possibility, and the difficulty of assessing the weight to be attached to an account related on behalf of someone else, make it likely that an initial caution was not required.

On that assumption, is the confession admissible? This is not a case where oppression could be relied on, but would a submission under **s 76(2)(b)** of **PACE** be likely to succeed? The words uttered by Mrs Benson might have amounted to something said which was likely, in the circumstances existing at the time, to render unreliable any confession that Mr Benson might have made in consequence. The words or action do not have to come from the police. In *Harvey* (1988), a woman heard her lover confess to a murder. As this may have led her to make a false confession to protect him, her statement was excluded. In Benson's case, part of the circumstances existing at the time included the fact that he had, probably recently, consumed alcohol. There appears to be no question of his having done so to such an extent that he was unable to appreciate the significance of questions, or of his own answers. But the probability that alcohol had recently been consumed might be thought to add to the likelihood of unreliability. It seems clear that the accused's own mental state may be part of the circumstances under **s 76(2)(b)** of **PACE**. Thus, in *McGovern* (1991), the physical condition and particular vulnerability of the defendant, who was six months pregnant and of low intelligence, were held to have been part of the background against which a submission should have been considered.[1]

If a submission under **s 76(2)(b)** fails, it is possible that one under **s 78** might succeed. *Mason* (1988) establishes that this section as well as **s 76** is applicable to evidence of confessions.

If the first confession is excluded, the second confession at the police station may be excluded also on the basis that it is tainted by the defects attaching to the first, as was the case in *McGovern* (1991). But in *Neil* (1994), the Court of Appeal said that whether a later interview, which is in itself unobjectionable, should be excluded is a matter of fact and degree. Exclusion is likely to depend on whether the arrangements for the second interview gave the suspect sufficient opportunity to exercise an informed and independent choice about what, if anything, to say.

Benson's need for another drink is not by itself likely to be of assistance. Under **s 76(2)(b)**, unreliability must come from something said or done by someone other than the defendant. Thus, in *Goldenberg* (1988), where it was argued that admissions were unreliable because the defendant was a heroin addict with withdrawal symptoms who would have done anything to be able to get more heroin, the Court of Appeal held that the unreliability of the confession had nothing to do with anything said or done by someone else, and so was beyond the scope of the provision. **Section 78** of **PACE** would, however, be available, and was used in similar circumstances in *Anderson* (1993), where the defendant was suffering from alcoholism.

But might Japp's response to the question about bail bring **s 76(2)(b)** into play? It is arguable that it would. **Paragraph 11.5** of **Code C** provides that if the person being interviewed asks the officer directly what action will be taken in the event of his making a statement, the officer may inform the person what action the police propose to take in that event. That is what Japp did. He implied that bail would probably be granted. But *this* was something said or done by someone other than the suspect. It was not improper, but it does not have to be to trigger **s 76(2)(b)** (*Fulling* (1987); *Harvey* (1988)). Once **s 76(2)(b)** has been triggered, all the circumstances can be taken into account (*Everett* (1988); *McGovern* (1991)), and these would include Benson's alcohol withdrawal symptoms. It is therefore possible that for this reason the second confession would be excluded under **s 76(2)(b)**.

---

1 See also *Everett* (1988).

QUESTION 28

Simon and Tim are jointly charged with the burglary of a valuable collection of paintings belonging to Ulrica. Simon was the first to be arrested and interviewed by the police. Vivian, a senior police officer, refused his request for a solicitor on the ground that to allow it would hinder recovery of the paintings. He then forced Simon to remain standing while he interviewed him, after cautioning him, between 11 am and 4 pm without a break. Finally, Simon said: 'I'll tell you what you want to know. I was involved in the burglary, but it was only because Tim threatened to kill me if I didn't help him. You'll find the paintings in the house where Wanda, Tim's girlfriend, lives.' Acting on this information, Vivian went to Wanda's house. When he discovered that she had gone away, he broke in unlawfully, ransacked the house, and recovered the paintings.

Tim was later arrested and taken to the police station. When interviewed by the police, he refused to answer any questions. He later instructed solicitors, and told them that he had not been involved in the burglary and that he had no knowledge of the paintings that were found in Wanda's house. He said that he now believed that they had been 'planted' there by Simon, who had a grudge against him because of an affair that Tim had had during the previous year with Simon's wife.

▶ Discuss the evidential issues arising.

Answer Plan
Take the defendants separately.

Simon
The first thing to do is to try to get his confession excluded. Try **s 76(2)(a)** of the **Police and Criminal Evidence Act 1984**, alternatively **s 76(2)(b)**. There's no point in discussing **s 78**; you are better off with **s 76** because of the burden placed on the prosecution by that section, and because it makes exclusion mandatory rather than discretionary. On these facts, any arguments available under **s 78** can be used equally well under **s 76**. Look for breaches of **Code C** and think about how you can use them to support arguments under **s 76**. On the assumption that the confession might not be excluded, you need to say something about its evidential status. You might add something about the burden of proof where a defence of duress is raised. **Section 76(4)** will be important for the discovery of the paintings. A brief discussion of **s 78** is appropriate to cover the unlawful entry that led to their discovery.

Tim
You need to discuss the effect of Tim's silence at the police station. Note the importance of discovering if he was offered legal advice. On the assumption that

he was, you need to describe how the judge will direct the jury in relation to **s 34** of the **Criminal Justice and Public Order Act 1994**. Another point to consider is whether Tim's theory about planting the paintings is something caught **by s 34**.

ANSWER

Although what Simon said to Vivian was partly exculpatory, it was also partly adverse because he admitted taking part in the burglary. It therefore comes within the definition of a confession in **s 82(1)** of the **Police and Criminal Evidence Act (PACE) 1984**. The first question to be considered is whether it could be excluded under **s 76**. Although **s 78** is theoretically available also, all the arguments for exclusion are relevant to **s 76**, and it is better for the defence to rely on **s 76** because of the burden of proof that it imposes on the prosecution, and because exclusion under that section is mandatory if the circumstances are appropriate, whereas under **s 78(1)**, exclusion is only discretionary.

By **s 76(8)**, oppression includes, among other things, 'inhuman or degrading treatment'. In *Fulling* (1987), Lord Lane CJ relied on a dictionary definition that included 'exercise of authority or power in a burdensome, harsh or wrongful manner . . . the imposition of unreasonable or unjust burdens'. He also emphasised the seriousness of the conduct needed to constitute oppression. This seems to be a borderline case. No violence was involved, although *Paris* (1992) shows that this is not an essential element. It is arguable that it was oppressive to question somebody forced to stand for five hours. There was clearly bad faith; Vivian must have known that by **para 12.6** of **Code C**, persons being questioned shall not be required to stand, and that by **para 12.8**, breaks from interviewing shall be made at recognised meal times and that short breaks for refreshment shall be provided at intervals of approximately two hours. There is nothing to suggest that the exceptional conditions referred to in that paragraph apply here.

If an argument under **s 76(2)(a)** fails, the same facts can be relied on under **s 76(2)(b)**. In addition, Simon could rely on the fact that he was wrongly refused access to a solicitor. Under **s 58** of **PACE**, delay is only permitted for limited reasons where someone has been arrested for an indictable offence and where the authorisation of an officer of at least the rank of superintendent has been obtained. Burglary is an indictable offence. We do not, however, know Vivian's rank. If he was not at least a superintendent, was the delay in access to legal advice authorised by someone who was? Even if the delay was authorised by an officer of appropriate rank, it is most unlikely that the **s 58(8)** condition applied. **Section 58(8)(c)** does indeed authorise delay where the exercise of the right will hinder the recovery of any property obtained as a result of the offence. But the Court of Appeal stated in *Samuel* (1988) that the right of access to legal advice was one of the most important and fundamental rights of a citizen. The court also said that where the police try to justify denial of access to a solicitor, that can be done only by reference to specific circumstances, including evidence about the person detained or the actual solicitor involved. The effect of this decision was summarised in **Annex B** of **Code C**, **para 3**. It follows that on these facts the authorised officer would have to have reasonable grounds to believe that Simon's solicitor would deliberately hinder the recovery of the stolen goods if he were allowed to have access to his client. There is no evidence whatsoever to support such a belief by Vivian. Provided causation can be shown, there is no reason why an argument based on **s 76(2)(b)**, relying on the denial of access to a solicitor as well as the matters relied on under **s 76(2)(a)**, should not succeed.[1]

If, by a remote chance, the confession is not excluded, its evidential status will have to be considered. Contrary to the traditional rule, it has been possible, at least since *Y* (2008), for a confession by one defendant to be evidence against any co-defendant whom it implicates. It was said in that case that such confessions should not be allowed as evidence against a co-accused as a matter of routine. But if a judge decides in a co-defendant's favour on this point, the former law will still apply, so that references to the co-accused will not be automatically excluded. Following *Lobban v R* (1995), the references to Tim will not be edited out unless Simon agrees. He is unlikely to do so because he will want to show that he raised his defence of duress at an early stage. He does not have the legal burden of proving this defence, but he has an evidential burden in respect of it (*Gill* (1963)).[2]

Even if the confession is inadmissible, the discovery of the paintings will be admissible under **s 76(4)** of **PACE**. It would be possible to argue that this evidence should be excluded under **s 78** because of the unlawful way in which the paintings were discovered. But although **s 78** is probably in principle available to protect process values regardless of reliability, in practice, where the reliability of evidence has not been affected by the impropriety of the way in which it was obtained, it is unlikely to be excluded. For example, in *Cooke* (1995), a case where rape and kidnapping were alleged, the question arose whether **s 78(1)** should be used to exclude evidence of a sample of hair that might have been improperly taken from the defendant. The Court of Appeal agreed with the trial judge's decision to admit the evidence, regardless of any possible assault. The fact of an assault on the defendant would have cast no doubt on the accuracy or strength of the evidence.

---

1 See also **Code C, Annex B**.
2 As a result of **s 114 CJA 2003** it seems that a confession may now be admissible in some circumstances as evidence against a person other than the maker. See *Y* [2008] EWCA Crim 10.

Tim faces the possibility of a direction to the jury under **s 34** of the **Criminal Justice and Public Order Act 1994** in respect of his silence at the police station. However, if he was not offered legal advice before being questioned no inferences from silence can be made: see **s 34(2A)**. If he was offered legal advice, and he relies at trial on facts that he did not mention to the police, it is possible that a direction would be given. His lack of involvement in the burglary and ignorance of the paintings are facts that might be caught. The defence could argue, following *Mountford* (1999) and *Gill* (2001), that the truth of these facts was the central issue in his trial, and that accordingly, a **s 34** direction should not be given. In *Gowland-Wynn* (2002), however, another division of the Court of Appeal rejected this approach and the law is therefore uncertain.[3] Tim's suggestion that Simon planted the paintings is a theory and not a fact and, as such, following *Nickolson* (1999), would not be caught by **s 34** unless he could reasonably have been expected to tell the police about the fact of Simon's grudge. If a **s 34** direction is given, the judge would have to follow the guidelines based on *Petkar* (2004). He must identify the facts on which Tim relies and which were not mentioned on questioning. He must identify the inferences which it is suggested might be drawn from failure to mention such facts, to the extent that they may go beyond the standard inference of late fabrication. The jury should be told that, if an inference is drawn, they should not convict wholly or mainly on the strength of it. They should be told that an inference should be drawn only if they think it is fair and proper, and it should be drawn only if the only sensible explanation for failure to mention facts relied on is that the defendant had no answers, or none that would stand up to scrutiny. Moreover, an inference should be drawn only if, apart from a defendant's failure to mention facts relied on, the prosecution case is so strong that it clearly calls for an answer by him. The jury should be reminded of the evidence on the basis of which they are invited not to draw any inferences from silence.

QUESTION 29

The police suspected that George and Harry were dealing in drugs. Without a warrant, they broke into a house occupied by the two men solely in order to look for evidence while George and Harry were away. They discovered a large quantity of cocaine. As a result of their discovery, George and Harry were arrested several days later and taken to the police station for questioning. Both men refused to answer any questions until they had received legal advice. When their solicitor arrived, she advised them to remain silent and accordingly they continued to refuse to answer any police questions. The police later placed them together in a cell in which a listening device had been installed in breach of the relevant regulations, and which recorded their conversation. At one stage, George was overheard saying to Harry: 'One thing's for sure, they can

---

3 See also *Chenia* (2003).

never prove we didn't have the stuff for our own use.' Harry replied: 'I wish I'd made as much out of it as you. I'd be in the south of France by now.' Then came the sound of two men laughing. Nothing further of significance was overheard.

▸ Discuss the evidential issues arising.

> **Answer Plan**
>
> The first point should be a familiar one – improperly obtained evidence and the use of **s 78(1)** of the **Police and Criminal Evidence Act (PACE) 1984**.
>
> You need to consider the exercise of the right to silence on legal advice, and the special direction that has to be given to the jury in such cases. Then we come to evidence obtained by bugging. You ought to be able to deal with this if you've studied the law relating to **s 78** efficiently. Finally, some thought is needed about the content of the conversation. Are there any confessions there? If so, how many? And by whom? Note yet again that the examiner is looking to see if you can *analyse* the information you are given.

ANSWER

The first question that arises is whether the cocaine discovered during the unlawful search will be admissible. The trial judge will have to consider whether, in view of the circumstances in which this evidence was obtained, he should exercise the discretion which he has under **s 78** of **PACE** to exclude evidence of what was found on the ground that its admission would so adversely affect the fairness of the proceedings that it ought not to be admitted.

It is implicit in **s 78(1)** that it is possible for the way in which evidence is obtained to result in its exclusion. This is particularly likely where the police have acted in bad faith. In *Matto v Wolverhampton Crown Court* (1987), the defendant was convicted of driving with excess alcohol. Police officers had requested a specimen of breath when they were on the defendant's property. This was unlawful and they knew it to be so. The specimen proved positive. The defendant was then arrested. At the police station, he provided another positive specimen. The appeal was allowed on the ground that because the police had acted in bad faith and oppressively, the Crown Court could have decided to exclude the evidence under **s 78** if it had directed itself properly.

However, in cases where improperly obtained real evidence has been considered by the Crown Court in a **s 78** application, it is usually admitted because any impropriety in obtaining it is far less likely to have affected its reliability than evidence of an improperly obtained confession. Thus, in *Cooke* (1995), the Court of Appeal pointed out that the vast majority of cases under **s 78** had concerned alleged confessions obtained in breach of the Codes. In that case, where a sample of hair had been obtained from the defendant in circumstances that may have been improper, the court held that the trial judge had properly decided to admit the evidence, despite the possibility that there might have been a technical assault on the defendant. This did not cast doubt on the accuracy or strength of the evidence.

Two features might make an application to exclude slightly more likely to succeed in this case. It seems very likely that the police were acting in bad faith, and it is clear that their entry was unlawful. But the offence is regarded as such a serious one that the discretion is still not likely to be exercised in the defendants' favour.

By **s 34** of the **Criminal Justice and Public Order Act 1994**, if either George or Harry failed to mention when questioned by the police any fact relied on as his defence in subsequent proceedings, and that fact was one that in the circumstances existing at the time he could reasonably have been expected to mention, the jury may draw such inferences from the failure as appear proper.

In *Argent* (1997), the Court of Appeal said that when considering whether a fact was one that a defendant could reasonably have been expected to mention, the court must take into account all relevant circumstances at the time of questioning, including the personal characteristics of the defendant. It was also said that legal advice is something the court might have to consider as one of those circumstances. Its significance was more fully considered in *Condron* (1997). In giving guidance, the Court of Appeal said that where a defendant says he failed to answer questions on legal advice, that bare assertion is unlikely to be regarded as a sufficient reason for failure to mention matters relevant to the defence. In practice, a defendant will have to go further and provide, either through his own testimony or that of his solicitor, the reasons for the advice.

If a direction is given under **s 34**, the judge should follow the guidelines based on *Petkar* (2004). He must identify the facts on which each of the defendants relies and which were not mentioned on questioning. He must identify the inferences which it is suggested might be drawn from failure to mention such facts, to the extent that they may go beyond the standard inference of late fabrication. The jury should be told that, if an inference is drawn, they should not convict wholly or mainly on the strength of it. They should be told that an inference should be drawn only if they think it is fair and proper, and it should be drawn only if the only sensible explanation for failure to mention facts relied on is that the defendant had no answers, or none that would stand up to scrutiny. Moreover, an inference should be drawn only if, apart from a defendant's failure to mention facts relied on, the prosecution case is so strong that it clearly calls for an answer by him. The jury should be reminded of the evidence on the basis of which they are invited not to draw any inferences from silence.

A special direction must be given, because the defendants' silence was on legal advice. In *Betts and Hall* (2001) the Court of Appeal held that adverse inferences could not be drawn from silence where the defendant had honestly relied on legal advice in his refusal to answer questions, and was not simply using the advice as a cloak behind which to hide. But in *Howell* (2003) the Court of Appeal held that genuine reliance on legal advice was not of itself enough to avoid the application of **s 34**. The Court said that what was reasonable depended on all the circumstances. Even where silence was advised, there must always be soundly based objective reasons for that advice. In *Knight* (2003) the Court of Appeal observed, *obiter*, that if there was any conflict between *Betts and Hall* and *Howell*, *Howell* was to be preferred. Although in *Robinson* (2003) another division of the Court of Appeal seemed to prefer the approach taken in *Betts and Hall*, it was later confirmed in *Hoare* (2004) and *Beckles* (2004) that *reasonable* reliance on legal advice is necessary to prevent the drawing of adverse inferences, and this is reflected in the amended Judicial Studies Board specimen direction on **s 34**.

In theory, the admissibility of evidence obtained by a trick can be challenged under **s 78(1)** of **PACE** but, for a long time, evidence obtained by eavesdropping has been admitted. In *Maqsud Ali* (1966), for example, a tape recorder was used to eavesdrop on a conversation between two suspects, and the evidence obtained was admitted. More recently, in *Bailey and Smith* (1993), the judge admitted evidence of confessions made by the two defendants and tape recorded during conversations between them while they were sharing a bugged cell at a police station after being arrested, charged and remanded in custody. The Court of Appeal upheld the decision to admit the evidence but said that this was a device to be used only in grave cases. Drug dealing for commercial gain is regarded as a grave offence, as was shown recently in *Khan* (1996) where the decision to admit evidence of drug dealing obtained by bugging private property was upheld by the House of Lords.

The exchange between Harry and George is ambiguous. Does it amount to a confession by either defendant? 'They can never prove we didn't have the stuff for our own use' is an observation that is at least partly adverse to both defendants in that it is capable of being interpreted as an admission that the drugs were in the possession of both Harry and George. Harry did not dissociate himself in any way from George's remark and may therefore be taken to have adopted it. On similar principles, a confession was admitted against both defendants in *Batt* (1995). Ashley and Kerry were convicted of robbery. One of them had appeared to be holding a gun that was partly concealed by material. While on remand in custody, they were sharing a cell. A police officer gave evidence that on one occasion Kerry had said to Ashley: 'They'll fuck themselves if they show that gun in court. It's not the one used.' The Court of Appeal held that this was evidence against Ashley as well as Kerry. Ashley had said nothing, but he had not dissociated himself from his companion's remark.

Harry's remark to George, 'I wish I'd made as much out of it as you', is capable of being interpreted as a confession to dealing and, on the principle just outlined, George's failure to dissociate himself from what was said is capable of being interpreted as an adoption of it.

Aim Higher

1. Make sure you are familiar with **Annex B** to **Code C** (dealing with the circumstances in which it is legitimate to delay a suspect's access to a solicitor). Even when candidates refer to **Annex B**, they should always bring out the fact that they appreciate fully its significance; reference to the contents of **note B3** in the **Notes for Guidance** is useful for this purpose.
2. Make sure you know when a statement in furtherance of a common purpose can be admitted against defendants other than the maker of the statement. Remember that 'narratives' can be confessions to the police, and so not in furtherance of the common purpose, but they can also be used by one member of an enterprise to keep others in the picture while the common purpose is being carried out.

Common Pitfalls

1. Many candidates try to set up an argument based on oppression when the facts obviously don't support it. Remember the partial definition in **PACE** and don't rely solely on the dictionary definition quoted in *Fulling*; make sure you note everything that was said about oppression in that decision.
2. Weak candidates often ignore or pay insufficient attention to **Annex B** of **Code C** when deciding whether there has been an improper delay in permitting a defendant access to his solicitor. Look at **note B3** in the **Notes for Guidance** and remember that if it is the duty solicitor he has asked for, it seems impossible for the conditions set out in **Annex B** to be satisfied.

Character Evidence I

INTRODUCTION

Character evidence is relevant mainly in criminal trials. Before the **Criminal Justice Act (CJA) 2003**, the common law recognised two ways in which such evidence could be relevant. It could be relevant to any witness's credibility, and it could also be relevant to the likelihood of a defendant's guilt. Whether an item of character evidence was relevant to one or both of these matters depended on the circumstances. Broadly speaking, evidence of a defendant's good character was relevant to both matters, and under *Vye* (1993) a direction to this effect became compulsory. The question whether a good character direction should be given or not, or given only in a qualified way, can arise either where the defendant has one or more previous convictions that can be regarded as not amounting to serious criminal behaviour, or where he has no convictions, but his evidence at trial discloses some criminal behaviour, though not that alleged by the prosecution. Students should note particularly the decisions in *Gray* (2004), *Goss* (2005), *Teeluck and John* (2005) and *Payton* (2006). Evidence of bad character was primarily relevant to guilt, where the prosecution was allowed to introduce it as part of its case against a defendant under the rules relating to similar fact evidence. Where such evidence was admitted only because of the way in which the defence was conducted, under rules contained in the **Criminal Evidence Act 1898**, it was generally meant to be relevant only to credibility. This distinction was not always easy to maintain in practice, and the **CJA 2003** does not preserve it. In former editions of this book it was easy to deal with these topics separately, because the sources of law for each were quite distinct. This is no longer the case, as the law relating to evidence of bad character is now governed by the provisions of **Part 11, Chapter 1** of the **CJA 2003**. To some extent, therefore, there is overlapping of the subject matter of Chapters 8 and 9 in this book, although the emphasis in Chapter 8 is on what used to be called similar fact evidence, and the emphasis in Chapter 9 is on evidence of bad character that becomes admissible by virtue of the way in which the defence is conducted. What is said here should be treated as an introduction to both chapters.

The relevant provisions where the prosecution wishes to adduce evidence of bad character as part of its case against a defendant are **s 101(1)(c)** and **(d)**. **Subsection (1)(c)** has to be read with **s 102**. Very broadly speaking, it covers the sort of evidence that was admissible before the **CJA 2003** as 'background' evidence. Examples can be found in *Fulcher* (1995) and *M(T) and Others* (2000). **Section 101(1)(d)** has to be read in conjunction with **s 103**.

The provisions that can be used to admit evidence of bad character by virtue of the way in which the defence is conducted are **s 101(1)(e), (f)** and **(g)**. These provisions must be read with **ss 104, 105** and **106** respectively.

Where evidence of a defendant's bad character is not admitted by agreement under **s 101(1)(a)** or elicited on behalf of the defendant himself under **s 101(1)(b)**, it is necessary to consider arguments that may be available to exclude it. You should note particularly **s 101(3)** and **(4)**, and **s 103(3)** and **(4)**. You should also consider the possibility of using the common law discretion, confirmed by *Sang* (1980), to exclude prosecution evidence where its prejudicial effect exceeds its probative value. This discretion appears to have been unaffected by the **CJA 2003**. Save in relation to **s 101(1)(d)** and **(g)**, which are covered by **subs (3)**, it may also be useful to consider the application of **s 78(1)** of the **Police and Criminal Evidence Act (PACE) 1984**, but it should be remembered that this provision applies only to evidence on which the prosecution proposes to rely.

The Court of Appeal has considered the new legislation on evidence of bad character on frequent occasions. Guidelines have been given in some cases to help trial judges to apply the statutory rules. Those laid down in *Hanson* (2005) are particularly important. There are several consolidated appeals where application of the legislation in particular cases can be studied; for example, *Edwards* (2006), *Renda* (2006) and *Weir* (2006). These are useful to read in order to get the 'feel' of the way in which the legislation is being applied, but it must be remembered that cases are likely to be decided very much on their own facts. It would be a mistake to regard these decisions as precedents in the strict sense.

One of the most important of the guidelines in *Hanson* concerns the direction that a judge should give to a jury where evidence of previous convictions has been admitted. For reasons of space, and to avoid too much repetition, I have not included this in all the model answers. However, in your examination you should remember to set it out in full if there is any possibility that previous convictions will be admitted. It will show the examiners that you have at least some familiarity with the *Hanson* guidelines, and that you recognise the growing importance in evidence law of the content of judicial directions in a summing-up. The judge in summing up should make these points to the jury:

(i) They should not place undue reliance on previous convictions. In particular, they should not conclude that the defendant has been untruthful or has committed the offence with which he has been charged merely because he has these convictions.
(ii) Whether the convictions do in fact show propensity is for them to decide.
(iii) If they do find propensity, they are entitled to take this into account when determining guilt. But it is only one relevant factor, and they must assess its significance in the light of all the other evidence in the case.

Checklist ✓

Students should be familiar with the following areas:

- relevance;
- **Part 11, Chapter 1** of the **CJA 2003**;
- *Sang* (1980);
- **s 78(1)** of **PACE**;
- **s 27(3)** of the **Theft Act 1968**;
- evidence of good character; note particularly the guidelines set out in *Gray* (2004) for cases where a defendant does not have an absolutely good character;
- the guidelines in *Hanson* (2005).

QUESTION 30

James is charged with indecently assaulting Kate in a large department store during the January sales. The case for the prosecution is that he approached her from behind and whispered in her ear, 'You look sexy. What about a drink?' It is alleged that he then fondled one of her breasts. James denies that he said anything to Kate, whom he had never met before. He admits that he might have touched her breast, but says that if he did, it was an accident. A crowd of shoppers had suddenly pushed him forward, and he had instinctively clutched at the person standing in front of him to ensure that he did not lose his balance and fall to the ground. James was carrying a briefcase at the time. When this was lawfully searched by the police after his arrest it was found to contain several magazines devoted to heterosexual pornography. James was convicted three months ago of a public order offence in connection with a political demonstration and was fined £50.

▸ Discuss the evidential issues arising.

> **Answer Plan**
>
> This appears to be a relatively simple set of facts, but in order to answer the question well you must analyse them carefully. There are two potential problems to be considered: the discovery of the magazines, and the significance of the previous conviction.
>
> *The magazines*
> The first question to consider is relevance. Remember how to construct an argument for relevance by finding an appropriate generalisation. Why is relevance so important? Note the dictum of Lawton LJ in *Turner* (1975). Take into account the possibility that, while logically relevant, the evidence may not be weighty enough to be legally relevant. Don't be satisfied with reaching the conclusion that the evidence is irrelevant and leaving the matter there. What if the judge decides it *is* relevant? What law will be applicable? It might be the common law, because the **Criminal Justice Act (CJA) 2003** applies only to evidence of 'bad character' within the meaning of **s 98** and **s 112**. Look at those sections. Do you think the discovery of the magazines might count as evidence of bad character for the purposes of the **2003 Act**? Can you get any guidance from some of the principles in *Hanson* (2005)? (You should memorise a summary of these.) The distinction drawn in *Weir* may be helpful. What opportunities for exclusion are there, (a) assuming the Act does not apply; (b) assuming that it does?
>
> *The previous conviction*
> Note the missing information that may well determine what happens at trial. Can the defence argue that James should be treated effectively as a man of good character? If so, what is the position about a *Vye* direction? (Don't forget to spell out for the examiner the contents of such a direction.) Could the prosecution make use of the previous conviction? Obviously it wasn't for a similar offence. How, then, could they use it? Have you studied the **2003 Act** sufficiently well to remember **s 103(1)(b)**?

ANSWER

The first question is whether the prosecution can rely on the magazines to support the case against James. Are they relevant at all? If they are, does their discovery amount to evidence of bad character within **s 98** of the **CJA 2003**?

It could be argued that they are relevant on the basis that a man with an interest in heterosexual pornography is more likely than a man without such an interest to commit an indecent assault on a woman. But the success of such an argument must be doubtful. Obviously, if a judge is not persuaded of the truth of the generalisation that would make the magazines relevant, they will be excluded. Relevance, as Lawton LJ said in *Turner* (1975) is a condition precedent to admissibility. A judge might decide that the evidence was logically relevant, but of insufficient weight to give it legal relevance. In those circumstances also it would be excluded. If a judge decides that it has both logical and legal relevance, it will have to be decided if it is evidence of 'bad character' within **s 98** of the **CJA 2003**.

By **s 98**, evidence of a person's 'bad character' is evidence of, or of a disposition towards, misconduct on his part. (It does not appear that the evidence has anything to do with the alleged facts of the offence, or that it is evidence of misconduct in connection with the investigation or prosecution of the offence.) 'Misconduct' is defined in **s 112** as 'the commission of an offence or other reprehensible behaviour'. Possession of the magazines presumably does not constitute an offence in itself. Might it count as reprehensible behaviour? In *Weir* (2006) a contrast was drawn between behaviour that was 'reprehensible' and that which was merely 'unattractive'. The distinction might well be drawn here. If possession of the magazines does not count as reprehensible behaviour, it will not amount to evidence of bad character within the meaning of **s 98**. In that case, the **2003 Act** will have no application and admissibility will be decided on ordinary principles. (It is assumed that a judge has decided it to be relevant.) The first of these is the common law principle, established in *Sang* (1980), that allows a judge to exclude prosecution evidence where its probative value is exceeded by its prejudicial effect. Reliance could also be placed on the discretion contained in **s 78** of the **Police and Criminal Evidence Act 1984**.

If it is thought that possession of the magazines does amount to reprehensible behaviour, the prosecution will argue that it is evidence of bad character that is admissible under **s 101(1)(d)** of the **CJA 2003**, on the basis that it is relevant to an important matter in issue between the defendant and the prosecution, because it shows a propensity in the defendant to commit offences of the kind with which he is charged (see **s 103(1)(a)**). At this stage it will be important for the court to consider some of the principles laid down by the Court of Appeal in *Hanson* (2005).

The starting point should be to bear in mind that Parliament's purpose in the legislation was 'to assist in the evidence-based conviction of the guilty, without putting those who are not guilty at risk of conviction by prejudice'. Where propensity to commit the offence is relied on as the basis for admitting evidence of bad character under **s 101(1)(d)**, it has to be considered whether the proceedings will be unfair if the evidence is admitted. The court has a duty, not merely a discretion, under **s 101(3)** to exclude evidence that is in principle admissible under **s 101(1)(d)** if it appears to the court that the admission of the evidence would have such an adverse effect on the fairness of the proceedings that the court ought not to admit it. If the evidence is admitted, the judge when summing up should tell the jury that whether possession of the magazines does show propensity is for them to decide. If they do find propensity, they are entitled to take this into account when determining guilt. But it is only one relevant factor, and they must assess its significance in the light of all the other evidence in the case.

The next consideration is James's previous conviction. There may be a persuasive argument for treating him as a person of good character for the purposes of this trial. In *Gray* (2004) the Court of Appeal discussed what should be done where a defendant does not have an absolutely good character. Among guidelines laid down was one stating that if a defendant has a previous conviction which, because of its age *or nature*, may entitle him to be treated as being effectively of good character, the trial judge has a discretion to treat him in this way. Another guideline stated that where the previous conviction is irrelevant in relation to the offence charged, the judge's discretion ought to be exercised in favour of the defendant. The conviction for the public order offence clearly falls into this category. If a defendant is treated as being effectively of good character, the judge must then give a full direction in accordance with the rules laid down in *Vye* (1993). That is to say, he must tell the jury that good character is relevant to a defendant's credibility and also to the likelihood of his having behaved as alleged by the prosecution. In James's case there may be a slight difficulty if it is decided that evidence of the magazines should be admitted as evidence of disposition. A judge might decide to qualify the *Vye* direction in some way. On the other hand, he might choose to refer to the evidence of the magazines but balance that reference by giving a full *Vye* direction.

If the defendant pleaded not guilty at the earlier trial, and gave evidence in his own defence, the prosecution might wish to rely on his conviction as evidence of a propensity to be untruthful because his evidence had been disbelieved. But the defence would rely on *Campbell* (2007), where the Court of Appeal said that the question whether the defendant has a propensity for being untruthful will not normally be capable of being described as an *important* matter in issue between the defendant and the prosecution so as to fall within **s 101(1)(d)**, because a propensity for untruthfulness will not, by itself, go very far towards establishing the guilt of the defendant. The only circumstances in which there is likely to be an *important* issue as to whether a defendant has a propensity to tell lies is when telling lies is an element of the offence charged. The prosecution, however, could argue that the Court of Appeal in other decisions, such as *Alobaydi* (2007), has been less forthright, and that the approach taken in *Campbell* makes a 'dead letter' of **s 103(1)(b)**.[1]

---

1 Mirfield, 'Character, Credibility and Truthfulness,' [2008] LQR 1.

QUESTION 31

Louis is charged with sexually assaulting Mary on a train journey between London and Plymouth. The case for the prosecution is that they had not met before, but were sitting next to each other, and that after a while Louis began a conversation by commenting on the fine weather. It is alleged that Louis touched Mary's breast during the conversation that followed. Louis denies the charge. He says that he might have touched Mary's breast, but says that if he did, it was only an accident when the train slowed suddenly and he lost his balance in his seat. Last year Louis was convicted of sexually assaulting Nellie, who had been sitting next to him on a coach journey between Bournemouth and London. On that occasion Louis had begun a conversation with Nellie, whom he had not previously met, and a little later had fondled her thigh. His defence, in support of which he gave evidence, was that he had not touched Nellie and that she had invented the whole incident.

▶ Discuss the evidential matters arising.

Answer Plan

You have to consider the relevance and admissibility of the earlier conversation and of the circumstances leading to it. Note the two possible arguments for admissibility under **s 101(1)(c)** and **(d)** of **CJA 2003**. You should consider arguments for exclusion and how use can be made of the *Hanson* guidelines. When dealing with propensity under **s 101(1)(d)**, note the two possibilities under **s 103(1)(a)** and **(b)**, but in connection with the latter you will need to consider the effect of *Campbell* (2007).

ANSWER

The question is whether the prosecution case can be supported by evidence of Louis's previous conviction and the circumstances that led to it. It can plausibly be argued that a man with a recent conviction for sexually assaulting a woman is more likely to be guilty of a further sexual assault on a woman than someone without such a conviction. It can also be argued that where features of the current allegations resemble features of the earlier offence, the likelihood of the defendant's guilt is increased. The previous conviction is obviously 'misconduct' within **s 112(1) CJA 2003**. It is therefore evidence of bad character within **s 98**, and its admissibility will be governed by **Part 11, Chapter 1** of the Act.

There are two possible arguments for admissibility. The first is that the evidence is admissible under **s 101(1)(c)** on the basis that it is important explanatory evidence as defined by **s 102**. It would have to be argued that without this evidence the court would find it impossible or difficult to understand other evidence in the case, *and* that its value for understanding the case as a whole is substantial. On these facts, the prosecution might argue that the court would find it difficult to assess properly the defendant's evidence of accident without knowing about the earlier offence, and that its value for understanding the case as a whole was for that reason substantial. But this assumes that assessing the weight of evidence is at least part of the process of understanding it. A judge might consider this questionable, and a safer course for the prosecution would be reliance on **s 101(1)(d)**.

Under this subsection the prosecution would say that evidence of the earlier conviction is relevant to an important matter in issue between the defendant and the prosecution, namely, that Louis touched Mary's breast without her consent and that his touching was sexual and not accidental. The prosecution will argue that Louis has a propensity to assault women sexually, and that in giving expression to that propensity he follows a similar course of action. Such evidence would rebut Louis's defence of accident and would fall within **s 103(1)(a) CJA 2003**. It might also be argued that the evidence shows a propensity to be untruthful, because on the earlier occasion Louis gave evidence in his defence and was disbelieved. However, this argument is unlikely to be put forward, or if put forward to succeed, because in *Campbell* (2007) the Court of Appeal said that the question whether the defendant had a propensity to be untruthful will not normally be an *important* matter in issue between the defendant and prosecution so as to fall within **s 101(1)(d)**. And in *Foster* (2009) the Court of Appeal approved an observation in *Campbell* to the effect that in general it is unhelpful to tell a jury that they can take bad character into account when deciding whether a defendant's evidence is truthful.

In considering whether to admit evidence of the previous conviction or to exclude it under **s 101(3)**, or under the statutory and common law preserved by **s 126(2)**, the judge will take into account the guidelines laid down in *Hanson* (2005), where the Court of Appeal said that there are three questions to be considered in circumstances like these. First, does the history of the convictions establish a propensity to commit offences of the kind charged? Secondly, does that propensity make it more likely that the defendant committed the offence charged? Thirdly, is it unjust to rely on the convictions, and will the proceedings be unfair if they are admitted? Importantly for this case, the Court said in *Hanson* that although there was no minimum number of events necessary to demonstrate propensity, a single previous conviction for an offence of the same description or category would often not be enough. But the Court also said that it might be enough if it showed a tendency to unusual behaviour, or where its circumstances demonstrated probative force in relation to the offence charged. Those circumstances were not to be confined to those showing striking similarity.

It could be argued on the facts given that both these conditions are satisfied. The previous conviction, it could be said, by itself shows a tendency to unusual behaviour. Even if sexual assault by itself is insufficient to show this, sexual assault on a woman previously unknown to the defendant, it could be argued, shows such a tendency, especially since the circumstances were unlike those where relations between strangers are more relaxed and where sexual tension may be heightened, as for example at a party or in a nightclub. The mode of commission of the previous offence, including starting a conversation with a stranger during a journey and taking advantage of the proximity afforded by public transport, tend to rebut the defendant's defence on the current charge. On the other hand, it would be pointed out on his behalf that the classic situation in which reliance is placed on a previous conviction is where the defence raised then was the same as that raised in answer to the current charge. That is not the case here. On the earlier occasion the defence was that the complainant had fabricated the whole story; the current defence is accident. The prosecution might then reply that the defence of accident has traditionally been one where the courts have been readier to admit evidence of similar facts, as can be seen from *Makin v Attorney General for New South Wales* (1894) and similar cases. On balance, it seems likely that the conviction will be held admissible.

QUESTION 32

Edgar is charged with indecently assaulting Fergus. Fergus, aged 15, was flying his kite at dusk in a public park when he was approached by a man who said that he had a collection of kites and invited Fergus to his house, which he said was nearby, to see them. Fergus agreed to go with him, but while they were walking together the man made suggestions of a sexual nature and then sexually assaulted him by placing his hand under Fergus's trousers. Fergus, somewhat hesitantly, picked out Edgar in an identification parade. Garry, aged 17, has made a statement to the police in which he says that he was in another public park in the same town shortly before the date of the assault on Edgar. He said that he was flying his kite when he was approached by a man who said that he had a collection of kites and invited him to his house to see them. Garry agreed to go with him, but while they were walking together the man made suggestions of a sexual nature to him. At this, Garry knocked him down and then ran away. Garry identified Edgar in an identification parade as the man who had approached him. Garry and Fergus attend the same school and know each other slightly. Rumours have been circulating at the school about a man who sexually assaults local boys. When Edgar's house is lawfully searched, no kites are found, but the police find a collection of homosexual videos, some leather masks and several pairs of handcuffs.

Edgar denies meeting Fergus and Garry and claims to have been mistakenly identified by them.
▶ Advise the prosecution on the evidential issues arising.

> **Answer Plan**
> First, you need to determine the relevance of Garry's evidence, ie, the probative job that it is intended to do. It is clearly evidence of the defendant's bad character; what argument for admissibility does the **Criminal Justice Act (CJA) 2003** provide? What are the possibilities for exclusion? Don't forget to deal with the possibility of some form of collusion, and with the problems of relevance arising from the search.

ANSWER

The primary question is whether the rather weak evidence that Fergus is able to give can be supported by the evidence of Garry. It is important that it should be supported because of the special danger that attaches to evidence of identification, and the consequent need for directions to be given to the jury in accordance with *Turnbull* (1977). According to the decision of the Court of Appeal in that case, a judge must warn the jury of the special need for caution before convicting on identification evidence. He must tell the jury the reason for having to give such a warning. Some reference should be made to the possibility that a mistaken witness can be a convincing one, and that a number of convincing witnesses can all be mistaken. He should direct the jury to examine the circumstances in which each identification was made. Although the Court of Appeal has not always been consistent, recent decisions such as *Donald* (2004) suggest that another essential ingredient of a *Turnbull* direction is that the judge should point out to the jury the weaknesses in any identification evidence. The judge should also direct the jury to consider whether the identification evidence is supported by any other evidence, and should identify for them the evidence that is capable of providing such support.

Garry's evidence is clearly evidence of Edgar's bad character within **ss 98** and **112(1)** of the **CJA 2003**. Although the events narrated by Garry were close in time, place, and in some circumstances to those narrated by Fergus, it seems unlikely that it will qualify as important explanatory evidence under **s 101(1)(c)**; it can hardly be said that without it the jury would find Fergus's evidence impossible or difficult to understand properly, as required by **s 102**.

But Garry's evidence could be relevant to an important matter in issue between the defendant and the prosecution – namely, the identity of the assailant – and therefore admissible under **s 101(1)(d)**. By **s 101(3)** the court must not admit evidence under **s 101(1)(d)** if, on an application by the defendant to exclude it, it appears to the court that its admission would have such an adverse effect on the fairness of the proceedings that the court ought not to admit it. This test is the same as that contained in **s 78(1)** of the **Police and Criminal Evidence Act (PACE) 1984**, and the decisions under that subsection show that the test can be satisfied where the prejudicial effect of an item of evidence exceeds its probative value. For example, in *Boyson* (1991) and in *Lee* (1996) this argument led to the exclusion of convictions tendered under **s 74** of **PACE**. Either under **s 101(3)**, therefore, or under the common law discretion confirmed by *Sang* (1980), it will be open to the defence to argue that Garry's evidence ought to be excluded.

So far as the weight of Garry's evidence is concerned, everything depends on the extent to which collusion is a likely danger, and on the improbability of similar features in the incidents being due merely to coincidence.

The relevant similarities are as follows:

(i) both the victims were teenage boys;
(ii) both were in public parks in the same town;
(iii) both events took place at dusk;
(iv) both events took place within a short time of each other;
(v) both boys were flying kites when they were approached;
(vi) both boys were told of a collection of kites and invited to view them;
(vii) both boys were subjected to indecent suggestions.

However, only Fergus was indecently assaulted. This may have some significance. In cases decided under the former law of similar fact evidence, such as *Johnson* (1995), the Court of Appeal said that a judge who has to decide whether each incident bears the signature of the accused should look at the nature and quality of any disparities that exist. But it was also said that the presence of some dissimilarities will not lead inevitably to exclusion. Item (vii) would be significant if the suggestions were sufficiently unusual.

It should be observed, though, that in *Somanathan* (2005) the Court of Appeal held that evidence admitted under **s 101(1)(d)** does not have to satisfy the former test for admissibility of similar fact evidence, which is now to be regarded as obsolete. Dissimilarities may therefore be less significant under the new law. The guidelines laid down by the Court of Appeal in *Hanson* (2005) included one to the effect that a single conviction will often not show propensity, but that it may do so where it shows a tendency to commit unusual behaviour, or where its circumstances demonstrate probative force in relation to the offence charged. Although the incident in relation to Garry did not result in a conviction, the same principle is likely to be applied, with the court taking the view that it does show a tendency to unusual behaviour on the part of the defendant. Further, the earlier incident has probative value in relation to the offence charged because it is evidence that tends to support the complainant's identification of the defendant. On the other hand, it was also said in *Hanson* that the judge must consider the strength of the prosecution case. If there is no, or very little, other evidence against a defendant, it is unlikely to be just to admit a defendant's previous convictions. Presumably the same principle applies where an earlier incident did not give rise to criminal proceedings.

There seems to be little risk of collusion in the ordinary sense because although the boys attend the same school, they know each other only slightly. However, in *DPP v Boardman* (1975), Lord Wilberforce referred also to a risk of falsity arising from 'a process of infection from media or publicity or simply from fashion', and in *Ryder* (1993) the Court of Appeal recognised the possibility of collusion in the sense of a witness's being unconsciously influenced by another. What is present on these facts is a common source of rumour that might have tainted the accounts of both boys and increased their similarity. However, by **s 109** of the **CJA 2003**, in the assessment of the probative value of evidence, the assumption must be made that it is true, unless it appears on the basis of any material before the court that no court or jury could reasonably find it to be true. It is very likely that the assumption of truth will be made in this case and that the possibility of even indirect collusion will be disregarded.

The absence of kites when Edgar's house was searched is ambiguous. It may show that the police have got the wrong man; on the other hand, the account of a kite collection may have been no more than a ploy to entice the defendant's victims to his house. Unless the leather masks and handcuffs can be connected with the indecent suggestions, their discovery will be irrelevant, and so inadmissible. The discovery of the videos is more difficult. If they are in Edgar's possession, they are capable of showing that he has a homosexual inclination. The probative value of this is that that it tends to confirm the identification by Fergus. What a coincidence it would be if the man *misidentified* by Fergus also had a homosexual inclination. A case that may support this argument is *Thompson v R* (1918), where a defence of mistaken identity was rebutted by proof of facts tending to show that the defendant was a homosexual with a taste for boys. For the defence, it could be argued that the possibility of coincidence is greater than was realised in 1918, since homosexuality is recognised now to be a more frequent phenomenon. It might also be argued that proof of a general homosexual tendency has little or no probative worth where a sexual assault on a boy under the age of 16 is alleged. The interesting question also arises whether possession of homosexual videos counts as evidence of bad character under **ss 98** and **112(1)** of the **CJA 2003**. If it does, the prosecution would have to establish that this evidence is admissible under **s 101(1)** of the Act.

QUESTION 33

Hector is charged on an indictment containing two counts of handling stolen goods. Count 1 alleges that on 1 February last year, he received 50 bottles of gin, knowing or believing them to have been stolen. Count 2 alleges that on 1 March last year, he received 500 cigars, knowing or believing them to have been stolen. Hector's defence to count 1 is that he purchased the gin honestly from a teetotal friend in the belief that his friend had received it as a gift. His defence to count 2 is that it was not he who had received the cigars, but his identical twin brother. Four years ago, Hector was convicted of handling 500 bottles of stolen whisky. His defence on that occasion, which he supported by giving evidence, was that he had purchased the whisky honestly from a teetotal friend in the belief that his friend had won it as a prize in a raffle. Hector continues to maintain that he received the whisky innocently and says that he was wrongly convicted by the jury.

▶ Advise the prosecution on the evidential issues that arise.

Answer Plan

This question is based on the special provisions of **s 27(3)** of the **Theft Act 1968**. Note particularly:

- the limited purpose for which evidence can be adduced under **s 27(3)**;
- the discretion to exclude, even though the section is available;
- the notice provision and time limit;
- limits on what can be given in evidence: *Fowler* (1988);
- **s 74(3)** of the **Police and Criminal Evidence Act (PACE) 1984**;
- the direction that should be given to the jury where there are several counts in the indictment.

ANSWER

The first matter that has to be considered is whether and to what extent the prosecution can rely upon Hector's conviction for handling whisky to support the present case against him. **Section 27(3)** of the **Theft Act 1968** provides, amongst other things, that where a person is being proceeded against for handling stolen goods, if evidence has been given of his having in his possession the goods that are the subject of the charge, evidence of a previous conviction for handling shall be admissible for the purpose of proving that he knew or believed the goods to have been stolen. In the present case, therefore, evidence of Hector's previous conviction will be admissible in relation to count 1, because on that count receiving is admitted and the only issue is guilty knowledge. Evidence of the previous conviction would not, however, be admissible in relation to count 2, where the live issue is whether it was Hector or his identical twin brother who received the goods. By **s 27(3)(b)**, the conviction must have been within the five years preceding the date of the offence charged. This condition is satisfied. There is also a further condition requiring that seven days' notice in writing be given to the defendant of intention to prove the conviction.

The judge has power to exclude **s 27(3)** evidence on the ground that its prejudicial effect outweighs its probative value (*Smith* (1976); *Perry* (1984)). Because the conviction will be relevant on one count only, the judge may very well exercise this discretion in Hector's favour. If he does admit the evidence, he will have to explain carefully to the jury the extent to which it is relevant (*Wilkins* (1975)).

The subsection does not permit details of the earlier conviction to be given; a bare recital of the conviction is all that is allowed. If the prosecution wants to adduce evidence of the details of the previous offence it must rely on **s 101(1)(d)** of the **Criminal Justice Act (CJA) 2003**. However, the effect of **s 73(2)** of **PACE** is that any certificate of conviction following trial on indictment must state the substance and effect of the indictment and conviction, including the type of property involved. In *Hacker* (1994), such a certificate was held by the House of Lords to be admissible in evidence, subject only to the judge's discretion to exclude it if its admission would prejudice the fairness of the proceedings.

It is possible that the prosecution would be permitted to adduce evidence of the circumstances of the previous offence under **s 101(1)(d)** because of the defence raised on that occasion. It could be argued with some force that the jury ought to know about the earlier defence that failed because it makes it most unlikely that, remembering his earlier experience, this defendant would have accepted a very similar story had he indeed been told it. It would be possible to argue more generally that the earlier offence shows a propensity to commit offences of the kind with which the defendant is currently charged, and also that the defendant has a propensity to be untruthful, since on the earlier occasion he pleaded not guilty and gave evidence in his defence that must have been disbelieved. This would make the earlier offence relevant to both counts. The defence could argue that, just as one swallow does not make a summer, so one conviction is not enough to establish a disposition. Such a submission could be supported by reference to the guidelines in *Hanson* (2005), one of which states that a single conviction will often not show propensity, but that it may do so where it shows a tendency to unusual behaviour, or where its circumstances demonstrate probative force in relation to the offence charged. On these facts a judge might well find that the circumstances of the previous conviction do have probative force, because they tend to make improbable the defendant's account of the innocent circumstances in which he received the gin. It could also be argued, relying on **s 103(3)**, that by reason of the length of time since the conviction it would be unjust to admit it in this case. But it seems that this argument is available only in relation to the use of a conviction under the **CJA 2003** to establish disposition to commit offences of the kind currently charged. It does not appear to be available if the conviction is relevant to some other matter that assists the prosecution, such as the significance on these facts of the earlier defence, or the defendant's propensity to be untruthful. The defence could, however, rely on **s 101(3)**, or on the common law discretion, confirmed in *Sang* (1980), to exclude prosecution evidence on the basis that its prejudicial effect outweighs its probative value.

It appears that if evidence of the earlier conviction is given, Hector will insist that it was wrongful. The ordinary rule, provided by **s 74(3)** of **PACE**, is that where it is proved that the accused has been convicted, he shall be taken to have committed the offence in question unless he proves the contrary. This raises the interesting possibility that the defendant might try to use the current trial to try to establish his contention in relation to the earlier conviction. Such an issue would clearly be collateral to the issue being tried, but to prevent the defendant from adducing evidence relating to matters considered at the earlier trial would turn the presumption contained in **s 74(3)** of **PACE** into a conclusive one for the purposes of the current trial, which, according to **s 74(3)**, it is not.

A final argument for the admissibility of Hector's previous conviction would be based on **s 101(1)(g)** of the **CJA 2003**: by putting the blame on his twin brother in relation to count 2 he has made an attack on another person's character. Under the former law, a defendant was free to attack the character of persons who were not co-defendants, witnesses for the prosecution, or deceased victims of the alleged crime without having his own bad character revealed. But the reference in **s 101(1)(g)** to 'another person's character' seems wide enough to include anybody. If this argument is accepted, the defence could argue that the evidence should be excluded, either under **s 101(3)** or under the common law discretion.

In *Highton* (2006) the Court of Appeal held that where evidence of bad character was admitted under any of the gateways established by **s 101(1)**, it was admissible for any purpose relevant to the case, and could therefore go to both credibility and propensity.

QUESTION 34

Steven, aged 18, has been charged with murder. The case for the prosecution is that on 3 May he raped and strangled Lynne, a classmate, after taking her in his car to an area known as Coppett's Wood where her body was afterwards found. Steven told the police that at Lynne's request he had given her a lift to a nearby railway station, had left her there, and had never seen her again. The prosecution have a statement from Jocelyne, another classmate of the accused. She said that she and Steven had made an arrangement to go bird watching on 3 May in Coppett's Wood. Jocelyne said that Steven had asked her to keep the arrangement secret. On the day in question, Jocelyne had changed her mind and had decided to go shopping with some other classmates instead. There is also police evidence that when they searched Steven's locker at school they found a collection of heterosexual pornographic magazines. Two weeks before the murder, Steven had been arrested for indecently exposing himself to two women in Coppett's Wood.

❱ **Advise the prosecution on the evidential issues that arise.**

Answer Plan
This question requires consideration of three items of evidence:

- Jocelyne's statement. You need to discuss its relevance. Remember the need to determine what probative job the disputed evidence is expected to do. Note the discussion of the generalisation on which the prosecution would need to rely. *Rodley* (1913) is a useful case to bring in by way of illustration. Don't forget to reach a conclusion, with reasons, for admissibility or inadmissibility.
- The magazines. Note the importance of the initial assumption that they had no special bearing on what had been done to Lynne. In practice, you would need to know the exact nature of these magazines, and you should indicate this to the examiner. Again, relevance is all important, and finding an appropriate generalisation that would establish this forms a significant part of the discussion.
- Indecent exposure. You will have to consider the relevance of these events in relation to **ss 101(1)(d)** and **103(3)** of the **Criminal Justice Act (CJA) 2003**, and also in relation to the relevant guidelines in *Hanson* (2005).

The final paragraph is an important one. Thinking in general is 'not to be conceived to "form a chain which is no stronger than its weakest link"', but as 'a cable whose fibres may be ever so slender provided they are sufficiently numerous and intimately connected' (Peirce, CS, *Collected Papers* 5, p 265). Much defence advocacy works on the assumption that this is *not* the case.

ANSWER

With regard to Jocelyne's statement, the main problem is one of relevance. Does the arrangement with Jocelyne tend to show that the accused was not telling the truth to the police about his encounter with Lynne? It might do so if it indicated that Steven had determined to take *some* girl, regardless of who it was, to Coppett's Wood that day for the purpose of sexual intercourse, to be obtained by force if necessary. It would then appear that when Jocelyne dropped out, Lynne was substituted as the victim.

It is useful to consider whether Jocelyne's statement would be thought to have significance if she had said nothing about a request for secrecy. Almost certainly it would not. But a person who asks another to keep an assignation secret usually does so because he does not wish others to know about it. One reason, but only one, why he might wish this is because he intends to do something unlawful, or at least improper, with his companion. But there might be innocent reasons for not wanting to be disturbed by others. Thus, if a bird watching exercise were planned, stillness and silence would be wanted.

On the assumption that Steven said nothing else to throw light on his request, the position would be that if Jocelyne were to testify, the jury would have before them a piece of evidence with very little probative value but which might easily mislead because of its tendency to invite speculation. Perhaps a similar problem arose in *Rodley* (1913). The appellant was charged with housebreaking with intent to rape. The prosecution called evidence to show that he had entered a house by climbing down the chimney and had been met by the father of his supposed victim. The appellant said that he had indeed intended to have intercourse with the daughter, but only with her consent. The prosecution also called evidence to show that later that night he had climbed down the chimney of another house and had had consensual intercourse with a woman living there. It was held that this evidence should have been excluded. It proved nothing at all about the real issue of the appellant's willingness to commit rape. On the other hand, it certainly showed a lustful disposition which may well have prejudiced the appellant in the eyes of the jury.

So here, Jocelyne's testimony would prove nothing about Steven's willingness to commit rape and murder, but it might prejudice him because it would leave the jury guessing and without the means to advance beyond that stage to a reasoned conclusion. It is likely, therefore, that her evidence would be excluded.[1]

In considering the pornographic magazines, it is assumed that the pornography has no marked resemblance to what was done to Lynne. Apart from this, the finding of these magazines will be relevant if, and only if, an appropriate generalisation can be found about the way things are in the world that makes them so. We must discard at once something like 'Most persons who rape and murder girls take an interest in pornography'. (This generalisation will be referred to as 'G1'.) While it might be the case that most persons who rape and murder girls do in fact take an interest in pornography, it is not the case that most persons who take an interest in pornography rape and murder girls. If G1 is used to establish relevance, you attain it only by assuming the truth of the very thing that the pornography is meant to prove – that Steven is a rapist and murderer.

---

1 Cf the Canadian case *Reference re R v Truscott* (1967); Le Bordais, I, *The Trial of Steven Truscott*, 1966.

Might a more useful generalisation be that people who take an interest in pornography are more likely to rape and murder girls than those who do not ('G2')? In the first place, although this *may* be true, it is not obviously so, and if the prosecution is going to rely on its truth to establish guilt they must be prepared to adduce expert evidence on the matter, for it would almost certainly be challenged by the defence.

But, supposing that G2 can be established, what is the probative value of the discovery? It must be almost nothing. The police evidence will have put Steven in a class of persons who are more likely to rape and murder girls than those not in that class. However, that class will certainly be a large one, and the question in relation to any individual in it will be how much greater his membership makes the likelihood of his having raped and murdered a particular victim. The possession of pornography is unlikely to increase significantly the probability that Steven committed this crime. Unless there is a resemblance between what appears in the magazines and what was done to Lynne, its discovery, even if relevant, is likely to be far more prejudicial than probative, and it will be excluded, either under *Sang* (1980) or under **s 78(1)** of the **Police and Criminal Evidence Act (PACE) 1984**.

The prosecution might wish to adduce evidence of the earlier incidents of indecent exposure. Again, relevance would seem to present difficulties. Is it the case that a man who indecently exposes himself to women is more likely than someone who does not do so to rape and murder a woman? It is far from obvious that this is so. If this evidence is regarded as relevant, it will certainly be evidence of Steven's bad character within **ss 98** and **112(1)** of the **CJA 2003**. But the guidelines in *Hanson* (2005) suggest that the evidence is unlikely to be admitted under **s 101(1)(d)**. If they are held to be relevant, the judge will have decided that they tend to establish a propensity to commit offences of the kind charged, and circumstances demonstrating probative force are not confined to those sharing striking similarity with the incident that is the subject of the charge. But there is little, if any, similarity between the current offences and the earlier incidents, and this is something that a judge may take into consideration when considering the fairness of the proceedings and **s 103(3)**. He may also take into account the respective gravity of the past and present offences. Further, it was said in *Hanson* that a judge must always consider the strength of the prosecution case. If there is no, or very little, other evidence against a defendant, which is the case here, it is unlikely to be just to admit previous convictions. On these facts, of course, there are as yet no convictions in respect of the earlier incidents, which Steven may well deny on the basis of mistaken identity.

In relation to all three items of evidence – Jocelyne's statement, the pornographic magazines, and whatever may be the evidence of indecent exposure – the prosecution might argue that all are items of circumstantial evidence and that they operate cumulatively. Like the strands in a cord, one might be insufficient to sustain the weight of the prosecution case, but three woven together may be of sufficient strength.[2] The answer to this is that circumstantial evidence must be evidence of relevant facts, and the objection in all three cases has been that the evidence in question is of irrelevant facts. Something that you have already decided to be irrelevant will not be made relevant by being added to something else that is irrelevant, although it is sometimes the case that what initially appears to be irrelevant may later be seen to be relevant in the light of some later discovery of relevant matter. Suppose, for example, that the magazines, contrary to the supposition in this answer, contained material that resembled what had been done to Lynne. They would then acquire more significance and would stand a greater chance of being considered relevant, and so admissible. The position would also change if it were discovered that Steven had no interest in bird watching, so that he would appear to have been lying to Jocelyne and to have had some hidden purpose in persuading her to accompany him to Coppett's Wood.

Aim Higher ★

1. If you are going to argue that evidence should be admitted under **s 101(1)(c)**, be sure that you base your reasoning on the facts of the case. The definition of 'important explanatory evidence' in **s 102** should be used as a test.
2. Always show familiarity with the relevant *Hanson* guidelines where there is a question of admitting evidence of bad character. Pay attention in particular to what was said about the number of convictions required to establish a disposition and the directions that should be given to the jury if previous convictions are admitted.

Common Pitfalls ✗

1. A surprisingly common pitfall is the attempt to apply **s 101** to non-defendants. Remember that there is an entirely different section (**s 100**) that applies to them.
2. Most candidates are aware that *Hanson* laid down guidelines for the operation of **s 101**, but fewer candidates are able to refer to individual guidelines when it might assist in answering a question. Use the facts that you are given in a problem question to suggest which guidelines would be likely to be relied on in court.

2 Cf Pollock CB in *Exall* (1866).

Character Evidence II

INTRODUCTION

This chapter continues the topic begun in Chapter 8, and you are referred to the introduction to that chapter for the background to the new law on this subject. This chapter concentrates, though not exclusively, on the ways in which a defendant's bad character can emerge as a result of the way in which the defence is conducted.

Checklist ✔

Students should be familiar with the following areas:

- relevance;
- spent convictions;
- **Part 11, Chapter 1** of the **Criminal Justice Act 2003**;
- *Sang* (1980).

QUESTION 35

Edna and Mavis are being tried in the Crown Court for theft. The case for the prosecution is that they are both guilty of shoplifting in the Ealing branch of Bromides, the well known chain of chemists. A store detective gives evidence and states that Edna and Mavis were together in the store. She says that Mavis was carrying a holdall and that she opened it to allow Edna to conceal in it a bottle of shampoo and a tin of talcum powder, the property of Bromides, for which neither defendant paid. Edna gives no evidence, but her counsel cross-examines the manager of the store, who is one of the prosecution witnesses, about a conviction that he had for indecent exposure when he was a student at university. Mavis gives evidence in her own defence and states that she was with Edna in the store, but was not herself involved in any shoplifting. She admits that when stopped outside the store she was carrying the holdall, but says that it belonged to Edna, who alone had been carrying it in the store. She said that Edna had given it to her to hold outside the store so that she, Edna, could more easily look for her season ticket, which she thought she had lost. Edna has a number of recent convictions for theft and for offences involving prostitution. Mavis has several recent convictions for theft. They all involved similar items stolen from other branches of Bromides.

▸ **Edna and Mavis are separately represented. Discuss the evidential issues that arise.**

> **Answer Plan**
>
> The following points need to be considered:
>
> ❖ the effect of Edna's failure to give evidence;
> ❖ the legitimacy of the cross-examination of the manager;
> ❖ the effect of the cross-examination of the manager on Edna;
> ❖ the possible prosecution argument about Edna's previous convictions;
> ❖ the effect of Mavis's denial of the store detective's evidence about the holdall;
> ❖ the effect of Mavis's evidence on Edna;
> ❖ the possible prosecution argument about Mavis's previous convictions.

ANSWER

Edna has chosen not to give evidence and the first question that arises concerns the extent to which comment can be made on this. By **s 35(3)** of the **Criminal Justice and Public Order Act 1994**, the court or jury, in determining whether the accused is guilty of the offence charged, may draw such inferences as appear proper from the failure of the accused to give evidence. Further, under the pre-1994 law, counsel for a co-defendant always had a right to comment on a defendant's failure to give evidence, and the judge had no discretion to prevent this (*Wickham* (1971)). The **1994 Act** has not altered this. Thus, Edna's failure to testify is likely to be the subject of comment by both the judge and counsel for Mavis.

The Court of Appeal emphasised in *Napper* (1996) the general rule that it should be open to a jury to draw adverse inferences when a defendant fails to testify, and said that attempts to marginalise the section are contrary to the spirit of its provisions. The judge, in any direction under the section, must tell the jury that: (1) the defendant is entitled to remain silent; (2) an inference from silence cannot prove guilt on its own; and (3) they must be satisfied that there is a case to answer before drawing any inferences from silence. (The judge must have thought there was, or the case would have already been stopped. But the jury may not believe the witnesses whose evidence was considered by the judge to raise a *prima facie* case.) The judge must also tell the jury that if they conclude that the silence can only sensibly be attributed to the defendant's having no answer, or none that would stand up to cross-examination, they may draw an adverse inference. The effect of this appears to be that the jury must not draw such an inference unless sure that there is no other explanation, consistent with innocence, to account for it. However, the defence will not be able to suggest innocent reasons for the defendant's silence that are unsupported by evidence at trial (*Cowan* (1996)).

The cross-examination of the manager by Edna's counsel may well have been improper. If the conviction was spent, it should not have been referred to without leave of the judge, who should not have given leave unless he was satisfied that the interests of justice required that this matter be put. Further, cross-examination of the manager is now governed by provisions relating to the bad character of non-defendants in **s 100** of the **Criminal Justice Act (CJA) 2003**. By **subs (1)**, such evidence is admissible, if not agreed, if, and only if, it is important explanatory evidence, or has substantial probative value in relation to a matter which is in issue in the proceedings and is of substantial importance in the context of the case as a whole. Even then, the leave of the court is required by **subs (4)**. On the facts, the conditions in **s 100(1)** are not satisfied, and the question should not have been put. Having put it, however, Edna is in the position of having made an attack on another person's character. Accordingly, evidence of her bad character is in principle admissible under **s 101(1)(g)** of the **CJA 2003**. The Court of Appeal held in *Highton* (2006) that wherever evidence of bad character is admitted, it is admissible for any purpose that is relevant in the case; the particular 'gateway' that allows admission does not affect this.

However, by **s 101(3)**, such evidence must be excluded if it appears to the court that its admission would have such an adverse effect on the fairness of the proceedings that it ought not to be admitted. The onus is on the defendant to raise the issue. In determining whether evidence of Edna's previous convictions should be admitted, the court will take into account the prejudice likely to follow from disclosure of the convictions for prostitution, and these may be excluded. The recent convictions for theft are in a different category. It might be objected that these convictions are likely to prejudice Ellen because the jury will jump to the conclusion that if she has committed theft before, she is likely to have done so again. However, even under the pre-2003 law the fact that a defendant's previous convictions were for the same or similar offences to that being currently tried was not inevitably a bar to adducing them. And under the new law it would have been possible for the prosecution to argue that Edna's convictions for theft were admissible under **s 101(1)(d)**, though it is difficult to predict the likelihood of success in such an application.

Mavis's evidence that she was carrying the holdall only outside the store contradicts the store detective's evidence, but this is not likely to be construed as an attack on the store detective's character under **s 101(1)(g)** because it is probably a matter about which the store detective could have made an honest mistake. However, Mavis's evidence is likely to have substantial probative value in relation to an important matter in issue between her and her co-defendant, Edna. It is not wholly clear what Edna's defence is, because she does not give evidence. But the evidence of Mavis clearly has the effect of placing the blame for any theft that took place on Edna. Edna will therefore be able to cross-examine Mavis about her previous convictions under **s 101(1)(e)** of the **CJA 2003**. There is no judicial discretion to exclude such cross-examination either under the Act or by virtue of the common law. The discretion confirmed in *Sang* (1980) applies only to prosecution evidence. Cross-examination of Mavis in these circumstances is very likely to be held relevant to guilt, not merely to credibility, and could therefore extend to the circumstances in which the earlier offences were committed.

It would have been open to the prosecution to rely on Mavis's previous convictions under **s 101(1)(d)**. **Section 103** expressly states that for the purposes of this provision, the matters in issue between the defendant and the prosecution include the question whether the defendant has a propensity to commit offences of the kind with which he is charged. Had the prosecution done so, it is unlikely, in view of the substantial similarity of the previous offences and the fact that they were recent, that a court, bearing in mind the guidelines in *Hanson* (2005), would have excluded them under **s 101(3)** or **103(3)**.

If the court had disallowed a prosecution application to adduce evidence of Mavis's convictions, the question would then arise whether the jury would be entitled to consider them in relation to the prosecution case against Mavis as well as in relation to Edna's defence. The Court of Appeal is at present divided on problems of this kind. In *Price* (2005) and *B(C)* (2004) it was held that there was no need to warn a jury not to consider, when dealing with the prosecution case against D1, evidence of D1's bad character adduced by D2 rather than by the prosecution. But the contrary was held in *Mertens* (2005) and in *Murrell* (2005). In *Robinson (Dennis)* (2006), which was concerned with a similar situation, the Court of Appeal said that a direction should not needlessly perplex the jury. The result appears to be that a trial judge has a good deal of discretion in the matter. If he decides that the sort of direction given in *Mertens* and in *Murrell* will encourage confusing mental gymnastics, he can safely follow the course approved in *Price* and *B(C)*; the Court of Appeal is unlikely to upset his decision.

QUESTION 36

Ian and Jason are both aged 26 and are charged with outraging public decency, the case for the prosecution being that they were seen engaging in oral sex on

Hampstead Heath by PC Plod. Both plead not guilty. Ian wishes to call Katie as a defence witness. She is prepared to say that she has known Ian since they were at university together seven years ago, and that during that period she and Ian have had regular, normal sexual intercourse. Ian plays football most weekends and he also wishes to call Larry, a fellow member of his football club, to say that Ian is well known among members for his dislike of homosexuals. Ian has a letter from his local vicar which states that Ian has sung in the church choir for the last five years. The vicar also writes that from his knowledge of Ian he is sure the allegation must be false. Ian has no previous convictions of any kind, but Jason has two recent convictions for soliciting in a public place for the purpose of prostitution.

(a) Discuss the evidential issues that arise in relation to admissibility.
(b) On the assumption that Ian and Jason both testify in their own defence, how should the judge direct the jury about their characters?

Answer Plan

The first part of this question requires you to consider what is admissible as evidence of good character. You should refer to the restriction imposed by *Rowton* (1865) and point out that the sort of evidence permitted in *Redgrave* (1982) is heard because of a concession only.

You should then consider generally the impact of Jason's previous convictions and conclude by referring to the ruling of the Court of Appeal in the case of *Vye* (1993).

ANSWER

The defence may call witnesses to testify as to the accused's good character. However, the right to adduce such evidence is restricted by the rule in *Rowton* (1865) that evidence of specific acts, or of the opinions of specific persons, is inadmissible to establish either good or bad character. In strictness, the only way in which character evidence can be given is by getting a witness to speak of the reputation of the accused among those who know him. In practice, this rule tends to be loosely applied.

However, so far as Katie's evidence is concerned, the court would have to consider first whether it was relevant at all. Assuming it is relevant, perhaps on the basis that a man in a regular heterosexual relationship is less likely than a man not in such a relationship to engage in homosexual activity, the court would then have to take into account the decision of the Court of Appeal in *Redgrave* (1981). In that case, the appellant had been charged with persistently importuning for immoral purposes in a public lavatory. The trial judge refused to allow him to call evidence of his relationships with a number of girlfriends which would, the defence hoped, establish that the accused had heterosexual rather than homosexual inclinations. The Court of Appeal acknowledged that in that sort of case, indulgence was sometimes shown to accused persons, but said that it was only an indulgence and not a right. Failure to extend it to any particular defendant could not form the basis of a successful appeal.

Lawton LJ said that the court was not trying to stop defence counsel from putting questions designed to show that the accused was happily married and had a normal sexual relationship with his wife. He went on to suggest that evidence of a sexual relationship with one woman, even though she was not married to the defendant, might be unobjectionable. But he emphasised that questions on such matters could be asked only with the indulgence of the court. Katie's evidence will not, therefore, be heard as of right, but only with the goodwill of the judge. It should be added that it is not clear on the facts that the relationship with Katie has the substantial quality that Lawton LJ seems to presuppose. If, when the facts were more fully investigated, it turned out, for example, that she was merely one regular sexual partner among several and that Ian had no special emotional ties to her, it is doubtful whether her evidence would be admitted.

By contrast, Larry's evidence does appear to be evidence of reputation and so is admissible under the rule in *Rowton*. Again, however, there may be an objection based on relevance. An overt dislike of homosexuals might have been adopted, consciously or unconsciously, to try to hide a man's own homosexual tendencies. So if the jury had this information it might lead to no more than inconclusive speculation of the sort that led to the rejection of evidence in *Blastland* (1986).

It seems clear that the evidence of the vicar, even if he were willing to attend court and give oral testimony, would be inadmissible under *Rowton* (1865). The fact that Ian sings in the church choir is today likely to be thought irrelevant to any question of character. In any case, testimony to this effect would not be testimony of Ian's reputation. The vicar's own opinion of Ian's innocence would certainly not be admitted.

Ian's counsel will, of course, be able to bring out the fact that his client is of previous good character in the sense of having no previous convictions recorded against him.

A zealous prosecutor might argue that Jason's previous convictions are admissible under **s 101(1)(d)** of the **CJA 2003** and in the light of the guidelines in *Hanson* (2005). It could be argued that the evidence is relevant because a man with such convictions is more likely to have a sexual encounter with another man in a public place than a man without such convictions. In reply, it could be argued that even if the evidence is admissible, it ought to be excluded under **s 101(3)** because of the prejudice that would be caused to Ian; his guilt could be seen as more likely if his co-defendant's history is revealed. If Jason pleaded not guilty and gave evidence in his defence on the earlier occasions, the prosecution could also argue that his convictions are admissible as being relevant to the question whether he has a propensity to be untruthful. They would, however, encounter a difficulty in *Campbell* (2007), where the Court of Appeal held that a defendant's propensity for untruthfulness will not normally be an *important* matter in issue between defendant and prosecution as required by **s 101(1)(d)**. Even if this objection could be overcome, the same argument for exclusion of the convictions under **s 101(3)** would apply.

Rules for the proper direction of the jury where good character is relevant were laid down by Lord Taylor CJ in the judgment of the Court of Appeal in the case of *Vye* (1993). They are as follows:

- A direction as to the relevance of good character to a defendant's credibility should be given where he has testified or made pre-trial answers or statements. Such a direction will clearly be appropriate in Ian's case, assuming that he testifies or has at least made some admissible pre-trial statement.
- A direction as to the relevance of good character to the likelihood of the defendant's having committed the offence charged is to be given, regardless of whether he has testified or made any pre-trial answers or statements. Again, such a direction will obviously be appropriate in Ian's case.

Where there are two defendants, one of good character and the other not, these principles still apply. The trial judge should either say nothing at all about the character of the defendant with previous convictions, or he should direct the jury that they have heard nothing about this and should not speculate.

Ian's position is therefore unaffected by the fact that Jason has previous convictions.

QUESTION 37

Alex and Bess are charged with the robbery of Philip. Philip testifies that he was attacked in a car park one evening by Alex and Bess, one of whom grabbed a gold watch from his wrist. Alex, wearing the uniform of a security company, testifies in his defence that Philip attacked him and Bess without warning, and that he hit back to defend himself and Bess. He says that the strap of Philip's watch probably broke in the struggle and denies stealing it. Bess gives no evidence. Alex has one recent conviction for robbery of a man whom he attacked in a car park. Bess has no previous convictions.

▶ **Discuss the evidential issues arising.**

> **Answer Plan**
>
> You should deal with the defendants separately. In relation to Alex, you need to consider whether evidence of his previous conviction can be given, either under **s 101(1)(f)** or **101(1)(g)**. You should also mention the possibility of an application under **s 101(1)(d)**. Don't forget to deal with arguments for exclusion as well, and remember that you may have to consider how far the evidence of the previous conviction can go. In this connection you have to consider the evidential value of the conviction. Is it relevant to credibility and to guilt, or only to credibility?
>
> When you deal with Bess's failure to testify, remember to set out at least the most important directions, based on *Cowan* (1996), that have to be given. How much of the *Vye* direction will it be proper to give?

ANSWER

There appear to be several opportunities for cross-examination of Alex under **Part 11, Chapter 1** of the **Criminal Justice Act (CJA) 2003**. First, it may be argued that he has given evidence of his own good character, either by his testimony that he hit back to defend himself *and Bess*, or by appearing in the witness box in the uniform of a security company.

On this basis the prosecution could submit that evidence of his bad character (the recent conviction for robbery) should be given under **s 101(1)(f)** to correct a false impression given by Alex. By **s 105(1)**, a defendant gives a false impression if he is responsible for the making of an express or implied assertion, which is apt to give the court or jury a false or misleading impression about the defendant. **Section 105(2)** lists the circumstances in which a defendant is to be treated as being responsible for an assertion. An obvious instance is where the assertion is made by the defendant while giving evidence in the proceedings: see **s 105(2)(a)**.

A problem may occur where a defendant gives evidence as a necessary part of his defence that incidentally has the effect of showing good character. The same problem arose under **s 1(f)(ii)** of the **Criminal Evidence Act 1898**, which allowed cross-examination of a defendant about previous convictions where he had given evidence of his good character. The provision was held to apply only where the defendant went beyond what was necessary to meet the prosecution case about the facts in issue.

For example, in *Malindi v R* (1967), the defendant was charged with conspiracy involving the use of violence against property. He gave evidence that at a meeting in his house at which violence was discussed, and which the prosecution relied on as part of its case, he had disapproved of violent action and advised against it. It was held by the Privy Council that this should not have brought **s 1(f)(ii)** into play: the defendant had restricted his evidence to his own account of an incident relied on by the prosecution. He had not asserted his own good character as an independent reason for making it unlikely that he had done what the prosecution alleged.

On this basis, Alex's evidence that he hit back to defend Bess, as well as himself, will not amount to giving evidence of his own good character. However, it may be that his wearing the security company's uniform would be so regarded, because it suggests that his employers regard him as a person of integrity. **Section 101(1)(f)** makes it clear that an assertion in this context can be implied, and this is confirmed by **s 105(4)**, which includes false impressions given by conduct other than the giving of evidence. By **subs (5)** 'conduct' includes appearance or dress. The legitimacy of the conduct need not be challenged. It is the claim to good character associated, rightly or not, with certain occupations at which **subss (4)** and **(5)** are aimed.

By **s 105(3)** a defendant may withdraw an assertion, but this may not be easy on the facts. If he does not, the defence might argue that the judge should exercise his discretion to exclude evidence of the previous conviction, either under **s 78(1)** of the **Police and Criminal Evidence Act (PACE) 1984** or under the common law confirmed in *Sang*.

If the judge allows cross-examination about the conviction, can questions extend to the similarities with the present charge? Cross-examination under **s 1(f)(ii)** of the **1898 Act** was relevant only to credibility, not to guilt. But this distinction was condemned by the Law Commission as unworkable in many cases. It was held by the Court of Appeal in *Highton* (2006) that whenever evidence of bad character is admitted, it is admitted for any purpose that is relevant to the case. The particular 'gateway' that allows the evidence to be admitted does not affect the use made of it. Once admitted under **s 101(1)(f)** of **CJA 2003**, the evidence of Alex's previous conviction for robbery can be used to assess his guilt as well as his credibility.

In *Hanson* (2005) the Court of Appeal said that there is no minimum number of events necessary to demonstrate propensity, but that a single previous conviction for an offence of the same description or category will often not show propensity. It may do so, however, where it shows a tendency to unusual behaviour, or where its circumstances demonstrate probative force in relation to the offence charged. Circumstances demonstrating probative force are not confined to those showing striking similarity. It is possible, therefore, that an application under **s 101(1)(d)** would be successful, bearing in mind the recent date of the previous conviction, and the fact that the robbery to which that related also took place in a car park. It could also be argued that evidence of the conviction was admissible under **subs (1)(d)** to rebut the defence that Alex was defending himself and Bess from an attack by Philip.

Alex's suggestion that the watch strap broke in the struggle does not, in itself, suggest that Philip was lying, as opposed to merely being mistaken in his testimony, and alone would not bring **s 101(1)(g)** into play. But the evidence that Philip was the aggressor clearly amounts to an attack on his character and would let in Alex's previous conviction, unless excluded by **s 101(3)** or the common law discretion.

As Bess gives no evidence, the judge will instruct the jury that they may, in determining whether the prosecution has proved its case, draw such inferences as appear proper from her failure to testify. However, the directions based on *Cowan* (1996) will have to be given. In particular, the judge must tell the jury that the defendant is entitled to remain silent; that an inference from silence cannot be the sole or main basis for convicting; and that the jury must be satisfied that there is a *prima facie* case to answer before drawing any inferences.

Assuming that Bess said nothing outside court that was evidence of the truth of its contents, the only limb of the *Vye* direction required (on the significance of her good character) will be that relating to the likelihood of her guilt.

QUESTION 38

Callum and Daniel are charged with the robbery of Ethan. Ethan testifies that he was attacked in a public park one afternoon by three men, two of whom were Callum and Daniel. The third man got away and was never caught. He says that one of the three men stole his wallet. Callum gives evidence in his defence to the effect that he and Daniel had been joined in the park that day by a third man, whom they did not know. He says that Ethan, who was drunk, attacked all three of them, and that he hit back to defend himself and Daniel. He denies stealing Ethan's wallet, and says that it probably fell from Ethan's pocket in the struggle. Daniel subsequently testifies in his defence that he had stopped to rest some distance behind Callum and the third man and did not see what happened when they met Ethan. When Daniel was interviewed by the police he said that he alone had robbed Ethan. But the trial judge refused to allow the prosecution to adduce this in evidence because it had been made in response to a promise by the police that Daniel would get bail if he confessed. Callum has several previous convictions for robbery. Daniel has a previous conviction for sexual assault and another for outraging public decency.

▶ Discuss the evidential issues arising.

> **Answer Plan**
>
> The best approach is to take each defendant separately and consider the arguments that the prosecution and the co-defendant might wish to use to reveal his previous convictions. These can be summarised as follows:
>
> | Callum | | Daniel | |
> |---|---|---|---|
> | Prosecution: | s 101(1)(d) | Prosecution: | s 101(1)(d) |
> | | s 101(1)(g) | Callum: | s 101(1)(e) |
> | Daniel: | s 101(1)(e) | | |
>
> In addition, you need to consider whether Callum can adduce evidence of Daniel's confession even though it is not open to the prosecution to do so.

ANSWER

The first question is whether the prosecution can adduce evidence under **s 101(1)(d)** of the **Criminal Justice Act (CJA) 2003** of Callum's previous convictions as part of the case against him. By **s 103(1)(a)**, the matters in issue between defendant and prosecution include the question whether the defendant has a propensity to commit offences of the kind with which he is charged, except where having such a propensity makes it no more likely that he is guilty of the offence. By **s 103(2)**, the propensity can be established by evidence that the defendant has been convicted of an offence of the same description as the one with which he is charged. There are no details of idiosyncratic features of Callum's previous robberies, and the question therefore arises whether propensity to commit a commonplace offence in a commonplace way makes it more likely that Callum is guilty on this particular occasion. On one view it does, because the propensity adds weight to Ethan's evidence against him. If this submission is upheld, the defence could argue that evidence of the convictions ought nevertheless to be excluded, either under **s 101(3)** or under the common law discretion, which *Sang* (1980) confirmed, to exclude prosecution evidence where the probative worth is outweighed by prejudicial effect. An important factor might be whether his convictions are recent or are spent under the **Rehabilitation of Offenders Act 1974**.

The previous convictions might also be relevant to Callum's propensity to be untruthful, which, by **s 103(1)(b)**, is capable of being a matter in issue between prosecution and defendant. However, this seems less likely since the decision in *Campbell* (2007), where the Court of Appeal said that the defendant's propensity for untruthfulness will not normally be an *important* matter in issue between defendant and prosecution as required by **s 101(1)(d)**. This approach was reaffirmed in *Foster* (2009), where the Court of Appeal approved an observation in *Campbell* to the effect that in general it is unhelpful to tell a jury that they can take bad character into account when deciding whether a defendant's evidence is truthful.

Whether reliance is placed on **s 103(1)(a)** or **(b)** or both, the court would take into account the relevant guidelines in *Hanson* (2005). These would include the 'starting point': Parliament's purpose in the legislation was 'to assist evidence-based conviction of the guilty, without putting those who are not guilty at risk of conviction by prejudice'. The age of a previous conviction may be a relevant consideration in deciding whether to admit it. An important factor might therefore be whether Callum's previous convictions are recent, or spent under the **Rehabilitation of Offenders Act 1974**. If evidence of Callum's bad character is given, the judge in summing up should make these points to the jury:

(i) they should not place undue reliance on previous convictions. In particular, they should not conclude that the defendant has been untruthful or has committed the offence with which he has been charged merely because he has these convictions;
(ii) whether the convictions do in fact show propensity is for them to decide;
(iii) if they do find propensity, they are entitled to take this into account when determining guilt. But it is only one relevant factor, and they assess its significance in the light of all the other evidence in the case.

Another prosecution argument would be that Callum has made an attack on Ethan's character by saying that he was drunk and attacked Callum and his companions. The fact that this is a necessary part of his defence is unlikely to prevent the operation of **s 101(1)(g)**. Even under the **Criminal Evidence Act 1898** that would not have been a reason for excluding cross-examination under **s 1(f)(ii)**, as the House of Lords decided in *Selvey v DPP* (1970). If **s 101(1)(g)** is held to apply in principle, the defence arguments for exclusion will be the same as those available in relation to **s101(1)(d)**. In *Hanson* (2005) it was said that pre-2003 authorities on what constitutes an attack on another person's character will apply to the extent that they are not incompatible with **s 106**, which contains provisions supplementing **s 101(1)(g)**.

Daniel may be able to cross-examine Callum about his previous convictions on the strength of **s 101(1)(e)**, on the basis that Callum's bad character has substantial probative value in relation to an important matter in issue between co-defendants. If this test is satisfied, the court has no power to exclude the evidence. Daniel would argue that **s 101(1)(e)** applies because Callum's evidence contradicts Daniel's case that he was some distance from the incident with Ethan and did not see what happened. On one view, Callum has simply provided the jury with another reason to acquit Daniel, so the matter in issue between the two defendants is not important. But under the former law, a line of authority based on *Crawford* (1998) supported the view that one defendant could give evidence against another for the purposes of **s 1(f)(iii)** where his testimony varied from that of his co-defendant so as to undermine the co-defendant's credibility, thus making the prosecution case against him more likely to be true. **Section 104** of the **CJA 2003**, which supplements **s 101(1)(e)**, says that evidence of bad character is admissible only if the nature or conduct of the defence is such as to undermine a co-defendant's defence. It is certainly possible that in interpreting **s 101(1)(e)** the court will follow the *Crawford* approach. If evidence of Callum's bad character is admitted only under **s 101(1)(e)**, and not under **s 101(1)(d)**, it is unclear whether the jury should be told to take it into account only when considering Daniel's defence, and not when considering the prosecution case against Callum. The Court of Appeal is at present divided on problems of this kind. In *Price* (2005) and *B(C)* (2004) it was held that there was no need to warn a jury not to consider, when dealing with the prosecution case against D1, evidence of D1's bad character adduced by D2 rather than by the prosecution. But the contrary was held in *Mertens* (2005) and in *Murrell* (2005). In *Robinson (Dennis)* (2006), which was concerned with a similar situation, the Court of Appeal said that a direction should not needlessly perplex the jury.

Daniel's previous convictions show no propensity to commit robbery, and their admissibility under **s 101(1)(d)** could be justified only on the basis that they might show a propensity to untruthfulness. Even this is not very likely; someone who has been untruthful about his sexual activity could be entirely reliable where other matters are concerned. If the condition in **s 101(1)(d)** were found to be satisfied, the likelihood of exclusion under **s 101(3)** or under the common law discretion would be substantial in view of the possible moral prejudice against Daniel when the nature of his previous convictions is revealed.

Callum might wish to adduce evidence of Daniel's previous convictions under **s 101(1)(e)** on the basis of the discrepancy between Daniel's evidence and his own. But Daniel's convictions could be relevant only to his credibility. Although at common law any kind of offence was relevant to credibility, the common law rules governing admissibility have been abolished by **s 99(1)** of the **CJA 2003**, and the nature of Daniel's convictions is unlikely to be considered to have any bearing on his credibility. The point has already been made that even if he pleaded not guilty and gave evidence at the earlier trials, this is unlikely to have any bearing on his credibility in very different circumstances. While a judge has no *discretion* to exclude evidence of bad character that is admissible under **s 101(1)(e)**, he would have a *duty* to exclude it if he was not satisfied of its relevance.[1]

---

1 Cf *Gadsby* (2006).

The final question that arises is whether Callum can adduce evidence of Daniel's confession. The relevant law is contained in **s 76A(1)** of the **Police and Criminal Evidence Act (PACE) 1984**, which provides in effect that where one defendant proposes to adduce evidence of a co-defendant's confession, the rules about admissibility are the same as those applying to the prosecution, save for the standard of proof. Callum is unlikely to be able to prove on the balance of probabilities that Daniel's confession was not obtained in consequence of anything said or done which was likely, in the circumstances existing at the time, to render unreliable any confession that might be made by him in consequence thereof. Accordingly, he will not be able to adduce evidence of Daniel's confession.

QUESTION 39

Liza, Mabel and Nellie are charged with committing burglary in a block of flats. Liza chooses not to give evidence in her own defence, but her counsel in cross-examination puts to one of the prosecution witnesses that her evidence against Liza is concocted out of spite because Liza has been having an affair with the witness's husband. Liza has three recent convictions for burglary.

Mabel gives evidence in her own defence and claims to have been elsewhere at the time the burglary was committed. When prosecuting counsel puts it to her in cross-examination that this is a lie, Mabel bursts into tears and shouts, 'I'm an honest woman! I've never told a lie in my life!'. Mabel was convicted two years ago of fraud and of assisting in the management of a brothel.

Nellie gives evidence in her own defence. She admits having entered the building and climbed the stairs, but says that she did so because she loves animals and wanted to rescue a kitten which she had seen stranded on a window ledge. Nellie has two spent convictions for burglary.

▶ Discuss the evidential issues that arise.

Answer Plan

It does not appear that any of the defendants has undermined another's defence. So, dealing with each defendant separately, the following points should be considered:

Liza
- ❖ **s 35** of the **CJPOA 1994**
- ❖ **s 101(1)(d)** of the **CJA 2003**
- ❖ **s 101(1)(g)** of the **CJA 2003**

Mabel
- **s 101(1)(d)** of the **CJA 2003**
- **s 101(1)(f)** of the **CJA 2003**

Nellie
- **s 101(1)(d)** of the **CJA 2003**
- **s 101(1)(f)** of the **CJA 2003**.

ANSWER

Liza's failure to give evidence is likely to bring into operation **s 35(3)** of the **Criminal Justice and Public Order Act 1994**. Under this provision the court or jury, in determining whether the accused is guilty of the offence charged, may draw such inferences as appear proper from the failure of the accused to give evidence. In any direction under **s 35** the judge must follow the guidelines based on *Cowan* (1996). He must tell the jury that the defendant is entitled to remain silent; an inference from silence cannot be the sole or main basis for a conviction; and the jury must be satisfied that there is a case to answer before drawing any inferences from silence. The judge must also tell the jury that they may draw an adverse inference only if they conclude that silence can only sensibly be attributed to the defendant's having no answer to the charge, or none that would stand up to cross-examination. However, the defence cannot suggest reasons for silence that are unsupported by evidence.

The prosecution could argue that evidence of Liza's previous convictions should be admitted under **s 101(1)(d)** as showing a propensity to commit burglary, and perhaps also a propensity to be untruthful if in any of the earlier cases she pleaded not guilty and gave evidence in her own defence. Although Liza gave no evidence on this occasion, a propensity for untruthfulness could still be relevant in light of the allegation made on her behalf against a prosecution witness. It would be open to the defence to argue, under **s 101(3)**, that the admission of this evidence would have such an adverse effect on the fairness of the proceedings that the court ought not to admit it. Alternatively, reliance might be placed on **s 103(3)**. However, such arguments would be likely to fail, as it is a recent history of convictions for the same offence, and, presumably, the prosecution has other cogent evidence to support its case against Liza. In the absence of other evidence, or if there were only weak evidence, the defence, relying on the *Hanson* (2005) guidelines, could argue that the judge has a duty to consider the strength of the prosecution case and, if there is no, or very little, other evidence against a defendant, it is unlikely to be just to admit previous convictions, whatever they are.

Through her counsel, Liza has made an attack on another person's character by suggesting that a prosecution witness's evidence has been concocted out of spite. Evidence of her bad character is therefore admissible in principle under **s 101(1)(g)** and **s 106(1)(b)** of the **Criminal Justice Act (CJA) 2003**. The Court of Appeal held in *Highton* (2006) that, if admitted through this 'gateway', the evidence would be relevant to propensity as well as credibility. It would be open to the defence to argue for exclusion under **s 101(3)**.

Could the prosecution adduce evidence of Mabel's previous convictions under **s 101(1)(d)**? Neither offence is of the same kind as the current offence. The offence of fraud almost certainly involved the telling of lies, so this would be admissible in principle to show a propensity to be untruthful, regardless of her plea or whether she gave evidence on that occasion. If she pleaded not guilty to the other offence and gave evidence in her defence that the jury must have disbelieved, those facts also would show a propensity to be untruthful. But in view of the availability of the conviction for fraud, and the moral prejudice that might attach to a conviction for assisting in the management of a brothel, a defence argument that this conviction should be excluded, either under **s 101(3)** or **s 103(3)** might be successful.

In Mabel's case the question also arises whether evidence of her convictions can be adduced under **s 101(1)(f)** in order to correct the false impression given when she said that she was an honest woman who had never told a lie. Her best course would be to withdraw the claim, which appears to have been made in the heat of the moment. If she does so, by **s 105(3)** she will not be treated as responsible for the assertion. If she fails to withdraw, it would be open to her counsel to argue that the evidence of her convictions should be excluded on the basis of the common law discretion confirmed in *Sang* (1980). At this stage the judge might distinguish between the two convictions and exclude the one for assisting in the management of a brothel because of the moral prejudice to which it might give rise. Arguably, **s 78(1)** of the **Police and Criminal Evidence Act (PACE) 1984** would also be available, but a doubt is created by **s 101(3)**, which confines the **s 78** test built into **s 101(3)** to **subss (1)(d)** and **(1)(g)**. Further, by **s 105(6)**, evidence is admissible under **s 101(1)(f)** only if it goes no further than is necessary to correct the false impression. Almost certainly, the conviction for obtaining property by deception would be regarded as sufficient for this purpose. As with 'gateway' **s 101(1)(g)**, evidence of bad character admitted under **s 101(1)(f)** can be relevant to both credibility and propensity (*Highton* (2006)).

Can Nellie's spent convictions for burglary be admitted under **s 101(1)(d)**? Depending on whether she gave evidence in her own defence on those occasions, the evidence could fall within **s 103(1)(a)** and **(b)**. True, both the convictions are spent, and this would invite argument for exclusion under **s 101(3)** or **s 103(3)**. It was said in *Hanson* (2005) that the age of a previous conviction may be a relevant consideration in deciding whether to admit it, but, as one of the consolidated appeals in *Hanson* showed, this will not be a conclusive argument. So far as **s 103(1)(b)** is concerned, *Campbell* (2007) suggests that the evidence is unlikely to be admitted: a propensity for being untruthful will not normally be an *important* matter in issue between defendant and prosecution as required by **s 101(1)(d)**.

It is unlikely that evidence of Nellie's spent convictions can be given under **s 101(1)(f)**. She has almost certainly not created a false impression by saying that she is an animal lover, for there is no reason why an animal lover should not be criminally inclined. Her explanation that she wanted to rescue the kitten is necessary to account for her presence on the premises. Even if that shows her character in a good light, it does so only incidentally and should not bring **s 101(1)(f)** into operation if the reasoning adopted under the **Criminal Evidence Act 1898** is followed. In *Malindi v R* (1967), the defendant, charged with conspiracy to use violence against property, testified that he had been present at a meeting during which violence had been discussed, but had disapproved and had advised against it. The Privy Council held that this had not brought **s 1(f)(ii)** of the **1898 Act** into operation because it did not amount to an independent assertion of good character.

QUESTION 40

Oscar is charged with burglary of Penelope's flat. He gives evidence in his defence and admits being in the flat on the day when the burglary took place. But he says he was there because Penelope had given him a key as they were lovers, and he had called in that evening on his way home in the hope of having sexual intercourse with her. In cross-examination, it is put to him by the prosecution that he entered by a window, not the door. Oscar replies: 'Anyone who says that is a liar.' Oscar has three previous convictions for fraud.

▸ Discuss the evidential issues that arise.

Answer Plan

You have to consider the various arguments that could be put forward to admit or exclude evidence of Oscar's previous convictions. Note that the facts do not reveal whether or not they are spent. Take arguments under **s 101(1)(d)** first, remembering **s 103(1)(b)**. Then consider **s 101(1)(g)**. Note that there are two aspects to this: whether Oscar has attacked Penelope's character, and the significance, if any, of what Oscar has said during cross-examination.

ANSWER

On what basis, if any, can the prosecution adduce evidence of Oscar's previous convictions? One approach would be to rely on **s 101(1)(d)** of the **Criminal Justice Act (CJA) 2003**, arguing that evidence of the convictions is relevant to two important matters in issue between the defendant and the prosecution: first, the question whether the defendant has a propensity to commit offences of the kind with which he is charged; secondly, whether he has a propensity to be untruthful.

By **s 103(2)**, a defendant's propensity to commit offences of the kind with which he is charged may be established by evidence that he has been convicted of an offence of the same category as the one with which he is charged. Categories of offences can be prescribed by order of the Secretary of State under **s 103(4)(b)**. But by **subs (5)**, a category prescribed by order must consist of offences of the same type. Fraud is not in the theft category prescribed by the **Criminal Justice Act 2003 (Categories of Offences) Order 2004**.[1]

However, the defendant has given evidence, and the prosecution may wish to establish a propensity to be untruthful under **s 103(1)(b)**. Convictions for fraud could be used for this purpose, but the view taken in *Campbell* (2007), that a propensity for being untruthful will not normally be an *important* matter in issue between the defendant and the prosecution would militate against admissibility. Nor do we know if the convictions are spent. The defence might want to rely on **s 103(3)** to argue that because of the length of time that has passed, it would be unjust to rely on them. Curiously, **subs (3)** applies only to evidence of a defendant's propensity to commit offences of the kind with which he is charged. But the defence could still rely on **s 101(3)** and on the common law discretion, confirmed by *Sang* (1980), to exclude prosecution evidence where the probative worth is outweighed by prejudicial effect.

Another argument for admitting the convictions could be based on **s 101(1)(g)**, relying on the fact that the defendant has made an attack on another person's character. By **s 106(2)**, evidence attacking another person's character includes evidence to the effect that the other person has behaved in a reprehensible way. Potentially this creates a problem on these facts. Is it reprehensible for a woman to have a sexual relationship with a person to whom she is not married? Do the personal circumstances and beliefs of Penelope have to be taken into account when deciding if Oscar's allegation is one of reprehensible behaviour? Probably these awkward questions can be avoided by arguing, if Penny denies the relationship, that the allegation necessarily implies that Penelope's evidence is deliberately false. It was established in *Britzman* (1983), for the purposes of the **1898 Act**, that a defendant could make an imputation on a

---

1 SI 3346, Sched Pt 1.

prosecution witness, and so expose himself to cross-examination about his own previous convictions, if what was alleged amounted in effect to an allegation of perjury. It is inconceivable that Penelope could have made an honest mistake by denying her affair with Oscar. His allegation would therefore amount to one of perjury, and so be an attack on Penelope for the purposes of **s 101(1)(g)**. Again, the defence could argue for exclusion under **s 101(3)**. Following the *Hanson* guidelines, as in all cases where evidence of previous convictions is admitted, the judge in summing up should make these points to the jury:

(i) they should not place undue reliance on previous convictions. In particular, they should not conclude that the defendant has been untruthful or has committed the offence with which he has been charged merely because he has these convictions;
(ii) whether the convictions do in fact show propensity is for them to decide;
(iii) if they do find propensity, they are entitled to take this into account when determining guilt. But it is only one relevant factor, and they assess its significance in the light of all the other evidence in the case.

The prosecution might also rely on Oscar's answer in cross-examination to the effect that anyone who says he entered Penelope's flat by a window is a liar. However, it is not clear that in saying this he has attacked another person's character. Unless there is a witness who has given evidence to this effect, the expression seems to amount to no more than a strong denial. Certainly under the **1898 Act** a distinction was drawn between using words such as 'lying' or 'liar' simply as strong denials, and using the words to allege perjury. For example, in *Desmond* (1999) a prosecution witness gave an account of events that differed significantly from that in his witness statement and, in doing so, implicated the defendant further. Defence counsel in cross-examination suggested to him that he was lying under oath, but the Court of Appeal held this to be no more than an emphatic denial of the charge.

Aim Higher ★

1. Where there are two or more defendants, you should be aware of the opportunities for admitting evidence of the bad character of one defendant on the application of a co-defendant. Always be ready to consider **s 101(1)(e)** and **(g)**.
2. If the question says that the defendant has a minor conviction for an offence unrelated to the current charge, always be ready to make the point that it is possible for him to be treated as a person of good character for the purposes of the trial. Be ready to refer to the guidelines in *Gray* (2004).

Common Pitfalls

1. Where a defendant is of good character the judge must nearly always give an unqualified *Vye* direction. But candidates who remember this often forget to explain the content of that direction.
2. Weak candidates often assume that a conviction cannot be referred to if it is spent. The fact of being spent is something that will often be relevant to the question whether it should be admitted, but it is not a conclusive argument for exclusion, as the **Rehabilitation of Offenders Act 1974** clearly shows.

10 The Course of Testimony

INTRODUCTION

You are likely to find the sort of problems in this chapter inserted as part of questions dealing with more central topics such as hearsay or character evidence. Another favourite of examiners is a question about a charge of rape, where points on recent complaints can arise as well as on the complexities of **ss 41–43** of the **Youth Justice and Criminal Evidence Act 1999**. It is well worth studying these sections carefully, together with the cases that have been decided about the restrictions they impose on the conduct of the defence.

Most topics concerning the course of testimony are well explained in textbooks, but a warning is needed about the finality of answers to collateral questions. The rule is sometimes expressed in this way, and sometimes by saying that when a witness in cross-examination answers questions on collateral matters, his answers are conclusive. There is quite a common misunderstanding that the effect of this is that once counsel in cross-examination gets a denial of the collateral matter that is being put, he may ask no further questions about it. This is not the case. Counsel may continue to question the witness about the collateral matter if he thinks he is likely to obtain any advantage in doing so. What he cannot do is call evidence in rebuttal if the witness persists in his denial. It is only in this sense that the witness's answers are 'final' or 'conclusive'.

You should note that, by **ss 119** and **120** of the **Criminal Justice Act (CJA) 2003**, where evidence of a witness's previous consistent or inconsistent statement is admitted, it is evidence of any matter stated of which oral evidence by the witness would be admissible. It is no longer relevant to credibility alone, as used to be the case. Note also the circumstances, set out in **s 120**, in which evidence of previous consistent statements is now admissible. An important change in the law extends the 'recent complaint' exception, formerly applicable only where the charge related to a sexual offence, to all offences where the person making the complaint is a person against whom the offence has been committed. Further, it is now irrelevant, so far as admissibility is concerned, that the recent complaint was elicited, for example, by a leading question, unless a threat or a promise was involved: see **s 120(8)**. The **Coroners and Justice Act 2009** has amended **s 120(7)** by removing the requirement in **subs (7)(d)** that the complaint should have been made as soon as could reasonably be expected after the alleged offence. The effect of this seems to be to leave it to the judge to decide whether a particular complaint was made too late to be of assistance to the jury, and thus irrelevant and inadmissible. It has already been held in *O* (2006) that **s 120(4)** and **(7)** allow evidence of multiple complaints to be admitted. But you should read that case for the reservations made on this subject. Clearly, evidence of complaint after complaint could be irrelevant, time-wasting and unfair.

Checklist ✔

Students should be familiar with the following areas:

- refreshing memory;
- unfavourable and hostile witnesses;
- previous consistent statements;
- cross-examination of the parties as to credit;
- *Edwards* (1991) and subsequent decisions;
- **ss 41–43** of the **Youth Justice and Criminal Evidence Act 1999** and *A* (2001);
- previous inconsistent statements;
- finality of answers to collateral questions.

QUESTION 41

Len is being prosecuted for assaulting Mick, who had identified Len to the police in a nearby street shortly after the attack and subsequently during an identification procedure. At his trial, Len claims that he has been wrongly identified. Mick has a recent conviction for handling stolen goods.

(a) Mick identifies Len in court as the person who attacked him. May he also give evidence of his previous identifications of Len in the street and in the identification parade?

(b) Len tells his counsel that Mick is a heavy drinker and that he can produce a witness, Olive, who will support this and who can say that she saw Mick drinking whisky in a public house on the evening when Mick alleged that he was assaulted by Len, but at a time before the alleged attack took place. In cross-examination, Mick denies being a heavy drinker and says that he had nothing at all to drink that evening. May Len's counsel call Olive to rebut these denials?

(c) Len also tells his counsel that a month before the alleged assault, he had quarrelled with Mick about a woman and Mick had threatened that he would 'get even' with Len some day. Len says that his cousin Percy was present at the time and can confirm this. What use, if any, can Len's counsel make of this information?

(d) Should Len's counsel put Mick's previous conviction to him? If he does so, and Mick denies it, what is likely to happen?

> **Answer Plan**
>
> The question raises the following points:
>
> ❖ evidence of previous identification;
> ❖ whether the evidence about Mick's drinking is collateral to the main issue;
> ❖ the rule concerning the finality of answers on collateral matters and the exceptions to it;
> ❖ cross-examination of prosecution witnesses as to character.

ANSWER

(a) Despite the general rule that excludes evidence of previous consistent statements (see *Roberts* (1942)), evidence of an earlier identification was admissible at common law to show that the witness was able to identify the accused at the time and to exclude the idea that any later identification in court was an afterthought or a mistake (*Christie* (1914)). The current law is contained in **s 120(4)** and **(5)**. Mick can give evidence of his earlier identifications of Len, provided he indicates that to the best of his belief he made the earlier statements establishing identification, and that to the best of his belief they stated the truth.

(b) The purpose of establishing that Mick is a heavy drinker and that he had been drinking before the attack is to suggest that his identification of Len could well have been wrong as his faculties were impaired, at least to some extent, by the alcohol that he had consumed. The identification is the central issue in the case and questions designed to show that it might have been impaired by alcohol will therefore not be regarded as dealing with collateral matters. Olive can be called to rebut Mick's denial that he had had anything to drink that evening. She may also give evidence of his heavy drinking if that is a matter within her own knowledge, or of his reputation as a heavy drinker under the rule in *Rowton* (1865). The question whether Mick is a heavy drinker is probably not a collateral matter. If true, it tends to make it more probable that he was drinking on the evening in question, and also that he drank enough to impair his ordinary powers to make an accurate identification.

(c) The quarrel with Mick is a collateral matter, but if Mick denies that it took place or that he threatened Len on that occasion, evidence may nevertheless be called in rebuttal because the effect of such evidence will be to show bias on the part of Mick against Len. Facts showing that a witness is biased against a party may be elicited in cross-examination and if they are denied, rebutting evidence can be called. Thus, in *Shaw* (1888), evidence was held admissible to show that on a previous occasion a witness had threatened the defendant (see also *Phillips* (1936)). Both Len and Percy can therefore be called to give an account of the incident during which Mick threatened Len.

(d) Two matters have to be taken into account when deciding whether to put this conviction to Mick. The first is whether evidence of Mick's bad character is admissible under **s 100** of the **Criminal Justice Act (CJA) 2003**, which relates to the bad character of non-defendants. It is possible that the prosecution will take the view that Mick's conviction should be revealed during examination-in-chief. It is for an offence of dishonesty, which could bear on his credibility as a witness, especially if he had pleaded not guilty and given evidence in his defence. If this view is not taken, the defence will have to convince the judge either that the evidence of the conviction is important explanatory evidence under **s 100(1)(a)**, which is unlikely, or that it has substantial probative value in relation to a matter that is in issue in the proceedings and is itself of substantial importance in the context of the case as a whole: see **s 100(1)(b)**. Whether these conditions are satisfied depends on the nature of Len's case. He appears to be saying that Mick has deliberately given false evidence incriminating him, in which case the conditions would almost certainly be satisfied. Leave of the court will still be necessary under **s 100(4)**. The second matter is that if Len adduces the evidence under **s 100(1)(b)** he will have made an attack on another person's character, which will allow evidence of his own bad character, if he has one, to be given under **s 101(1)(g)**. But since he has almost certainly brought this provision into play by his claim that Mick is a person whose testimony has been affected by a grudge, this additional attack is unlikely to have any separate significance.

If the conviction is put and Mick denies it, it may be proved against him by virtue of **s 6** of the **Criminal Procedure Act 1865**. Proof would be made by producing a certificate of the conviction under **s 73** of the **Police and Criminal Evidence Act 1984**. But it is likely that counsel for the prosecution would forestall the need for this by making a formal admission of the fact, since the information will have come from him in the first place.[1]

---

1 The prosecution has a duty to disclose to the defence any previous convictions recorded against their witnesses. See *Paraskeva* (1983).

QUESTION 42

Amy is prosecuted in the Crown Court for assaulting Bella, her neighbour. She pleads not guilty. The case for the prosecution is that Amy punched Bella during a quarrel in the street, causing Bella to fall and break her leg. When Amy was interviewed by the police, she told them that Bella's allegation was untrue and that on the occasion in question Bella had been about to hit her, but fell after tripping over a paving stone.

Consider the evidential issues that arise in each of the following circumstances:

(a) Amy gives evidence in her defence. During cross-examination, she states for the first time that at the time of the fall Bella was drunk. Counsel for the prosecution says: 'You've just made that up a moment ago, haven't you?' Amy replies: 'No, I haven't. The truth is, that woman needed half a bottle of gin before she could get up in the morning.' Defence counsel later wants to call Amy's cousin, Eddie, to give evidence that shortly after the incident, Amy spoke to him about it and said: 'It was that bitch Bella's own fault. She was out of her mind with drink as usual.'
(b) Amy calls her husband, Charlie. He wants to refresh his memory about the incident, which he observed, from a diary that Amy keeps.
(c) After Charlie has given evidence, Amy's brother, Dan, is called. He is asked about the incident, which he observed, but says: 'I'm sorry. I'm trying hard to remember, but it's just gone out of my head.'

Answer Plan

Part (a) involves an allegation of recent fabrication; you should refer to *Oyesiku* (1971). It also raises the possibility that the prosecution might want to rely on **s 34** of the **Criminal Justice and Public Order Act 1994**. Don't forget to set out the *Petkar* direction. Part (b) is a straightforward question about the use of memory-refreshing documents. Part (c) raises a number of possibilities. You should discuss the law relating to hostile and unfavourable witnesses, refreshing memory during the course of giving evidence, and the possibility of using **s 23** of the **Criminal Justice Act 1988**.

ANSWER

(a) The general rule is that evidence of a statement previously made by a witness which is consistent with his present testimony is inadmissible. Thus in *Roberts* (1942), a trial for murder where the defence was that a gun had gone off by accident, the accused was not allowed to call evidence to show that two days after the incident he had told his father that the death had resulted from an accident.

Exceptionally, however, evidence of such a statement can be adduced under **s 120(2)** of the **Criminal Justice Act (CJA) 2003**, in order to rebut a suggestion that the witness's oral evidence has been fabricated. At common law such evidence was admissible to rebut an allegation of *recent* fabrication, which is the allegation on these facts. By **s 120(2)**, the earlier statement will be evidence of the truth of its contents. In *Oyesiku* (1971), for example, counsel for the prosecution challenged the evidence of the accused's wife on the basis that she had concocted a story with her husband after his arrest. It was held that the defence should have been allowed to show that she had made a previous consistent statement about the events to her solicitor at a time when she had had no opportunity to discuss matters with her husband because he was then still in custody.

Amy was presumably interviewed by the police and failed to mention Bella's drunkenness at that stage. The prosecution could therefore ask the judge to give a direction under **s 34** of the **Criminal Justice and Public Order Act 1994**. If he does so, he must give directions on the lines set out in *Gill* (2001) and *Petkar* (2004), that is to say, he must identify the fact on which the defendant relies and which was not mentioned on questioning. He must direct the jury that it is for them to decide whether in the circumstances that fact was something that the defendant could reasonably have been expected to mention. He should tell them that if they think it was, they are not obliged to draw any inferences, but that they may do so. Further, he must tell the jury that a suspected person is not bound to answer police questions, that they must not convict solely or mainly on an inference drawn from silence, and that the jury must be satisfied that there is a case to answer before they can draw any adverse inferences from silence. Finally, he should tell the jury that they can draw an adverse inference only if they are sure that the defendant was silent because he had no answers, or none that would stand up to investigation.

(b) By **s 139(1)** of the **CJA 2003**, a person giving oral evidence in criminal proceedings may, at any stage in the course of doing so, refresh his memory from a document made or verified by him at an earlier time if he states in his oral evidence that the document records his recollection at that earlier time, and that his recollection of the matter is likely to have been significantly better at that time than it is at the time of his oral evidence. Accordingly, Charlie can refresh his memory from the relevant entries made by Amy in her diary, provided he verified them at an earlier time. A witness who has used such a document must produce it for the inspection of the opposing party, who can cross-examine on it. It seems clear from *Senat v Senat* (1965) that counsel inspecting a document that has been used to refresh a witness's memory is not confined in cross-examination to those parts which were used for memory-refreshing purposes, provided it is relevant to go beyond them. But if cross-examining counsel does go beyond them, either party can apply to have the diary made an exhibit in the trial so that in due course the jury can take it into account as a whole when assessing the evidence. If the diary is made an exhibit, the entries used to refresh the witness's memory will, by **s 120(3)** of the **CJA 2003**, be evidence of any matter stated of which oral evidence by the witness would be admissible.

(c) If Dan is simply suffering from a lapse of memory, he can refresh his memory from any written statement that he made earlier: see **s 139(1)** of the **CJA 2003**. If Dan is not suffering from a lapse of memory, he may be a hostile witness, that is to say, a person who is not desirous of telling the truth to the court at the instance of the party calling him. A witness ruled hostile by the judge can be cross-examined by the party calling him, with a view to showing what he said in his written statement on an earlier occasion. The power is provided by both statute and common law. By **s 3** of the **Criminal Procedure Act 1865**, the advocate calling the witness may, by leave of the judge, 'prove that he has made at other times a statement inconsistent with his present testimony'. If the witness, as seems to be the case here, does not provide enough 'present testimony' to be inconsistent with the previous statement, he can still be treated as hostile and cross-examined on the statement by virtue of common law (*Thompson* (1976)). It is possible that Dan is 'hostile' because he is afraid to testify on Amy's behalf. If that could be proved, it would be possible to apply to have the statement put in as a piece of documentary hearsay under **s 116(2)(e)** and **(4)** of the **CJA 2003**. By **s 119(1)**, such a statement will be admissible as evidence of any matter stated of which oral evidence by the witness would be admissible.

QUESTION 43

Konrad, aged 19, is charged with raping Letitia, aged 18. Letitia says that she met him for the first time in a public house, and that he invited her back to his flat for coffee when the pub closed at 11.00 pm. She says that after drinking coffee he tried to kiss her. She resisted, whereupon he flew into a rage, hurled her to the floor, and raped her. When he had finished, he shouted, 'Get out! You're a whore!' When Letitia arrived home at about 3.00 am, she was met by her father, Herbert, who said, 'What time do you call this? I've been waiting up for you since 10.30. You'd better give a good account of yourself or you're out of this house for good tomorrow morning!' Letitia burst into tears and said, 'I've been attacked.' Herbert replied, 'I've told you time and again to come home early. I hope this teaches you a lesson. Now get to bed; I'll speak to you again tomorrow.' Letitia went to college as usual the next day, but she was looking so tearful that her tutor, Megan, asked her what the matter was. She then told Megan that she had been raped by Konrad. Megan persuaded her to go to the police. She made a statement, and shortly afterwards Konrad was arrested.

At the police station Konrad said that he did not want legal advice. He was interviewed under caution, and at first denied meeting Letitia, but later in the same interview he admitted meeting her and having sex with her. 'But,' he said, 'she was the one who started it. She was all over for me, just begging for it. I should never have had anything to do with her.' Konrad wishes to give evidence in his own defence, and to call Naomi to say that she had often seen Letitia in public houses trying to pick up men. Konrad also wishes to call Omar, who can give evidence that earlier in the evening of the alleged rape he had been in the same public house where Konrad later met Letitia. He said that Letitia, whom he had known only by sight, had approached him and persuaded him to have sex with her in one of the pub lavatories.

Konrad has no previous convictions.

◗ Discuss the evidential matters arising.

> **Answer Plan**
> The following points should be covered:
>
> ❖ Admissibility of what Konrad said to Letitia.
> ❖ Can Herbert give evidence of what Letitia told him?
> ❖ Can Megan give evidence of what Letitia told her?
> ❖ Warnings that should be given to the jury.
> ❖ The significance of Konrad's initial lie.
> ❖ Admissibility of Naomi's evidence.
> ❖ Admissibility of Omar's evidence.
> ❖ Significance of Konrad's good character.

ANSWER

Letitia will be able to give evidence of her encounter with Konrad. There are no problems of admissibility. Konrad's words of invitation are not adduced as evidence of the truth of their contents, but as evidence of the fact that they were uttered by him, as an explanation of her decision to accompany him to his flat. His parting words are obviously adduced as evidence of his general violence towards her and are obviously not adduced as evidence of the truth of their contents.

The first substantial question is whether Herbert can give evidence that Letitia told him that she had been attacked. This will be admissible, if at all, as a previous consistent statement of the victim of a crime under **s 120(4)** and **(7)** of the **CJA 2003**. By **s 120(7)(c)** a complaint about conduct that would, if proved, constitute part of the offence is enough. So probably Letitia's statement that she had been attacked, though lacking in detail, will be enough to be admitted. However, the complaint, by **s 120(7)(e)**, must not be made as the result of a threat, and Herbert's suggestion that she might have to leave home may constitute a threat and so make her statement inadmissible.

Even if the complaint to her father is inadmissible, the complaint made to Megan will be admissible. It will almost certainly count as a complaint that was made 'as soon as could reasonably be expected' after the alleged offence. Letitia obviously felt unable to explain to her father in detail what had happened, and the Court of Appeal in *Valentine* (1996) recognised that victims of sexual offences often need time before they can bring themselves to tell what has been done to them, and some will find it impossible to tell a parent. In *O* (2006) the Court of Appeal said that evidence of more than one complaint can be admitted under **s 120**. In particular, where a later complaint is made in different circumstances and to a different party, it can be admitted. So Letitia's complaint to her father, if admissible, will be no bar to the admissibility of her later complaint to Megan.

By **s 120(4)** the complaint is evidence of the matter contained in it, and so is not merely relevant to the complainant's credibility. But the jury must be warned that the complaint cannot amount to independent confirmation of Letitia's evidence because the evidence and the complaint come from the same source (*Islam* (1999)). Evidence of Letitia's distress, observed by both Herbert and Megan, will be admissible to show consistency with her description of the incident but does not amount to independent confirmation (*Islam* (1999)). In appropriate cases the judge should warn the jury of the risk that distress may have been fabricated (*Romeo* (2004)). Whether a warning should be given in this case will largely depend on the defence evidence and the arguments put forward on Konrad's behalf.

In his interview under caution Konrad lied at first about meeting Letitia. The prosecution can rely on this as evidence indicating guilt, but the judge must direct the jury as laid down in *Lucas* (1981) and *Burge and Pegg* (1996). The jury must be warned that the mere fact that the defendant has lied is not in itself evidence of guilt because defendants may lie for innocent reasons. Only if the jury is sure that Konrad did *not* lie for an innocent reason can his lie support the prosecution case. (It is assumed that Konrad in his interview admitted the initial lie. If he did not do so then or later, the jury would first have to be satisfied beyond reasonable doubt that he did lie.)

Konrad's later admission of sexual intercourse, combined with the assertion that Letitia consented, amounts to a 'mixed' statement, which is admissible as evidence of the truth of all its contents, exculpatory as well as inculpatory (*Aziz* (1996)).

Konrad can, of course, give evidence in his own defence, but Naomi's evidence is unlikely to be admissible. It is unclear what she means when she says that she has often seen Letitia trying to pick up men. The facts observed by Naomi may not amount to sexual behaviour at all, in which case they will be irrelevant. If they do amount to sexual behaviour they will be excluded under **s 41** of the **Youth Justice and Criminal Evidence Act 1999** unless they can be brought within the exceptions in **s 41(3)(b)** or **(c)**. (The issue is clearly one of consent, as opposed to honest but mistaken belief in consent, so **s 41(3)(a)** does not apply.) There is no evidence that any of Naomi's observations took place within the twelve-hour period on each side of the alleged offence – the time limits supported by the House of Lords in *A* (2001). Nor is there any evidence of features of Letitia's behaviour that might satisfy the test of similarity in **subs (3)(c)**.

The admissibility of Omar's evidence is uncertain. The incident clearly falls within the contemporaneity test contained in **subs (3)(b)**. But the opening words of **s 41(3)** require that any evidence or question about a complainant's sexual behaviour should relate to a relevant issue in the case. The question, therefore, must be whether Letitia's sexual encounter with Omar is relevant to the question of whether she consented to intercourse with Konrad. The prosecution might argue that just because she consented to sex with Omar, it does not necessarily follow that she consented to sex with Konrad. This is right. But evidence does not have to be conclusive to be relevant. As Lord Steyn said in *A (No 2)* (2002), all that is required for an item of evidence to be relevant is that it should have *some* tendency in logic and common sense to advance or defeat the proposition in issue. What the prosecution would have to argue is that her consent to have sex with one customer in the pub, whom she did not know, does not make it to any degree more likely that she was consenting when she had sex with another customer from the same pub, whom also she did not know, only a few hours later. Test it this way. Is evidence about Omar capable of giving rise to a reasonable doubt about whether she consented to sex with Konrad? If it is, then it is relevant and should be admitted. It is likely that Omar's evidence would be admitted.

Because Konrad has no previous convictions he will be entitled to a direction in accordance with *Vye* (1993). His good character is relevant to his credibility as a witness and also when considering the likelihood that the allegations against him may be true.

Aim Higher ⭐

1. You must be completely familiar with the situations in which **s 41** of the **Youth Justice and Criminal Evidence Act 1999** applies. In particular, you must be able to say whether or not consent is an issue; and you must be able to distinguish between the test of contemporaneity provided by **s 41(3)(b)** and the test of similarity under **s 41(3)(c)**.
2. Where the defence wants to refer to similar allegations made in the past by a complainant which have failed to be substantiated for one reason or another, it's very important to know the recent cases which set out what has to be established before such evidence can be admitted. You need to show familiarity, e.g., with *T* (2001), *E* (2005), *M* (2009) and *D* (2009).

Common Pitfalls

1. Candidates frequently muddle the old law about 'recent complaints' and the new law under **s 120 CJA 2003**. In particular, you should remember that under the Act such complaints are not rendered inadmissible because prompted by a leading question; they are evidence of the truth of their contents; they are not confined to a single complaint, or to complaints of sexual offences.
2. One of the most frequent errors is to assume that **s 41(3)(b)** and **(c)** of the **Youth Justice and Criminal Evidence Act 1999** both apply tests of contemporaneity. Remember that only **s 41(3)(b)** applies that test; **s 41(3)(c)** applies a different test, namely, a test of similarity.

Opinion Evidence

INTRODUCTION

From the standpoint of the examination candidate, opinion evidence is a tricky subject to prepare. Your examiners may show little or no interest in it, so that an opinion point comes in, if at all, only as a minor part of a question dealing largely with other matters. On the other hand, it would be possible to devote a whole problem to the subject. It would even be possible – though surely not very interesting – to invite candidates to write an essay on some aspect of opinion evidence, for example, the current state of the so called 'ultimate issue rule'. Of course, you should keep up to date with any proposals for law reform in this area, as you would in any other. But let's assume that you have ruled out the possibility of an essay question, or at least of doing it should one turn up. How should you cope with opinion evidence as part of a problem?

In the first place, you should be careful in analysing exactly what it is that the expert is prepared to say. Break it down into a number of separate propositions if need be, because some may be more readily admissible than others.[1]

Next, you need to clarify the basis on which the opinion has been formed. For example, how much is a psychiatrist relying on what a defendant has told him? If he relies too much, he may find himself simply repeating what the defendant has said; that, obviously, would be open to the objection that it infringed the rule against hearsay.

Very often, the examiner will be vague about both these matters – exactly what the expert *is* saying and the basis for his opinion – and it will be for you to point out the difficulties.

Where you are dealing with the expert opinion of a psychiatrist or psychologist you should look at the issue to which it is directed. The reason is that evidence from either which does not amount to evidence of mental abnormality may be admitted to show,

---

1   For an example of close analysis leading to rejection of psychiatric testimony, see *Hurst* (1995).

for example, the reliability of a confession. But where the issue in question is that of *mens rea*, it is most unlikely to be admitted. See *Coles* (1995). Presumably, it is felt that to allow such evidence to be given would lead to experts deciding the issue that should properly be left to the jury. Alternatively, there may be a fear that a stage would soon be reached where experts were called on each side, the jury would be left no wiser and the expense and length of proceedings would have been increased for nothing.

Although your problem is likely to involve experts who make a living from their expertise, you may have to advise in relation to a layman who appears to be giving an opinion. Don't forget that an amateur may be an expert or that an opinion can be given by a non-expert if it is simply a short way of describing facts: see **s 3(2)** of the **Civil Evidence Act (CEA) 1972** and *Davies* (1962).

Checklist ✔

Students should be familiar with the following areas:

- opinion used as a way of conveying the sense of facts perceived;
- when expert psychiatric testimony is needed;
- who may give expert testimony;
- expert opinion on ultimate issues;
- expert evidence and the rule against hearsay – *Abadom* (1983); **s 30** of the **Criminal Justice Act (CJA) 1988**; **s 1(1)** of the **CEA 1972**;
- advance notice procedures in civil and criminal cases.

QUESTION 44

David and Jonathan are charged with murdering Salome, a prostitute. The prosecution case is that she was beaten and kicked to death by both the accused.

(a) David's defence is diminished responsibility. He says that he was one of Salome's regular clients and he acted as he did immediately after Salome said that if he did not give her £500,000 she would tell his wife of their relationship. David wishes to call Goliath, a psychiatrist. Goliath has prepared a report in which he says that he has examined David, that David described his horror at the blackmail attempt and became very emotional when speaking of his wife; in Goliath's opinion, David loves his wife dearly and would have been devastated by the break up of their marriage. Goliath adds that in two other cases in his experience, the sudden shock of a blackmail threat led to violent physical retaliation. He states that this observation has been explained in several privately circulated papers by psychiatrists who have described experiments in which they observed patterns of bodily chemical reactions which appeared to be peculiar to blackmail victims. Goliath concludes his report by saying that in his professional opinion David is not insane within the M'Naughten Rules, but was suffering at the relevant time from diminished responsibility within **s 2** of the **Homicide Act 1957**. May Goliath testify as to all or any of these matters?

(b) Jonathan's case is that he had been with David and Salome on the occasion in question, but that he had had nothing to do with the attack. He says that when he saw what David was doing, he went into a state of shock and ran to the house of his girlfriend, Jezebel, a short distance away. Jezebel is a member of the police force. May Jonathan call her to say that when he arrived at her house, he was in a state of shock? He also wishes to call Zadok, a psychiatrist, who has examined him and who is prepared to state that in his opinion, Jonathan is a truthful man who has a peculiar horror of any sort of violence as a result of having been bullied at school. Will Zadok's evidence be admissible?

Answer Plan

(a) Since the expert's evidence is directed towards providing a defence of diminished responsibility for David, it is a good idea to outline briefly what this defence requires. The first paragraph does this, and shows that this is a case where expert evidence will be admissible in principle. But now you have to point out that there may be difficulties about the admissibility of what this expert is prepared to say. To do so effectively, you must break up what Goliath wants to say into separate heads, as follows:

- David's reaction to the blackmail attempt;
- David's reactions when speaking of his wife;
- Goliath's opinion that David loves her dearly;
- Goliath's opinion about the effect on David of the break up of his marriage;
- Goliath's description of his own experience of similar cases;
- his reference to the psychiatric experiments reported in privately circulated papers;
- his opinion as to David's sanity;
- his opinion that David was suffering from diminished responsibility.

(b) The first matter to be considered is whether Jezebel's evidence is expert testimony at all. You then need to break up Zadok's opinion thus:

- his opinion that Jonathan was truthful;
- his opinion about Jonathan's capacity for violence.

ANSWER

(a) By **s 2** of the **Homicide Act 1957**, a person who kills another shall not be convicted of murder if he was suffering from such abnormality of mind as substantially impaired his mental responsibility for his acts. It is for the defendant to prove that he comes within the section. The requirement that some abnormality of mind be established makes it clear that this is the sort of case where expert opinion evidence is receivable. As was said in *Turner* (1975), the purpose of such evidence is to provide the court with information that is outside the experience and knowledge of a judge or jury. In *Dix* (1982), Shaw LJ said that while **s 2** of the **Homicide Act** did not in terms require that medical evidence be adduced in support of a defence of diminished responsibility, it made it a practical necessity if that defence was to begin to run at all. The question of admissibility in this case will therefore turn on the nature of the testimony that it is proposed that Goliath should give.

It appears that the first thing that Goliath wishes to do is to report the reactions of David when speaking of his wife, and to give his own opinion that David loves her dearly. He adds that David would have been devastated by the break up of his marriage, but whether this is an opinion formed as a result of what David told him directly, or as a result of what Goliath inferred from other things said by David, is unclear.

So far, it seems that nearly all this evidence would be inadmissible. To the extent that Goliath was repeating what David said to him, the evidence would be excluded by the rule against hearsay, although the fact that David became emotional when speaking of his wife would be admissible.[1] The questions of whether David loves his wife and what would have been his reaction to the break up of their marriage are not ones where the jury would require the special assistance of a psychiatrist. Thus, in *Turner* (1975), the Court of Appeal held that the trial judge had rightly excluded psychiatric evidence that the defendant had had a deep emotional relationship with his girlfriend, which was likely to have caused a blind explosion of rage after her confession of infidelity. As Lawton LJ said, the fact that an expert witness has impressive scientific qualifications does not by that fact alone make his opinion on matters of human nature and behaviour within the limits of normality any more helpful than that of the jurors themselves.

---

1 What is relevant is David's state of mind at the time of the offence. Light can be thrown on this by David's emotional reaction when talking to Goliath about his wife, but not, according to English law at any rate, by his account to Goliath of what his state of mind was at the time when he killed Salome. If David wants this to go before the jury, he will have to testify.

Then Goliath wishes to say that in two other cases in his experience the sudden shock of a blackmail threat led to violent physical retaliation, and he refers to the experiments of other psychiatrists by way of explanation. The basic question here is the same: does the jury need the assistance of this scientific evidence to determine the particular matter under consideration? At this stage, Goliath's evidence is directed to the issue whether it is more likely than not that when David killed Salome he was suffering from such abnormality of mind as substantially to impair his mental responsibility.

Is Goliath prepared to adopt the explanation of his colleagues as his own? Unless he is, there is not much point in referring to their opinions. Assuming that he does, the argument for admissibility is stronger than in relation to his earlier opinions because this is something that would not be within the ordinary knowledge of jurors. In *Abadom* (1983), the Court of Appeal decided that an expert is entitled to draw on the work of others as part of the process of arriving at his conclusions. The fact that the work is unpublished is immaterial. Goliath may therefore rely on the privately circulated papers in forming his opinion and, as the court pointed out in *Abadom*, he ought to identify them so that the quality of his opinion may be assessed.

However, it remains necessary to be cautious about admissibility. If the judge took the view that the scientists had merely been describing ordinary human reactions in scientific terms, he would very probably conclude that their discoveries would not assist the jury. The evidence would then be excluded.

Lastly, Goliath wishes to say that David was not insane, but was suffering from diminished responsibility. The question of David's sanity is not in issue, so the first part of this opinion would be irrelevant, and therefore inadmissible. Although experts may sometimes give opinions on the ultimate issue in a case, this is not one of them. The defence provided by **s 2** of the **Homicide Act 1957** involves more than a simple medical issue concerning the accused's state of mind. There is also the question of substantial impairment of responsibility and this is essentially for the jury to decide (*Byrne* (1960)).

However, in *DPP v A and BC Chewing Gum Ltd* (1968), Lord Parker acknowledged that although the question 'Do you think he was suffering from diminished responsibility?' was strictly inadmissible, it was allowed time and again without objection. Thus, on the assumption that there is some admissible evidence that Goliath can give, it is likely that he would also be allowed to say that in his opinion, David was suffering from diminished responsibility.

(b) Jezebel may certainly give evidence of Jonathan's physical and emotional condition when he arrived at her house; no special expertise is required to do this. If she wishes to give evidence that he was in a specific medical condition known as 'a state of shock', the fact that she is not medically qualified need not prevent her from doing so. It would be enough that she had acquired the necessary medical knowledge as part of her police training and experience. *Silverlock* (1894) is authority for the proposition that an appropriate professional qualification is not essential for an expert witness. In that case a solicitor who had studied handwriting as a hobby was allowed to give evidence as a handwriting expert.

Zadok will not be able to give his opinion that Jonathan is a truthful man. *Toohey v Commissioner for Metropolitan Police* (1965) establishes that medical evidence will be admissible to show that a witness suffers from some disease, or defect or abnormality of mind that affects the reliability of his evidence. But subject to this, it appears that only in the most exceptional cases will psychiatric testimony be admissible concerning the truthfulness of the accused.[2]

Two problems arise in connection with Zadok's opinion about Jonathan's capacity for violence. The first is whether it is in principle admissible at all. There is little to suggest that English courts are likely to follow the example set by the Supreme Court of Canada in *Lupien* (1970), which held admissible evidence showing that the defendant had a temperament that would have made his participation in a particular form of conduct very unlikely. In *Reynolds* (1989), the Court of Appeal took the view that psychiatric evidence about personal traits, such as the habit of fantasising, was inadmissible because the jury could use its common sense about such matters. It is likely that a court would regard an aversion to violence in the same light.

Even if this basic problem can be overcome, a second one remains: on what basis was Zadok's conclusion reached? If it was merely on what Jonathan said to him during a consultation it would be likely to fall foul of the rule against hearsay. At least in *Lupien* (1970) the defendant had been subjected to psychiatric tests for the purpose of determining the issue in question.

---

2   One such case was *Lowery v R* (1974), where two co-accused blamed each other for a murder and the Privy Council held that the trial judge had properly admitted the evidence of a psychologist, who had carried out tests on both defendants, to show that the testimony of one was more likely to be true than that of the other. Nothing of the kind arises here; David accepts that he killed Salome and has not tried to implicate Jonathan.

OPINION EVIDENCE

Aim Higher ★

1. Make sure that you can break down summaries of an expert's proposed evidence into its constituent propositions. Candidates who try to advise on a statement as a whole are likely to become muddled because only some parts may be admissible.
2. Show that you know it is necessary to adduce evidence to establish the provenance of an item of real evidence in respect of which an expert gives an opinion. For example, if a witness wants to say that he examined glass taken from a shoe and found that it corresponded with the type of glass used in the window of a house that had been burgled, there must be proof that the glass which was sent for examination had been taken from a shoe which the defendant had been wearing.

Common Pitfalls

1. Do not assume that a professionally qualified witness will always be able to give evidence within the area of his expertise. The courts take the view that the jury can usually reach the answer to some questions without the aid of expert evidence; e.g., in assessing the truthfulness of a witness.
2. Don't forget that the rule against hearsay is relaxed in favour of an expert witness, who is allowed to rely on knowledge obtained by reading and hearing about what others in the same field have discovered. Reference should now be made to **CJA 2003, s 118(1), paragraph 8**.

Privilege and Public Policy

INTRODUCTION

The first thing to get straight is the difference between these two concepts. A *privilege* is a right that the law gives to a person allowing him to refuse to testify about a certain matter, or to refuse to produce a document or piece of real evidence. *Public policy* (often now referred to as 'public interest immunity') comes into the picture where it is thought that the disclosure of evidence would be damaging in some way to the general good. The most obvious example is where national security would be compromised if the evidence in question had to be given, or the disclosure made.

There are four privileges that you ought to study. The first is the privilege against self-incrimination. One theoretical topic that could come up as an essay question is whether such a privilege should exist at all. You should note that this is not the same question as whether the accused should have a right to silence. Some writers do refer to 'the privilege against self-incrimination' in the broad sense of a 'right to silence', but this is confusing and it will be better if you keep the two ideas distinct.

The classic context for the operation of the privilege against self-incrimination is a *civil* action where one of the witnesses is being cross-examined about conduct that would amount to a criminal offence. For example, suppose I sue a storage company for the loss of my valuable furniture which was in store with them, and it is my case that the furniture was destroyed when the company deliberately set fire to the premises to collect on an insurance policy. In those circumstances, the privilege might well be invoked at some stage of the hearing by a witness for the company who was being cross-examined.

You should note the increasing number of statutory exceptions to this privilege.

Legal professional privilege is also of considerable importance. Note the various circumstances in which this applies, especially those cases where the communications are not directly between lawyer and client, but between lawyer and third parties on behalf of the client.

This privilege can be 'waived' by accident. What happens is that, in any large action, the task of preparing documents for disclosure is so great that quite often one side shows the other privileged documents by mistake. By **r 31.20** of the **Civil Procedure Rules 1998**, inadvertently disclosed privileged documents may only be used with the consent of the court. Some knowledge of the former law that governed the granting of injunctions to restrain the use of such documents is likely to be helpful in judging whether consent will be given.

Two more privileges ought to be studied. One is the limited privilege that has been given in respect of a journalist's sources. (See **s 10** of the **Contempt of Court Act 1981**.) The other is the privilege that attaches to 'without prejudice' statements. With the latter, remember that if the negotiations result in agreement, there is no longer any need for 'without prejudice' protection. It follows that, if there is any subsequent litigation concerning that agreement, you are free to use the documents marked 'without prejudice' as evidence of the agreement and its terms (*Tomlin v Standard Telephones and Cables Ltd* (1969)). But note also *Rush and Tomkins Ltd v GLC* (1989), which makes evidence of negotiations inadmissible in any subsequent litigation connected with the same subject matter. This is particularly likely to affect a situation where a main contractor reaches a settlement with one of several sub-contractors.

Public policy questions are not ones that many candidates answer well, and unless you have also studied public law it is, perhaps, better to avoid the topic in the examination. I have nevertheless suggested in the checklist some areas with which you might make yourself familiar. The subject of police informers is interesting, topical and not too difficult to master. It is also a subject that might feature as part of a wider question.

Checklist ✔

Students should be familiar with the following areas:

- the privilege against self-incrimination;
- legal professional privilege;
- **s 10** of the **Contempt of Court Act 1981**;
- 'without prejudice' statements;
- public policy considerations involving national security, affairs of state, and the proper functioning of government and its services;

- public policy considerations in respect of information in the possession of the police relating to the investigation of crime;
- public policy considerations in respect of confidential or personal statements made in official reports or inquiries.

QUESTION 45

'The fact that evidence which is relevant and otherwise admissible may be excluded by public policy or privilege gives to the two subjects an appearance of similarity that is misleading. The rules and their operation are quite distinct, and any superficial identity of result is more than outweighed by substantial and far reaching differences.'

▶ Discuss.

Answer Plan

Sometimes, the examiner sets quite a lengthy quotation as the subject for an essay. To write an effective essay, it is of course vital that you should read the quotation carefully, probably at least twice, in order to determine exactly what it means. All too often I have read scripts where it seemed as if the candidate had glanced at the quotation, had seen that it had something to do with public policy, and had assumed he would pass if he regurgitated his lecture notes on *Conway v Rimmer* (1968), etc. I emphasise again that the examiner is looking for an argument, not an exposition of basic law. If you fail to provide an appropriate response, you will fail the question.

What is this particular quotation about? First, the writer refers to the fact that the rules of both privilege and public policy have the effect of excluding evidence that would otherwise be relevant and admissible. To that extent, the two sets of rules appear to be alike, but, he goes on, the fact that the rules have the same *result* does not mean that there are any other similarities. Similarity of result need not involve similarity in the way the result is reached. This is certainly true in some matters; is it true in this case? In other words, what are the differences and similarities between the rules relating to privilege and those relating to public policy?

It probably strikes you that the idea contained in the quotation is basically correct. But it is not very interesting to say so at once, and the key to producing a really competent answer is to argue a little *against* the idea contained in the quotation. This is done here by arguing that there is not only a similarity in outcome, but a similarity in the way the rules are operated.

You can then move on to make obvious points about waiver, use of secondary evidence and persons entitled to make the claim. You conclude by agreeing with the proposition contained in the quotation. But you do so with reservations, and have shown some independent thought on the subject.

In summary, therefore, the essay is constructed as follows:

- difference between outcomes and the means of achieving them;
- argument for similarity of means based on the balancing of potential harms;
- place of balancing interests in privilege and public policy;
- potential differences between privilege and public policy: waiver and use of secondary evidence;
- persons who can claim privilege and raise issues of public policy;
- concluding remarks on the quotation.

ANSWER

Similarity of outcomes does not necessarily involve similarity in the way the outcomes under consideration were achieved. Dr Crippen died by hanging and Louis XVI lost his life by means of the guillotine. The outcome in each case was the same: death. However, the procedures preceding those outcomes and the methods by which death was achieved were vastly different. It does not, therefore, appear to be a very impressive argument for similarity between the rules relating to privilege and those relating to public policy that they achieve the same outcome.

However, it can be argued that there is more than identity of outcome, and that in fact there is similarity in the way the rules are operated. If a claim to privilege succeeds, it does so because when you balance the harm that will follow if the privilege is upheld against the harm that will follow if it is not, the latter is found to be greater. Yet this is the very same principle that operates in the sphere of public interest immunity.

When privilege is being considered, this balancing exercise operates in a way about which it is difficult to generalise, but which may best be described as 'oiling the wheels of the administration of justice'. For example, for each party to have his case presented as well as possible within our adversarial context, it is necessary that the lawyers on each side be fully acquainted with all the relevant facts. To achieve this, it is vital that the client should be able to trust the lawyer. This could not be the case if what he said to his own lawyer could be used against him, and this gives rise to rules about legal professional privilege.

The fact that justice can be done by disputants themselves, and not only by courts, is recognised by rules that encourage parties to settle their quarrels without recourse to litigation. So, for example, we find that there are rules that say that admissions made by parties while trying to reach a settlement cannot afterwards be proved against them if negotiations break down and the matter has to go to court.

On another level, there may be public interests that conflict with the doing of justice in a particular case. Thus, the public interest in the detection of crime or in the maintenance of national security may require non-disclosure of certain matters, even though this may harm an individual litigant by depriving him of vital evidence.

In both types of case, there is a balancing of interests. Is the interest in rectitude of decision outweighed by the interest in keeping the administration of justice working as well as possible, both inside and outside the courts? Is the interest in doing justice to the parties in a particular case outweighed by some wider public interest? So far, it seems that although the situations giving rise to such problems of balancing may be very different, the principle that is operating in each case is essentially the same. Have we found a common feature other than outcome that would disprove the contention expressed in the passage quoted?

Closer examination suggests that although the balancing of interests is indeed a feature common to both the law of privilege and the law relating to exclusion on grounds of public policy, this does not disprove the contention. The reason for this is that it is too common a feature of evidence law, for it can be used to account for all the ordinary rules of exclusion, such as those governing hearsay evidence or evidence of the accused's criminal propensity. The public may be said to have an interest in the full disclosure of relevant information in a criminal trial, but it also has an interest in rectitude of decision. This latter interest may be served better by concealing some information, because, if it were disclosed, its capacity to mislead the jury would increase the chances of mis-decision. Thus, it may be said that a balancing exercise takes place in which greater weight is given to one interest rather than the other, depending on the amount of harm likely to result.

On the other hand, there appear to be quite strong arguments to justify the contention expressed in the passage quoted.

Matters covered by public policy are those where the safety or well being of citizens generally is concerned. Privilege, by contrast, covers matters that directly affect only the particular litigant or witness. This gives rise to differences in the way in which the law deals with two subjects: waiver and the use of secondary evidence.

A party or witness who has a privilege may always waive it voluntarily and, in such a case, the once privileged document or testimony will be treated in the same way as any other evidence in the case. But, because public policy objections exist, in theory, for the benefit of citizens generally there is some difficulty with the idea that objections of this type can be waived. Thus, in *Rogers v Home Secretary* (1973), Lord Simon said that once the public interest which demands that evidence be withheld has been found weightier than the public interest requiring courts to have access to all relevant material, the evidence cannot in any circumstances be admitted. It is not a privilege that may be waived, either by the Crown or by anyone else.

However, in *Alfred Crompton Amusement Machines Ltd v Customs & Excise Commissioners (No 2)* (1974), Lord Cross thought that waiver could be allowed if a person or party, such as an informer, for whose benefit the objection was made volunteered to testify or disclose the evidence. One way of analysing such an odd situation would be to say that it was not a case of waiver at all, but one where the public interest had just disappeared, because the interest in question is that of protecting a person from having to disclose certain information *against his will*.[1] This approach was adopted by the Court of Appeal in *Savage v Chief Constable of the Hampshire Constabulary* (1997), where it was held that a police informer could waive his anonymity in order to sue the defendant on an alleged contract to make payments to the claimant in return for information.

The courts have recently brought the operation of public interest immunity more closely into line with that of privilege in respect of waiver. An important distinction used to be that, while a privilege could be waived, a claim to public interest immunity could not. As Lord Scarman said in *Air Canada v Secretary of State for Trade* (1983), when the Crown puts forward a public interest immunity objection, it is not claiming a privilege but discharging a duty. Similarly, in *Makanjuola v Commissioner of Metropolitan Police* (1992), Bingham LJ said that public interest immunity 'is not a trump card vouchsafed to certain privileged players to play as and when they wish'. He added that it could not, in any ordinary sense, be waived, because although rights can be waived, duties cannot. On that approach, it followed that

---

[1] Lord Denning has on several occasions said that there could be waiver of objections based on public policy. In *Campbell v Tameside Metropolitan Borough Council* (1982), he proposed a distinction between claims affecting documents which must be kept secret on such grounds as those of national security or the preservation of diplomatic relations, and documents in a lower category which are kept confidential in order that persons should be candid in their reports or for other good reasons. In these latter cases, he suggested, immunity should be capable of being waived either by the maker or by the recipient of the document.

where a litigant held documents in a class that was *prima facie* immune, he should (save in a very exceptional case) assert that they are immune and decline to disclose them. The ultimate decision about where the public interest lay was not for him, but for the court.

However, this approach, coupled with a claim to immunity based on the class into which a document fell, rather than on its specific contents, led to undesirably wide public interest immunity claims by ministers. The practice was criticised in the Scott Report,[2] and the central government has now effectively abandoned class claims.

Further, in *R v Chief Constable of West Midlands Police ex p Wiley* (1995), the House of Lords held that a class claim cannot be made in respect of documents compiled as part of the investigation of a complaint against the police, and it seems likely that class claims generally will be reduced in future. After *ex p Wiley*, it is clear that if a minister believes that the overriding public interest requires government documents to be disclosed, he is not obliged to request immunity for them. It appears that ministers must now consider, before making a claim for public interest immunity, whether the public interest is better served by disclosure than by concealment. It looks very much as if they are expected to exercise a discretion in deciding whether or not to waive public interest immunity.

The second main difference between information affected by privilege and information affected by public policy is in relation to the use of secondary evidence.

When public policy requires that information be concealed, the documents which are the immediate subject of the exclusion are obviously affected but, in addition, it is not possible to prove their contents by secondary means. Privilege, however, attaches only to an original document or communication. Subject to the possibility of protection under the law relating to confidentiality, secondary evidence is in principle admissible. Thus, an opponent may be able to prove facts contained in a privileged document by producing a copy, or by calling a witness to give oral evidence of its contents.

A final point of distinction between claims based on privilege and claims based on public policy is that in the case of privilege the claim must be made by the person who is entitled to the privilege, but an objection made on grounds of public policy may be made by someone who is not even a party to the proceedings. The court may even do so of its own motion.

---

2 *Report of the Inquiry into the Export of Defence Equipment and Dual-Use Goods to Iraq and Related Prosecutions*, **1996, HC 115, 15 February**.

Thus, it can be seen that, despite superficial similarities in both effect and operation, there are significant differences between the rules relating to privilege and public policy and between the ways in which those rules operate.

> **Aim Higher**
> 1. Writers differ in the way they use the expression 'privilege against self-incrimination'. If the expression occurs in an essay question you should, if necessary, make clear to the reader the sense in which you are taking the expression for the purposes of your answer.
> 2. You need to be familiar with the ways in which legal professional privilege can operate. In particular, you should be careful to note the circumstances in which it can apply between legal advisers and persons other than the lay client.

> **Common Pitfalls**
> 1. Candidates are often unaware that there are two kinds of legal professional privilege and that the rules governing them are slightly different. You should note carefully the distinction between 'legal advice privilege' and 'litigation privilege'.
> 2. It is commonly said that legal professional privilege will not protect a communication to facilitate crime or fraud. But many candidates are unaware of cases such as *Crescent Farm v Sterling Offices* (1972) and *Barclays Bank plc v Eustice* (1995) which show that 'fraud' is widely interpreted in this context.

QUESTION 46

Answer BOTH parts of this question:

(a) Francis is being prosecuted for possession of cannabis, which has been found at his house. When the police raided the premises, they discovered a small quantity of the drug wrapped in silver paper at the bottom of a pile of underclothes that lay on the floor. Francis denies the charge. He says that he is an asthmatic and unable to smoke, but that writers, artists and students are frequent callers at his house and that any one of them could have dropped the package. He suspects that the police were tipped off by George. George has been employed by Francis as a general handyman for the last eight years. In the past, he has been sentenced to terms of imprisonment; he is now an alcoholic and has often made false allegations against Francis when drunk.

May the defence require the police to disclose the name of their informer?

(b) Harry is being prosecuted for supplying drugs. The only evidence against him is that of four police officers. Two officers, Ian and John, give evidence that while keeping watch in private premises, they observed Harry selling drugs. Two others, Kate and Larry, give evidence that while keeping watch in an unmarked police vehicle, they also observed Harry selling drugs.

May the defence cross-examine Ian and John to discover the exact location of their observation point in order to test the quality of their observations? May they cross-examine Kate and Larry to discover the colour, make and model of their vehicle and the times of their alleged surveillance?

Answer Plan

This is a straightforward question involving cases on the public interest in non-disclosure of information concerning police investigations.

Part (a) deals with the traditional problem of the informer. The basic rule stated in *Marks v Beyfus* (1890) must be your starting point; it will be useful to refer to what Lawton LJ said in *Hennessey* (1978) about the reason for that rule. Don't rush things; deal with the basic rule first and turn to the exception only after that. Then comes the factual problem: is disclosure necessary to show the accused's innocence? The point is best made here by a comparison of *Agar* (1990) and *Slowcombe* (1991). Don't forget though to provide your own conclusion on the facts of this question; the cases you have cited are useful illustrations of a principle, but no more.

Part (b) is even more straightforward and is designed to test the candidate's knowledge of *Rankine* (1986), *Brown* (1987) and *Johnson* (1988).

ANSWER

(a) The basic rule is that in public prosecutions witnesses may not be asked, and will not be allowed to disclose, the names of informers or the nature of the information given. Thus, in *Marks v Beyfus* (1890), an action for malicious prosecution, the Director of Public Prosecutions, who had been called as a witness, refused on grounds of public policy to give the names of his informants or to produce the statement on which he had acted in directing the earlier unsuccessful prosecution of the plaintiff. His objection was upheld by the trial judge, and the plaintiff was unsuccessful in his appeal. Lawton LJ stated in *Hennessey* (1978) that the rationale of the rule is that informers need to be protected, both for their own safety and to ensure that the supply of information about criminal activities does not dry up.

However, in *Marks v Beyfus* (1890), Lord Esher qualified this basic rule by stating that it could be departed from if the disclosure of the name of the informant was necessary or right in order to show the prisoner's innocence. In such a case, one public policy would be in conflict with another, and the policy that said that an innocent man should not be condemned when his innocence could be proved had to prevail. However, it is for the accused to show that there is a good reason for disclosure (*Hennessey* (1978)).

An example of a case where disclosure was considered appropriate is *Agar* (1990). In that case, a prosecution for possession of drugs, the Court of Appeal said that the trial judge should have ordered the informer's disclosure because it was necessary for the support of the accused's defence that the informer and the police had acted together to frame him.

But it may well be the case that knowledge of the informer will not affect the defence, and then disclosure will not be ordered. An example is *Slowcombe* (1991). Following a tip off, the defendant had been arrested in possession of a shotgun outside a sub-post office. He claimed to have been recruited by V, and to have been told by him that there was an accomplice working in the post office who would hand over the money, but that the gun was necessary for the sake of appearances. The defendant argued accordingly that he was not guilty of conspiracy to rob, but only of conspiracy to steal. The judge refused a defence application to ask a police officer whether their informer had been V. The Court of Appeal upheld this decision. If V had not been the informer, the defendant's story could still have been true. If it had been V, this would not establish that the defendant had been told that only a theft was planned. V could have conspired with the defendant to commit robbery, but then have turned informer. Disclosing the name of the informer could contribute little or nothing to the issue the jury had to consider: might the defendant's explanation have been true?

The issue in the case of Francis is whether his explanation for the presence of the cannabis might be true. Knowing that George was the informer can contribute nothing to the resolution of this question. If Francis were to suggest that George planted the cannabis and then tipped off the police, the position would be different, but that does not appear to be his case.

It is unlikely, therefore, that the defence application would succeed.[1]

(b) It was held in *Rankine* (1986) that the rule in *Marks v Beyfus* (1890) also protects the identity of persons who have allowed their premises to be used for police observation, and the identity of the premises. Even if the accused argues that identification of the premises is necessary to establish his innocence (as it surely would be in this case), the judge may still refuse to allow the question to be put. For example, in *Johnson* (1988), where the accused was charged with supplying drugs, the only evidence against him was supplied by police officers who had kept observation from private premises. The defence applied to cross-examine about the exact location in order to test whether the officers could have seen what they said they did. The trial judge nevertheless ruled that the exact location should not be revealed and the Court of Appeal upheld this decision.

But the prosecution must have first provided a proper evidential basis to support their claim for protection of identity. In *Johnson* (1988), Watkins LJ stated the following as minimum requirements:

❖ the police officer in charge of the observations must testify that he had visited all the observation places to be used and ascertained the attitude of their occupiers, both as to the use to be made of them and to possible subsequent disclosure;
❖ a police officer of at least the rank of chief inspector must testify that immediately prior to the trial he visited the places used for observation and ascertained whether the occupiers were the same as when the observation took place and, whether they are or not, the attitude of those occupiers to possible disclosure of their use as observation points.

In *Johnson* (1988), the prosecution called evidence as to the difficulty of obtaining assistance from the public and the desire of the occupiers, who had been occupiers throughout, that their names and addresses should not be disclosed because of fear for their safety. Assuming that similar evidence is available in this case, the defence will not be permitted to cross-examine Ian and John about the exact location of the premises which they used.

But the object of keeping the identity of the premises secret is to protect the owner or occupier. Where this consideration does not apply, cross-examination may be permitted on detailed aspects of surveillance. Thus, in *Brown* (1987), where officers gave evidence that they had kept observation from an unmarked police vehicle, it

---

1 But for what happened in the case on which this question is based, see Farson, D, *The Gilded Gutter Life of Francis Bacon*, 1993, Chapter 12.

was held that the defence was entitled to information relating to the surveillance and to the colour, make and model of the vehicle.

The defence will therefore be entitled to ask Kate and Larry about these matters.

QUESTION 47

Cedric was employed by AB Ltd, a company engaged in the manufacture of meat pies. One day, his hand was caught in a mincing machine and he suffered grave injuries, because of which he decided to sue AB Ltd for compensation. When AB Ltd learned of the accident, they obtained a report from an independent safety expert in accordance with their usual practice when accidents occurred on their premises. Copies of this report were sent to the board of directors and to the legal department of the company.

Cedric wrote a letter to Derek, his solicitor, setting out his account of the accident in which he admitted that he had not complied with safety regulations when operating the mincing machine because he had been 'chatting someone up' at the time. Enid, Derek's secretary, took a photocopy of this letter and gave it to her lover Fabian, who is a director of AB Ltd.

Cedric wishes to obtain a copy of the safety expert's report. He suspects that his employers may have obtained a copy of his letter to Derek and is afraid that they may use it against him. Advise Cedric.

Answer Plan

A relatively straightforward question about privilege. You need to discuss the following points:

- the safety expert's report – legal professional privilege in relation to third party communications;
- whether Cedric's admission is privileged;
- whether AB Ltd will be allowed to use the photocopy of the letter sent by Cedric.

ANSWER

Communications made between a party or his legal advisers and a third party will be privileged provided the dominant purpose in making the communications was to obtain or provide advice in connection with pending or contemplated litigation. The requirement that advice in such a connection be the dominant purpose of the communication was established by *Waugh v British Railways Board* (1980). In that case, the claimant sued the defendants under the **Fatal Accidents Act 1976** in respect of the death of her husband, which had occurred in a railway collision. Her advisers wished to obtain discovery of an internal report prepared by the defendants for submission to the railway inspectorate and the ministry. Another object of the report was to provide information for the Board's solicitor to enable him to advise the Board. The House of Lords held that the Board was not entitled to claim privilege in respect of this report. To attract such privilege, preparation for the purposes of intended or contemplated litigation had to be 'at least the dominant purpose' for bringing a document into existence. But the report in *Waugh* had been prepared not only for the purpose of litigation but for other major purposes in relation to the safe running of railways. Submission to the solicitor had not been shown to be the dominant purpose of making the report; therefore it was not privileged.

Whether such a document is privileged will turn on the facts of each individual case. But, on the facts given, it looks as if assistance in litigation was only one of the objects of AB Ltd in obtaining the safety expert's report, and that the maintenance of safe working practices was equally important. The report is thus unlikely to be privileged.

All communications between solicitor and client made for the purpose of giving or receiving legal advice are privileged (*Waugh v British Railways Board* (1980)). It is clear that the letter that Cedric wrote to Derek was privileged for this reason.

However, privilege attaches only to the original letter sent by Cedric. In principle, secondary evidence of a privileged document is admissible. Thus, in *Calcraft v Guest* (1898), it was held that the defendant was entitled to put in evidence copies that he had made of certain proofs of evidence. By **r 31.20** of the **Civil Procedure Rules 1998**, inadvertently disclosed privileged documents may only be used with the consent of the court. But, this document has not been *inadvertently* disclosed. Use of a document that is an admissible piece of evidence may be restrained on the ground that it contains confidential information. In *Lord Ashburton v Pape* (1913), the plaintiff opposed the defendant's discharge from bankruptcy. The defendant obtained by trickery a number of relevant documents from a clerk in the employment of the claimant's solicitors. Having obtained them, he took copies. The Court of Appeal held that the plaintiff was entitled to an injunction requiring the defendant to deliver up all originals and restraining him from making any use of the copies or of the information that he had obtained. Provided the privileged documents or copies of them have not already been used as secondary evidence in the litigation, the party entitled to the privilege will be able to obtain a similar injunction (*Goddard v Nationwide Building Society* (1987)).

Cedric's solicitors will therefore be able to obtain an injunction restraining the use by AB Ltd of the photocopy that was given to Fabian and of the information contained in it.

Revision 13

INTRODUCTION

So far, each chapter has dealt very largely with one topic in the law of evidence. Essay questions in an examination are usually on a specific topic, but that is not generally the way in which examiners set problem questions. In these you are very likely to be given a scenario that will test your knowledge of the law more widely. It is important to get some experience in answering questions of this kind, and the object of this chapter is to provide this opportunity.

First, you have to choose the questions that you want to do. This means that you have to read all of them, carefully, at the beginning of the examination. You might think that, having made your decision, you should plunge at once into writing an answer to the first question of your choice. But this is not the best way to proceed. Almost certainly, you know more evidence law than you think you do. But you probably cannot recall it all at once. So you need to give your brains the best opportunity to recall what you know. You can do this by planning your answers to *all* the questions that you intend to answer before writing a full answer to any of them.

How does this help? I expect that you have sometimes had the experience of trying to remember something in ordinary conversation. Perhaps you are telling a friend about an old film that you once saw and liked. You can remember some of its details, and perhaps its title, but you cannot remember who starred in it. Ten minutes later you are talking about something completely different – and suddenly you remember the name that you were trying to recall earlier. What seems to happen is that subconsciously your brain carries on its task of recall even though you have, apparently, dismissed the subject from your mind. This is what can happen in examinations. If you alert your brain by making as thorough a preparation as you can of questions 4–7 at the start, when you are writing your full answer to question 4, you may very well find that something comes into your head about some law you could not at first remember in connection with question 6. It will be the work of a moment to add this to your answer plan for question 6, and then continue writing your full answer to question 4. You will not, of course, find that you have been distracted from question 4 because you will already have on rough paper an answer plan to follow for that question.

Moral: at the very start of the examination make as good an answer plan as you can for *all* the questions that you intend to answer.

Next, how should you tackle a problem question? After you have read it through once, go through it again and break it up mentally into defendants and pieces of information. (I am assuming that the problem is about evidence in a criminal trial.) It's a good idea to deal with each defendant separately, and to consider the significance for evidence law of each piece of information that you are given. That means that you should be thinking initially about its relevance for the case as it affects a particular defendant and any co-defendants. In criminal problems, it helps to put yourself in the shoes of counsel for the prosecution and then in those of counsel for the defence. For example, you might ask yourself of a piece of information, 'If I were prosecuting, why would I want this information to go before the jury?' And then, 'If I were counsel for the defence, what arguments would be available to me to get this piece of information excluded?'

But, as I have said before in this book and elsewhere, evidence law is not concerned only with questions about the admissibility of evidence. It is also concerned with directions that a judge should give during his summing-up to the jury about how to treat specific items of evidence that have been admitted, but which for various reasons require careful handling. If, for example, identification evidence has been admitted, a *Turnbull* direction will be required. And don't think you can satisfy the examiner by saying that, and no more. The examiner wants to see if you know what a *Turnbull* direction should contain. What directions should be given if **s 34** of the **Criminal Justice and Public Order Act 1994** applies? Don't just mention *Petkar*; find some means of remembering what points were made in that case, and summarise them for the examiner. Where this sort of memory work is needed, try to make a list of key words, one for each point that the judge should make, and turn the initial letters of those words into a single word that you can remember. The army used to be good at this sort of thing. When I was at school, we were taught in the Combined Cadet Force how to give an order to fire at a specific target. You had to specify the group of soldiers whom you wanted to carry out the order; you had to specify the range of fire; you had to indicate where they should be firing; and you had to indicate the target. Group – Range – Indication – Target: GRIT. We all remembered it then, and I can remember it now, even though after leaving school I never had to give an order to anyone to fire a gun at anything. Work out something on those lines to help you remember the contents of judicial directions. It's quite fun to try, and the very process of trying should help to fix the details in your mind. A variant of this system is to use the initial letters of your key words to make up a memorable sentence. For example, 'Every good boy deserves flogging.' It's memorable because it's nonsense. But it helps you to remember the sequence E, G, B, D, F, and if you have studied music you will know the significance of that.

One way to use the questions in this chapter would be to read the question and then without looking at the answer plan, try to work out your own plan. Then compare it with the plan in the book, look up what you have forgotten, and finally write your answer without reference to books or notes in roughly the time that you would have to answer a question in the examination. (Don't forget to deduct your initial preparation time when working out the time available for each question.)

Here, then, are three more questions, but of a kind more like the ones that you will encounter in your examination.

QUESTION 48

Edward and Frank are charged with the murder of Godfrey. The case for the prosecution is that all three were sharing a house, and that one evening there was a quarrel, during which Godfrey was stabbed with a knife that has not been found. In the ambulance on the way to hospital Godfrey said to Hilda, a paramedic, 'They told me they hated me. I heard them talking about poison. I didn't think they'd use a knife.' Godfrey lost consciousness a few minutes later and was certified as dead on arrival at the hospital. When the police lawfully searched the house where all three had been living, they seized a computer in Frank's bedroom. On later examination it was found to have been used to download pornography and information about various poisons.

Edward declined legal advice and was interviewed under caution by the police. He denied being present in the house when Godfrey was stabbed and said that he had been playing darts with friends in a local public house. The police later discovered that this alibi was false.

Frank was interviewed under caution in the presence of his solicitor. He denied having anything to do with the attack on Godfrey, or with the pornography and information about poisons that had been downloaded on his computer. He said that everyone in the house used the computer, as did people who came to stay from time to time. He said that he had been having a shower, had heard nothing, and discovered the stabbing only later.

The prosecution wishes to call Jerry, a next-door neighbour, who says that he knew Godfrey well and that at about the time when the attack took place he had heard

Godfrey shout, 'Don't, Edward! Oh please, don't!' Then about thirty seconds afterwards he heard Godfrey shout, 'I'm dying!'

▶ Discuss the evidential issues arising.

> **Answer Plan**
>
> You should consider the following points:
>
> ❖ The admissibility of what Godfrey said to Hilda. You will need to break this up into separate sentences because the same rules do not apply to all three. Consider first, in relation to each, whether Godfrey could himself have given evidence on the same lines if he had survived. Then consider what difference is made by the fact that the information comes from Hilda. Remember to look out for multiple hearsay.
> ❖ The relevance of what Godfrey said.
> ❖ The effect of Edward's lie about his alibi.
> ❖ The admissibility of Jerry's evidence. Again, break up what was said. Different rules may apply.

ANSWER

The first question concerns the admissibility of Hilda's evidence about what Godfrey said to her in the ambulance. It is not clear to whom Godfrey was referring, but one possibility is that he was referring to Edward and Frank. 'They told me they hated me.' If Godfrey had survived that attack he could have given evidence of this. The words uttered by the speakers were statements relating to their contemporaneous emotions, and so would have been admissible as evidence from Godfrey under the *res gestae* exception to the rule against hearsay preserved by **s 118(1), para 4(c)** of the **CJA 2003**. Hilda will herself give hearsay evidence under **s 116(2)(a)** to the effect that Godfrey told her of these earlier statements made to him. This part of what Godfrey said will therefore be multiple hearsay as evidence from Hilda and reliance will have to be placed for admissibility on **s 121(1)(c).**

Godfrey, had he survived, could also have given evidence that he had overheard a conversation about poison. This would not have been caught by the rule against hearsay. The object of adducing the evidence would have been to show the speakers' interest in poison, not to establish that what they said about any particular poison was true. It was for a similar reason that in *McIntosh* (1992), a paper containing calculations of the price and weight of drugs found in the possession of the defendant was held admissible, although not in his handwriting. This part of what Godfrey said will therefore be first-hand hearsay when it comes from Hilda. 'I didn't think they'd use a knife' would be admissible as first-hand evidence of

Godfrey's mental state and so admissible either under **s 116** or as *res gestae* under **s 118(1), para 4(c)**.

The defence might question the relevance of some or all of what Godfrey said. The prosecution would argue that hatred can be a motive for murder. It can be inferred from the next two sentences that the persons who used a knife had earlier been talking about poison. The contents of the computer show that Frank could have been one of those talking about poison who later used a knife. According to Frank, the computer was available to everyone, so Edward could have been another. (The pornography will be irrelevant and so inadmissible.)

Edward has been caught out in a lie about an alibi. The prosecution can rely on this as evidence of guilt, but the judge must direct the jury as laid down in *Lucas* (1981) and *Burge and Pegg* (1996). The jury must be warned that the mere fact that a defendant has lied is not in itself evidence of guilt because defendants may lie for innocent reasons. Only if the jury is sure that Edward did *not* lie for an innocent reason can his lie support the prosecution case. The jury must first be satisfied, of course, that Edward did lie to the police.

Jerry's evidence will be relevant and admissible. The first part does not amount to hearsay evidence because Godfrey's object in making his first utterance was not to cause another person to believe any matter, but to beg that person to stop whatever he was doing. The statement 'I am dying' was probably intended to cause another person to believe that fact, but Jerry's evidence about it will be admissible under **s 116(2)(a)**. There is no need to rely on the more complicated rules of *res gestae* preserved by **s 118(1), para 4(a)**.

QUESTION 49

Advise on the correctness of the following rulings, which were made in the course of three separate trials.

(a) 'The defendant is charged with unlawfully and maliciously wounding his neighbour's son, who was aged 15 at the time. The prosecution wished to call the defendant's wife to give evidence against her husband. They are now separated, but she does not wish to give evidence against him. The law here is quite clear. You remain married until decree absolute of divorce. That decree has not been granted; indeed divorce proceedings haven't even been commenced. It follows that she is entitled to stay out of the witness box. But at an earlier stage in the proceedings she did give a witness statement to the police, and the prosecution has now applied to have that statement admitted as hearsay. It is by no means the only evidence against the defendant in this case, so we are not concerned with what the European

Court has been saying about such a situation. Before the **Criminal Justice Act 2003** the prosecution's application would be bound to have failed. But the new legislation has changed that, and my powers under **s 114** are very wide. So I grant the application. It seems a very sensible way of dealing with the problem.'

(b) 'In this case the defendant is charged with murder. He relies on self-defence in answer. If that is made out, of course, he will be acquitted. However, at this stage the question that arises is whether it is right for the jury to consider this defence at all. It's true that he doesn't bear a legal burden of proof in respect of it, but he does have an evidential burden to discharge. I have listened carefully to his evidence, but I remain unsatisfied that he has discharged that burden. I am not satisfied on the balance of probabilities that this is a defence the jury could find to have been established. So in due course I shall direct them that, as a matter of law, they need not consider a defence of provocation.'

(c) 'The complainant, a mature woman, makes the very grave allegation of rape against this defendant, who is aged only 19 and of hitherto impeccable character. The defence wishes to cross-examine her about a similar complaint which she made a year ago about another young man. It is said that after she made the complaint she refused to co-operate with the police in the inquiries that they very naturally instituted. The defence also wishes to cross-examine her about a recent conviction for assault. In that matter she was charged, pleaded not guilty, but was found guilty after giving evidence in support of her defence. In other words, she lied recently on oath and the defence argues that the jury are entitled to know this. In my judgment, both applications should succeed. If there's any suggestion that she's the sort of woman who makes false allegations of sexual offences, the matter must be examined. Fairness to the defendant demands it. Her conviction for theft after giving evidence in her own defence is clearly relevant to her credibility, and of course in cases of this kind, where it is so often the word of one person against another, the credibility of the parties is absolutely central.'

Answer Plan

The first thing is to check that none of the judicial rulings is from a civil trial. It is amazing to see the number of candidates who ignore this simple precaution and start talking of a civil trial in terms of **PACE**, **CJA 2003** and so on. Alas, they score nothing for their attempts. In this case you are all right: all three rulings come from criminal trials.

The next matter to understand is that it is vital to read each ruling carefully, preferably several times. It goes without saying that you tread on thin ice if your experience of written English is too limited. A large part of a lawyer's task is dealing with words, and this is particularly true of a criminal lawyer concerned with finding grounds for an appeal. If you are not good at analysing language you start at a considerable disadvantage. You cannot, of course, analyse what has been said unless you understand it completely.

Next, you must pay attention to the general instruction at the beginning of the whole question. In this case, it is to advise on the correctness of the rulings. That is what you must do. This sort of question is not an invitation to write in general terms about the law that should govern the ruling, let alone about totally different areas of law. Make sure that you avoid this peril by expressing in the very first sentence of each part of your answer the conclusion you have reached about whether the ruling was correct. For an example, see the model answer below.

With these matters in mind, you should consider the following points:

(a) The compellability of spouses under **s 80** of **PACE**. Is this a specified offence where a spouse is compellable? The answer is clearly that it is. So she was compellable, but the judge thought she wasn't. Where does that leave his decision to admit her statement? *R v L* (2008) will get you forward in your answer to some extent, but that was a case where the spouse was not compellable. This judge seems to have made a decision to admit the evidence, presumably under **s 114(1)(d)**, on a false premise. You are entitled to point out as well that he appears to have done so without considering the factors applicable to admissibility under **s 114(1)(d)**, which are set out in **subs (2)**. In this case, **(g)** is obviously relevant.

(b) It is necessary to understand the context in which this ruling must have been given. Obviously, it is not part of the summing-up itself. It must be the result of prosecution and defence submissions about what the summing-up should contain. Submissions of this kind are quite usual, and are often made these days at the invitation of the judge. It will obviously be necessary to refer to *Lobell* (1957). You must then consider the correctness of what the judge has said in the light of that decision. He has summarised its effect correctly, but has he applied it correctly?

(c) Deal with the defence applications separately. The first, to cross-examine about a previous complaint, has been considered in a number of cases, and reference can be made to *T* (2002), *M* (2009) and *D* (2009). The second, to cross-examine about the previous conviction, requires you to apply **s 100 CJA 2003**. (*Not*, please note, **s 101**.)

ANSWER

(a) The judge was wrong to rule that the wife was not compellable, as the offence involved injury to a person who was at the material time under the age of 16 and was therefore a specified offence under **s 80(3)**. Although it was held in *L* (2008) that a judge has power to admit the witness statement of a non-compellable witness under **s 114(1)(d) CJA 2003**, that decision is unlikely to be extended to cover a situation where an incorrect decision has been made about whether a potential witness was compellable. In these circumstances it is clear that the judge took into account a matter that ought not to have been taken into account (the non-compellability of the wife), or alternatively, failed to take into account the matter of compellability that he should have taken into account. It is a classic case of *Wednesbury* unreasonableness and the Court of Appeal would have no difficulty in setting the ruling aside. The argument for a successful appeal is even stronger if we consider that the judge has apparently failed to consider the matters that have to be considered under **s 114(2)** if there is to be admissibility under **s 114(1)(d)**. Of particular concern here is item **(g)**: whether oral evidence of the matter stated can be given and, if not, why it cannot.

(b) The judge was wrong to withdraw the defence of provocation from the jury. According to *Lobell* (1957) a defendant has an evidential burden in respect of this defence, but this means no more than that there must be some evidence before the jury that is capable of supporting the defence. It is for the judge to decide whether a defendant has satisfied this evidential burden, but this judge was wrong in reaching his conclusion because he treated the evidential burden as if it were a burden of *proof* that had to be satisfied to a certain standard. There is a further point of criticism arising from his statement that this was not a defence which 'the jury could find to have been established'. The words quoted suggest that he is reaching his decision on the basis that the defendant has in fact a *legal* burden to establish his defence, which is contrary to the decision in *Lobell* that he began by summarising accurately. The argument could be strengthened by reference to the third sentence in the ruling: 'If that [i.e., the defence of self-defence] *is made out*, of course, he will be acquitted.' The words suggest that throughout this ruling the judge was not focused clearly on where the legal burden of proof lay. An appropriate form of words would have been, 'If that *might reasonably be true*, of course, he will be acquitted.'

(c) The judge was in error in both decisions. It is clear from *T* (2002) that cross-examination about a previous complaint is not allowed unless there is a proper evidential basis for asserting not only that the accusation was made, but that it was false. In *M* (2009) the Court of Appeal said that a proper evidential basis is something less than a strong factual foundation for concluding that the complaint had been false, but there must be material from which such a conclusion could properly be drawn.

The failure to pursue a complaint is *by itself* unlikely to meet that requirement. In order to allow cross-examination about the previous conviction under **s 100** it was necessary under **subs (1)(b)** to show that it had substantial probative value in relation to a matter in issue in the proceedings, *and* of substantial importance in the context of the case as a whole. While it can plausibly be said that in this sort of case the credibility of the complainant when giving evidence on oath is central, it may be doubted whether a single conviction following her own defence evidence can be said to have *substantial* probative value in relation to the matter now in issue. Nor is it very convincing to say that her earlier conviction in those circumstances has substantial importance in relation to the context of the case as a whole. It may be significant that under **s 101** a defendant's previous convictions were said in *Campbell* (2007) to be unlikely to be admitted as relevant to his credibility because the question whether the defendant has a propensity for being untruthful will not normally be capable of being described as an *important* matter in issue between the defendant and the prosecution under gateway (d). Under **s 101** the test is higher: the evidence must be of *substantial* probative value and importance. The *Campbell* argument has correspondingly greater force when applied in relation to **s 100**, and the cross-examination should not have been allowed.

QUESTION 50

Harry and Irma, both aged 18, had known each other for some years. The case for the prosecution is that they both went to the same party, and towards the end of the evening Harry offered Irma a lift home in his car, and she accepted. It is alleged that at some stage Harry stopped the car, dragged Irma into a field, and raped her. Irma says that she was so stunned by what had happened that afterwards she got back into the car with Harry and let him drive her home. Jack, her elder brother, says that when Irma arrived there was mud in her hair and on her clothes. He said to her, 'Irma, what have you been up to? Mind you tell me the truth, or I shall have to report this to Mother.' Irma replied, 'Oh Jack, that bastard Harry raped me in a field!' Jack gave a written statement to the police, but has since gone back-packing abroad and cannot at present be traced. When Harry was interviewed by the police he said, 'I'll tell you everything. She was going on and on about how she was excited at the thought of sex in the open air. When we reached a field she tried to stop the car. We nearly had an accident. I did have sex with her, but I'd never have done so if she hadn't been begging for it.' Jack wishes to call Ken and Larry to say that a short while ago they had sex with Irma on separate occasions, and that she had insisted on having sex in the open air. She had sex in a park with Ken, and with Larry she had sex on a building site.

▸ **Discuss the evidential issues that arise.**

> **Answer Plan**
>
> Four matters need to be discussed:
>
> ❖ Jack's evidence. If he is available in time for Harry's trial, will he be able to give evidence of what he heard and saw? What directions would the judge have to give to the jury about this evidence? If he is not available, can the prosecution use the written statement that he gave to the police?
> ❖ Harry's interview with the police. Is it admissible? What is its evidential status?
> ❖ Can Ken and Larry be called to give evidence for the defence?

ANSWER

If Jack is available at Harry's trial he would in principle be able to give evidence of Irma's physical condition when she came home. But it does not look as if this would assist the prosecution to any degree. Harry has admitted having consensual sex with her in a field, and her muddy condition is as consistent with that as with rape. On the other hand, the prosecution may be able to adduce evidence of what she told Jack. It could be argued that her allegation against Harry falls within **s 120(4)** and **(7) CJA 2003**. The only problem might be with **subs (7)(e)**; the defence could argue that Jack's words, 'Mind you tell the truth, or I shall have to report this to Mother' constituted a threat that would make her allegation inadmissible under that subsection.

If the words are held not to constitute a threat, the question arises whether the prosecution can use the written statement made by Jack if he is still unavailable at the time of Harry's trial. The provisions that would make a written statement by him admissible in principle can be found in **s 116(2)(c)** or **(d)**. However, **s 121** would also apply, because the significant part of Jack's evidence involves the report of an oral statement made to him by Irma. To allow the statement containing this to be given in evidence would be to allow multiple hearsay. The only condition of admissibility that might apply in this case would be **s 121(1)(c)**, and it may be doubted whether a statement confirming the oral evidence of Irma would be regarded as having such a high value that the interests of justice would require it to be admitted. If evidence of Irma's complaint were to be given, whether orally or by way of Jack's written statement, it would be the judge's duty to warn the jury that an earlier complaint by a rape complainant cannot provide independent confirmation of the complainant's own evidence (*Islam* (1999)).

Harry's interview with the police will be admissible. Insofar as it contains an admission that he had sex with Irma, it will be admissible as a confession under **s 76(1)** of the **Police and Criminal Evidence Act (PACE) 1984**. Insofar as it contains exculpatory matters – she was a willing, indeed an eager, partner – it will be admissible by virtue of the principle settled in *Pearce* (1979) that the prosecution must in fairness adduce evidence of exculpatory as well as inculpatory statements by the accused. What Harry produced was a 'mixed' statement, which, following *Sharp* (1988) and *Aziz* (1995), will be treated as evidence of the truth of all its contents, though the judge may point out that the exculpatory part should not be given the same weight as the inculpatory part.

Whether Ken and Larry can be called for the defence will depend on the application of **s 41** of the **Youth Justice and Criminal Evidence Act 1999**. The basic rule laid down in **s 41(1)** is that there can be no evidence or cross-examination about any sexual behaviour of the complainant without the leave of the court, which can be given only under **subs (3)** or **(5)**. **Subsection (5)** is inapplicable here. The defence is consent; there is no suggestion that it is anything else, such as an honest belief where consent did not in fact exist. The evidence of Ken and Larry can be given, therefore, only if it falls within the exceptions contained in **subs (3)(b)** or **(c)**. It does not sound as if the events involving Ken and Larry can be admitted under **subs (3)(b)**. In *A* (2001) members of the House of Lords observed that 'at or about the same time' would not normally be construed so as to refer to a time much more than 24 hours before or after the alleged offence. Reliance would have to be placed on **subs (c)**, which imposes a test of similarity. Although, as was observed in *A*, the test is not the old test of *striking* similarity that was once applied in similar fact cases, it was at least doubtful whether a preference for sex in the open air would be held sufficiently unusual to meet the requirement of the subsection. *A* decided that **s 41(1)(c)** was to be construed in accordance with the **Human Rights Act 1998** so as to allow evidence to be given where its exclusion would deny a defendant his right to a fair trial. But the evidence in *A* was of the *defendant's* previous sexual relationship with the complainant. A complainant's relationship with other men is very unlikely to be admitted under the principle acknowledged in that case. It is unlikely, therefore, that Ken and Larry will be allowed to give evidence.

Index

accomplices 79, 85, 192
accused persons *see* defendants/accused persons
admissibility 5, 12, 14; confessions 104–11; hearsay evidence 63, 64
alcohol 29, 112, 113–14, 119, 164, 165, 191
alibi evidence 18, 57, 87, 199, 201
ambiguity 28, 31, 78, 103
arson 25, 27
assault 164–6, 167–9; grievous bodily harm 22, 24–5, 93

bailment 112, 114
bailment for reward 28
bias, witnesses 166
Birch, D. 74
blackmail 176–7, 179
burden of proof *see* proof, burden and standard of burglary 84–7, 115–18, 156–9
Bywaters, Freddie 4–5

character evidence 97, 120, 123–5; cross-examination 143–6, 150, 151, 154–5, 156, 159, 160–1; directions to jury 123, 124–5, 128, 132, 146, 149, 152, 155, 157; failure to testify at trial 100–4, 144–5, 152; previous convictions 68, 123, 124–5, 128, 129–31, 133–4, 135–7, 145, 146, 148–9, 151–4, 155, 157–61; relevance 123, 126–8, 132–3, 136–7, 138, 139–40; sexual offences 125–34, 137–41, 146–9; witness credibility 166, 172
children 45; indecent assault 52–3; presumption of legitimacy 35, 37, 40–1, 42; as witnesses 34, 40, 79
civil cases 37, 38, 39–40; proof, burden and standard of 17, 18, 24, 25–31
civil partners, as witnesses 34, 42–3, 45
classification of offences 19–20
common purpose statements 64, 69–70, 98–9

competence and compellability of witnesses 38–40, 42–5, 203, 204
confessions 97; admissibility 104–11; directions to jury 102, 107, 111, 118, 120, 121; exclusion of 97, 99–100, 105–7, 109, 110–11, 113–14, 115, 116, 117, 119–20; hearsay 64, 66–7, 70, 86; impact on case as whole 98–9; improperly obtained 118–20, 121–2; oppression 99, 103, 105–6, 109, 116, 119; recognition of 98
consent: privilege and public policy 184, 195; sexual offences and 82, 83, 130, 139, 171–2, 207
conspiracy 64, 150–1, 159; to defraud 57, 70; to steal 192
contract(s): exclusion clauses 25–7, 28; freedom of 9
corroboration 79, 85
criminal cases 37; burden and standard of proof 17, 24–5, 27, 37; competence and compellability of spouses 38, 39, 42–5
criminal offences 19–20, 183; *see also* individual offences
Crippen, Dr 3–4
cross-examination 163, 166, 167, 168–9, 202, 205, 207; character evidence 143–6, 150, 151, 154–5, 156, 159, 160–1; hazardous evidence 78; hearsay 50, 51–2, 53, 57, 67; privilege and public policy 183, 191, 193–4

dangerous driving 38–40
death, presumption of 35–6, 40–2
deception, obtaining property by 111–14, 158
defences: diminished responsibility 176–7, 178, 179; duress 18, 48, 117; mental illness/disability 18, 22, 24; and offences, distinction between 20–1; self-defence 18, 22, 25, 202, 204
defendants/accused persons: detention of 87, 106; failure to answer police questions 86–7,

107–8, 109–10, 111, 115–16, 118–19, 120–1; failure to testify at trial 100–4, 144–5, 152; giving evidence 150, 151, 202; lies 80, 166, 168, 171; oppression 99, 103, 105–6, 109, 116, 119; presumption of innocence 19, 20, 21–2, 31, 33–4, 37; previous convictions 68, 123, 124–5, 128, 129–31, 133–4, 135–7, 145, 146, 148–9, 151–4, 155, 157–61; reverse burden of proof 19–22, 31

Dennis, I 19, 20, 21
detention of suspects 87, 106
diminished responsibility defence 176–7, 178, 179
directions to jury 1, 14, 68–9, 70, 168, 171, 172; burden and standard of proof and 17–18, 23–4, 25; character evidence 123, 124–5, 128, 132, 146, 149, 152, 155, 157; confessions 102, 107, 111, 118, 120, 121; hazardous evidence 78–80, 83, 85, 87, 91, 93–4
drug offences 8–9, 13–15, 101, 118–22, 190–4; hearsay evidence 60–1, 68–71
duress defence 18, 48, 117

eavesdropping 121
essay questions 197–9
evidential burden of proof 17
exclusion clauses 25, 27–8
exclusion of evidence 7, 8–9; improperly obtained evidence 13, 118–20, 121–2; *see also* confessions; hearsay evidence
exculpatory statements 69, 99, 101, 105, 107, 207
expert evidence 51, 140, 175–7, 178–80, 194, 195

fair trial right 10, 50–2, 207
fraud 27, 158, 159, 160

generalisations 4–5, 16, 126–7, 139–40
grievous bodily harm 22, 24–5, 93

handling stolen goods 134–7
hazardous evidence 77–8, 81–7; corroboration 79, 85; warnings to juries 78–80, 83, 85, 87, 91, 93–4; *see also* identification evidence
health and safety at work 19–20
hearsay evidence 47–8, 63–4; drugs offences 60–1, 68–71; exceptions to rule against 47, 48, 57, 63–4, 70, 72, 74; human rights issues 49–52, 54, 74–5; manslaughter 71–3; 'multiple' 55, 64, 67, 76; murder 55–62, 65–8; rationale for rule against 52–5; *res gestae* statements 63–4, 72, 74, 75, 86, 200–1; 'safety valve' exception 48, 54–5, 57, 63, 74; statutory reforms 73–6
hostile witnesses 167, 169
human rights issues: burden of proof and 18–22, 29, 31; fair trial 10, 50–2, 207; thearsay 49–52, 54, 74–5

identification evidence 57, 58, 79–80, 87, 88–91; mistaken identification 92–5, 131–4; video 80, 88, 89, 90, 95; voice 53, 55, 58, 59, 61, 94, 95
improperly obtained evidence 13, 118–20, 121–2
indecent assault 51, 52–3, 125–34
indecent exposure 138, 140–1
industrial accidents 194–6
informers 184, 188, 190–4
inheritance, presumption of death and 35–6, 40–2
innocence, presumption of 19, 20, 21–2, 31, 33–4, 37

joint enterprise 64, 98–9
journalists' sources 184
judges: discretion 57, 63, 74–6, 79; *see also* directions to jury
judicial notice 10–12

language, problems with 78
legal professional privilege 183–4, 186, 194–5
legitimacy, presumption of 35, 37, 40–1, 42
lies 80, 166, 168, 171
local knowledge 11

mala in se and *mala prohibita* 19–20
manslaughter 71–3
maximum penalties 21
medical evidence 22, 55, 178, 180
memory: mnemonics 198–9; testimony and 167, 168–9
mental illness/disability defences 18, 22, 24; diminished responsibility 176–7, 178, 179
mistaken identification 92–5, 131–4
mixed statements 66, 83, 99, 171–2, 207
murder 3–5, 86, 104–7, 199–201, 202; burden and standard of proof 22, 23–4; character evidence 137–41; hearsay evidence 55–62, 65–8; opinion evidence 176–80

negligence 25, 27–8, 37, 38

oaths 40, 53, 205
offensive weapons 18, 22, 24
opinion evidence 175–81; expert evidence 51, 140, 175–7, 178–80, 194, 195
oppression 99, 103, 105–6, 109, 116, 119
outraging public decency 146–9

Parliament 6, 20
Peirce, CS 138
photofit likenesses 47, 88, 90
photographs 88, 89–90; as tool of oppression 104, 105
planting of evidence 115, 116
police: failure to answer police questions 86–7, 107–8, 109–10, 111, 115–16, 118–19, 120–1; informers 184, 188, 190–4; surveillance 191, 193–4
presumptions 33, 34–8; of death 35–6, 40–2; of innocence 19, 20, 21–2, 31, 33–4, 37; of legitimacy 35, 37, 40–1, 42; trebuttable 33, 36, 42; of regularity 37
previous convictions 68, 123, 124–5, 128, 129–31, 133–4, 135–7, 145, 146, 148–9, 151–4, 155, 157–61
previous statements 167–8, 169, 170–1
privilege 185–90, 194–5; against self-incrimination 183; journalists' sources 184; legal professional 183–4, 186, 194–5; secondary evidence 189; waiver 188–9; without prejudice statements 184
proof, burden and standard of 17–18, 22–5; civil cases 17, 18, 24, 25–31; human rights issues 18–22, 29, 31
public policy (public interest immunity) 183, 184, 185–90; informers 184, 188, 190–4; surveillance 191, 193–4

rape 81–4, 95, 117, 137–41, 163, 169–72, 202, 205–7
rebuttal: presumption of law 33, 36, 42; testimony 163, 164, 165, 166, 168; refreshing memory 167, 168–9
regularity, presumptions of 37
relevance of evidence 4–5, 6–10, 14–15; and admissibility 5, 12, 14
res gestae statements 63–4, 72, 74, 75, 86, 200–1
reverse burden of proof 19–22, 31

robbery 39, 121–2, 149–56
Roberts, P 35, 75

searches 13, 14
selection of evidence 77
self-defence 18, 22, 25, 202, 204
self-incrimination, privilege against 183
sentencing, maximum penalties 21
sexual offences: indecent assault 51, 125–34; indecent exposure 138, 140–1; outraging public decency 146–9; rape 81–4, 95, 117, 137–41, 163, 169–72, 202, 205–7
shoplifting 143–6
silence: failure to answer police questions 86–7, 107–8, 109–10, 111, 115–16, 118–19, 120–1; failure to testify at trial 100–4, 144–5, 152; privilege against self-incrimination 183
special knowledge 11
spouses, as witnesses 34, 38, 39, 42–5, 203, 204
standard of proof see proof, burden and standard of
statements: common purpose 64, 69–70, 98–9; exculpatory 69, 99, 101, 105, 107, 207; and matter stated 47–8; mixed 66, 83, 99, 171–2, 207; previous 167–8, 169, 170–1; res gestae 63–4, 72, 74, 75, 86, 200–1; without prejudice 184
statutory offences 19–20, 21

Tapper, C 35
testimony 163–4; failure to testify at trial 100–4, 144–5, 152; lies 166, 168, 171; rebuttal 163, 164, 165, 166, 168; refreshing memory 167, 168–9; see also cross-examination, statements
Thayer, JB 6, 7
theft 22, 107–11; burglary 84–7, 115–18, 156–9; handling stolen goods 134–7; robbery 39, 121–2, 149–56; shoplifting 143–6
Thompson, Edith 4–5
tracker dogs 58, 60
trust 77
Twining, W 5, 33

video identification 80, 88, 89, 90, 95
video link 54, 67
video recordings, as evidence 131, 134

violent disorder 87–92
voice identification 53, 55, 58, 59, 61, 94, 95

warnings to jury *see* directions to jury
Wigmore, J 5, 6, 7–8, 53
without prejudice statements 184
witnesses: bias 166; competence and compellability of 38–40, 42–5, 203, 204; corroboration 79, 85; credibility 166, 172; in fear 75; hostile 167, 169; police informers 184, 188, 190–4; unreliable 79

wounding 201–2; burden and standard of proof 22, 24–5; compellability of spouses 203, 204

Zuckerman, A 35, 75